Restoration Glass:
A Vision for Healthy Conflict

*How Place, Stories, and Critical Thinking
Create a Culture of Reconciliation*

By

KIMBERLY ANN MAZZOCCO HART

Published by hope*books
2217 Matthews Township Pkwy
Suite D302
Matthews, NC 28105
www.hopebooks.com

hope*books is a division of hope*media

Printed in the United States of America

First paperback edition.
Paperback ISBN: 979-8-89185-302-7
Hardcover ISBN: 979-8-89185-148-1
Ebook ISBN: 979-8-89185-149-8

Headshot photo by sarahburnsphotography.com

Scripture taken from the New King James Version®. Copyright © 1982 by Thomas Nelson. Used by permission. All rights reserved.

hope*books
hopebooks.com
Because the world needs your hope-filled
words now more than ever.

"In *Restoration Glass*, Kimberly Hart has given us a blueprint for engaging in healthy conflict by weaving together the three strands of place, stories, and critical thinking and she does this by beautifully weaving her own story into her writing. She also reminds us that in this time of deep division, it is crucial to remember that we are all created in the Image of God and the power of story and myth to remind us of this truth. Hers is an optimistic, hopeful voice that provides real answers for how we can begin to heal the fractures in our nation by remaining curious and engaging in thoughtful conversations with those whom we disagree."

—THE REV. EDIE HOLTON, Vicar
St. Luke's Episcopal Church, Brownsville, Maryland

"This book reminds us that we are all part of the family of human beings, and unless we learn to hear each others' stories and to see one another as having dignity and worth, we risk deepening our divisions until the only way forward seems to be one of violence. I saw this happen firsthand in former Yugoslavia in the 1990s and have no wish to see history repeat itself. We may not all be at the center of the great debates of our time, but we all have the responsibility of creating a healthy culture in which those debates can be conducted with mutual respect and goodwill."

—BOJAN RUVARAC (SERBIA), Director, Renewing Our Minds
Forum for Leadership and Reconciliation

"In *Restoration Glass*, Kimberly Hart weaves together personal experience, historical reflection, and thoughtful analysis to offer a compelling vision for how we can transform conflict into opportunities for reconciliation. Drawing from the metaphor of the wavy, imperfect panes of glass in her historic home, she invites us to shift our perspectives and see beauty where we once saw disorder.

Kimberly shows us the power of slowing down, listening, and engaging with those who challenge our views. This book is both timely and timeless, offering a roadmap for navigating the fractured landscape of our polarized political and social world, reminding us that reconciliation is possible when we choose to see through a new lens."

—PASTOR JIMMY SWOGGER
Oakland Church of God, Distant, PA

"For those burned or burned out by the incessant political combat that dominates so much of our public spaces and private lives, Kimberly Hart has written an insightful and accessible book that gives readers the practical tools they need to rebuild a culture of grace and solidarity. As both an encouragement and how-to guide in creating hospitable and healing spaces, *Restoration Glass* is a must-read."

—CHERIE HARDER, President
The Trinity Forum

"In *Restoration Glass,* Kimberly Hart offers a hopeful vision and essential toolbox on how we can co-create a culture of reconciliation through the power of hospitality, story, and critical thinking. This must-read book can help us heal and overcome so much of the toxic polarization that afflicts our culture and politics and build Beloved Community together."

—ADAM TAYLOR,
President Sojourners

To *Nora, Jack, Gabriel, and Teddy,* who remind me every single day of the good, the true, and the beautiful. Our world will be all the brighter, kinder, and more reasonable for having you in it.

To my partner and best friend, my husband, *John,* for all the sweet and heartfelt "words of encouragement" I never seem to accept and for being my co-host, inspiration, faithful listener, and receiver of all my waterfalls of words and ideas, including my crazy suggestion that we buy a farm and a 200-year-old house with wavy glass windows.

To my parents who read me "just one more" story a million times over and let me ask a million questions every day, showing me how to open my home to the wild, the weird, and the wonderful without hesitation.

To my teachers who encouraged me to think deeply and never accept the easy answer (and let me think I was getting away with reading under my desk…)

To all the family, friends, and strangers who showed me the power of sharing stories and sharing Place with love and welcome.

To friends and colleagues who demonstrate every day the power of place, stories, and thoughtfulness, bringing hope and light to the darkest places of the world.

Be kind. Listen first and speak last. Read stories and tell stories. Welcome both friend and stranger into your space. Think deeply and critically and always seek to draw closer to the Truth. The world is a beautiful place.

Table of Contents

Introduction

I posed a question on social media the other day. I asked, "How many political memes have you shared versus how many *conversations*—about anything—have you had with someone with whom you disagree politically?" The silence was telling. And discouraging. I've been angry—and sad—to see many of the teachers who inspired and encouraged me use hateful, prideful words about people with different political opinions. I've tried to engage them directly, but they rarely answer. The memes continue, and I wonder how I can make a difference.

Our 1820 home—christened Friendly Hall by the original family—has many windows. Large, twelve-paned, six over six, two hundred-year-old windows. From them, I can look out over our fields and trees, seeing the light shift from the barest rose of dawn to the blinding gold of sunset. I can watch the moon rise over South Mountain, and I can see the rain as it waves across Elk Ridge. When the light changes or the wind rises, I instinctively glance to the window to see what has happened outside. Yet a quick glance will often tell me little. Our windowpanes are not the clear, flat panes of today's windows: Our windows are old, and much of the original blown glass remains.

Glass made with this technique today is called restoration glass. Like the window glass of centuries past, restoration glass is mouth-blown glass, imperfect, wavy, and bubbly. We've broken only one windowpane since we made Friendly Hall our home, and though we could choose to replace it with plain, clear glass, we will continue to use restoration glass. Why? Of course, we wish to honor the age and style of the house, but more, we have come to love the view and its perceptive-shaping story of what is good and true and beautiful.

Our "north parlor" has two north-facing windows, one to either side of the fireplace. For reasons we have not been able to uncover, the east window is as large as a door, a six-over-six paned window. As I sit at my desk, I can look to the garden, the fields of wheat or corn, and the hills beyond. Yet the view just outside is slightly less majestic. What was once a lovely bed of lilacs and other flowering shrubs is now terribly overgrown. Having had to remove one dying old lilac, we failed to remove the entire stump. That area, just outside my colossal window, is now a tangle of pokeweed, honeysuckle vine, stiltgrass, and other unidentified green. When we walk outside and examine that patch, my blood pressure rises. It destroys the view! It's ugly, unkempt, disorderly! But when I see that same disarray from inside, through the wavy panes of restoration glass, I see it transformed. Like an impressionist painting seen from across the room, the edges are softened, the colors blurred into one another. I no longer see mess but beauty in the many shades of green. Our wavy windows require us to slow down as we pass, to take a second look, to check our perspective. The ugly becomes beautiful and time less pressing. Restoration glass does not just preserve the past, the history of our home; it gives us a new way of seeing the present. Imagine if we could experience a similar perception shift in the way we see our world today.

In the United States (and increasingly throughout the developed world), we find ourselves more and more isolated from those who are unlike us: "the Other." Once again, the world teeters where but a breath more of unreasoned anger and alienation could send us plummeting to the depths of violence. We are frustrated that we cannot make ourselves heard in a world of constant noise from social media, 24/7 news cycles, and on-demand TV. We are also less likely than ever to really hear anything that contradicts our own beliefs. It's never been easier to read the words, listen to soundbites, and see the video clips, but do we really hear what "the Other" is saying? Do we absorb challenges to our assumptions and beliefs, ponder them, and seek to understand the other human being who is desperate to be heard? Are we even willing to take the time needed to challenge our perceptions and see things differently?

In 2017, Deb Roy, Director of the MIT Center for Constructive Communication and former chief media scientist at Twitter, discovered through a series of small town forums that social media was directly responsible for a breakdown in communication. People in small towns literally stopped talking to one another after seeing their neighbors' posts online.[3] Conversations that once occurred naturally in everyday life are no longer happening because we get advance notice of opinions and beliefs we do not like. That neighbor who votes so inexplicably differently from you is also the snack mom on your son's Little League team. Once, you would only know of her voting habits if she had a yard sign or bumper sticker. Even then, you would only know her general political leaning unless she also spoke out more directly regarding her political beliefs—whether via letter to the editor or diatribe at the team picnic. So, you would talk to her at games. You would chit-chat about school or gas prices or the coach's baseball jargon or where to find the cheapest white baseball pants that aren't see-through. Now, you are both members of the neighborhood Facebook group where she posts about various political topics, shares memes, and maybe rants about the odd issue or two. You are clearly very different from her, and before you've even had an in-person conversation, you feel certain you are unlikely to get along. Instinctively, without even conscious thought, you avoid that mom at the games and stick to the mom from your son's class who shares your beliefs. While that other mom may bring good snacks, she also believes all that crazy stuff on the "other" side. And you really don't think politics belong at a Little League game.

Once, those Little League fields, like local pubs and markets, churches, libraries, and coffee shops, were "third places." A third place is a sort of neutral ground, familiar, comfortable, and open to all. Third places are those sites where people run into one another, chit-chatting lightheartedly about life and news and events of the day. They might be the front stoops in an urban neighborhood of rowhouses or the front porches in a small town. They allow people to congregate without the burdens and expectations of work or the intimacies of home yet still connect with one another. At the advent of the internet, there was great hope that it would be the next great third place. And for a while, it almost was. In the early days of online forums and message boards, people would gather to "chat" about topics of common interest. To post on The Bronze, a posting board for fans of *Buffy the Vampire Slayer*, you had to follow the simple list of rules that included "basic netiquette guidelines" of the internet world of 1997: *"Posting in capital letters is equivalent to shouting; if you dis-*

agree with a post, make sure that you attack the post and not the post-er..." Those rules now feel almost nostalgic. Does anyone really expect others to "attack the post and not the poster?"

Why? Why do we find it so easy to SHOUT our opinions online? Why do we not feel that we should moderate our tone, listen to others, and think carefully about what is being said? We cannot merely blame the medium. You can still find positive third places online. And we see that same behavior, that same divisive speech in our in-person encounters as well. We label the news with which we disagree as fake or biased, from the *Faux News Network* to the *Clinton News Network*. We assume that people who watch one more than the other are misinformed and that we are the ones who know the truth. But do we?

How do we create space to be heard, and how do we create space–literal, virtual, cognitive, emotional, and figurative–to hear "the Other?" Can we still find ways to metaphorically hang out in the local general store and exchange views on the news of the day in ways that bring light and not heat to the conversation? Can we create spaces where we can meet with people of varying backgrounds and lifestyles and views and truly engage with them in responsible and productive ways? I believe we can—and we must.

I've always been hopeful about the existence of such space. Though I haven't always found it, I am a firm believer that most of us crave it, that we all have a human longing for connection. Looking back over my life, I see three primary strands that have shaped my optimism: place, stories, and critical thinking. Each strand alone cannot resolve our cultural inability to process and respond to conflict and restore community, but woven together, they form a rope that can haul us out of this chasm of discord. We can all relearn the art of each strand and the skill to weave them together.

I've lived in or visited a kaleidoscope of towns and countries throughout the world, and in every place, I've found the same restorative perspective shaping powers of place, stories, and critical thinking. The beauty of the warm welcome of true hospitality, the serenity of nature, and the cultivation of community breathe life into empty spaces, creating what author and songwriter Andrew Peterson describes as "Places with a capital P, places that honor the community's history, the sacredness of creation, and our basic human need for beauty and nature."[4] Within those Places, we find ourselves able to build community as we relate stories, sharing a foundation and cultural rootedness that binds us together, developing our imaginations, and growing empathy for others. We both firmly ground ourselves in a family, a place, and a culture through our knowing and telling of stories, but also we stretch ourselves in our ability to understand and know the stranger—even the enemy. That stretching expands our minds and gives us the room to question our most deeply held beliefs. We gain the creativity to think of solutions, the empathy to understand the positions of others, and the humility to know we do not always know the best answer. From family feuds around the dinner table to working meals with peacebuilders in the Middle East, the threads that wove the strongest ties were those of place, story, and critical thinking.

Through the work of the Fairlight Forum, we are weaving those together on our land, Fairlight Farm, in the Pleasant Valley region of central Maryland. Professionally, as well as personally, we welcome those who see one another as "the Other," helping to create a space to hear and to be heard. We use the beauty of nature to help set the stage for people to tell their stories. We guide them in the conversations that seek truth, asking questions with vulnerability and humility. This work of hospitality, stories, and thoughtful challenging of beliefs has been done before in our home.

In 1864, a young woman named Josephine Boteler refused to care for her suffering enemy. Lost to time are her reasons, but we can certainly speculate that three years of war, of armies battling across her family farm, of soldiers wearing the same uniform as the wounded young man in front of her burning her church to the ground, had left her tired. Afraid. Angry. Her family had been made to pay over and over again for their allegiance to the Confederacy, and this captured Union captain did not deserve her compassion. Seeing yet another enemy on her doorstep, Josephine cried out, "Just let the damn Yankee die!" And yet, she didn't. Somehow, in the days and weeks that followed, as she cared for his wounds, the young Miss Boteler began to see Captain Lapham as first a fellow human being, then later as Daniel, a friend. By 1867, Josephine Boteler and Daniel Wade Lapham were wed. They were willing to open their minds and eventually their hearts to one another, and from enemies, they became beloved partners.

Today, I live in the house where they met, broke bread, broke past hurt to share their stories, broke down walls to open their minds, and eventually fell in love. I walk those fields, stand in awe in the ever-changing play of light across those parallel ridges, and dream of creating a place where their story of reconciliation is but one of many. If we want to see that unity and hope flourish in our world today, let us explore how we can all do those small things that bring about great change.

I was barely seventeen when I left western Pennsylvania for Cambridge, Massachusetts and MIT. I was shy, but I was also conditioned to never turn down an offer when someone welcomed you to their home. So, when the daughter of one of my high school teachers invited me to spend the weekend with her family in a Boston suburb, I automatically accepted. Debbie and Chris, with their preschool son Nick, became my home away from home. I learned from them how to host with warmth and openness. When I was in their home, I wasn't a stranger but a friend from my first step across their threshold. They did have an absolutely lovely home with a cute backyard on a tree-lined suburban street. I slept under a heavy down comforter and ate mouthwatering home-cooked meals from sturdy and handsome stoneware dishes. But the welcome wasn't in the dishes or the thread count of the sheets or even in the stew and homemade fudge. The welcome was in the offering of themselves and their home. The welcome was in the opening of their hearts to me at a time when I needed the occasional refuge.

As I graduated and began to travel, I experienced an almost unimaginable assortment of welcomes. From children rushing home from school to teach their American guest more Tagalog words to a young Syrian soldier in Beirut tenderly showing off my infant daughter to his homesick buddies, I've been blessed with a form of hospitality nearly everywhere I've gone.

When I've been met on my travels, whether work or personal, with hospitality, a space has been created for connection, dialogue, and community. Sometimes, that means your infant is being babysat by a middle-aged Bosnian woman who gives her her first haircut because she wants to help a busy mom. (It took months for that to grow out!) Or that same young toddler being kept entertained by a group of young Albanian men so deeper conversations could be had that included me. Thanks to them, I didn't have to chase a wriggling, busy little girl but could sit at the table and learn more about how these students wanted to change the nature of politics in their young democracy. Some of them remain friends twenty years later.

The little things matter when it comes to welcoming others. It is not the setting but the noticing. While trying to have an informal dinner meeting in Sarajevo, a restaurant manager noticed my daughter getting restless, so he scooped her up and told me to continue my conversation. They were quickly surrounded by a group of grizzled men, making her laugh, talking to her in Serbian, and laughing in turn at her gibberish. Later, I was told they were a group of famous Bosnian writers who regularly met at this restaurant. They will never know the gift they gave to me—not just of the time to finish our conversation, but also of relationship. I will never meet them, and they, I am sure, do not remember an evening spent entertaining an American toddler, but it was a moment of community, of the hope and love that resided in a country still reeling from war.

As individuals and as a family, we have been the recipients of hospitality that has changed the trajectory of our lives. Those little moments of welcome that open up windows of the possible—that let us see how community can be built and nourished. We have tried to live lives of hospitality in return. We've extended an open invitation to our church for Christmas dinner for anyone who wasn't traveling "home" for the holidays. In a transient city like D.C., that is not an insignificant number.

We've also hosted a few dinners for the Student Leadership Network, which brings college students into D.C. each year for the National Prayer Breakfast. One year, we hosted a dinner for a large group that was all young men. When they entered our house, they stood awkwardly in the doorway, ill at ease and trying to be on their best behavior. We had prepared our house for guests—had cleaned a little more thoroughly than usual, fluffed the cushions, set the table nicely…It wasn't a fancy house. I had wrestled a bit with our invitation to host, knowing that other families who hosted were often wealthier, had bigger homes, nicer furniture, and fancier décor. But I wanted these students to feel that they were special, that we truly welcomed their presence. To do that, I took the time to prepare a space that was as welcoming as I could make it—clean, neat, well-lit, with comfortable places to stand or sit without having to dodge matchbox cars and LEGO bricks. I wanted to create an environment of ease. I wanted those young men to walk in and feel loved, that they mattered enough as college kids that a family made their home lovely for them, made a special meal just for them.

Hospitality creates a space for community. In those spaces, we can be vulnerable. We can share our thoughts knowing we are safe from harm. When our bodies relax, our minds relax. We find it easier to relate to others, even strangers. In a world where one internet search for cloth napkins leads to an endless parade of "suggested for you" social media sites on home décor and entertainment, it is hard to remember that hospitality is about welcoming others, not about perfect place settings.

Once we have re-envisioned our role in hospitality and place, once we set the stage for dialogue, we must then consider what helps us to actually have those conversations. I think the answer lies in forming a foundation of stories and building on that with critical thinking. I speak not only from my education at MIT and Columbia Law School and my experience in law, advocacy, and peacebuilding but also from my own personal life.

I found God at MIT. Crazy, I know. Or is it? After a childhood marinated in the magic and wonder of story, I found my way to God in a place of science, with wonder, questioning, and deep, critical thinking. Stories taught me about people, emotions, places, and events far beyond my life in rural western Pennsylvania. Stories fed my imagination and kept my curiosity alive well past childhood. I learned empathy as I lived in the characters I read, seeing the world through their eyes, understanding their motivation, their biases, their emotions. MIT helped ground that imagination in logic and reason, to use what I imagined of the world to inform my thoughts for problem-solving and creating. At MIT, I met scientists who not only led their respective fields in making discoveries about the world, chasing ideas from theory to hypothesis to theory, questioning, investigating, examining, and concluding, but they also believed deeply in a Creator of the world they studied so closely. As I read and explored and questioned, I found that the God who lived in the stories of my childhood was also in the science I was studying, also in the warmth and hospitality I experienced. God lived in the thoughtful pursuit of all three: stories, space, and science.

As I went out into the world as a lawyer, I held to two guiding verses:

> "And you shall know the truth, and the truth shall make you free." (John 8:32)
>
> "He has shown you, O man, what *is* good; And what does the Lord require of you but to do justly, to love mercy, and to walk humbly with your God?" (Micah 6:8)

I vowed to seek the truth in all that I did. To question, to wonder, to try to see from another's point of view. The law, I believed, was one tool to uncover that truth. The adversarial nature of the law is not to create enemies of your legal opposition, but to create an environment that seeks to reach a conclusion that comes as close to truth as possible. As I tell my Mock Trial students, who are always concerned about defense attorneys defending people they know to be guilty, the law is there as a tool to seek truth, and the job of the defense attorney is to ensure that the prosecuting attorney does their very best to achieve that.

As I pursued my advocacy career, I drew upon my love of stories to not only pursue truth but to do justice while loving mercy. When looking at the complexity, horrors, and chaos of both the present and the past in the Holy Land, one must use the lessons of stories to enter into the experiences of those living that tragedy. To see the truth, do justice, and be merciful is impossible without empathy and the ability to seek solutions by thinking creatively. That thinking must be informed by logic, and personal biases must constantly be checked.

As I met with those who were doing the very hard work of seeking peace in the Holy Land, I was treated to incredible hospitality, where those who should be enemies met at the table as friends and partners. They shared stories—hard stories of lives shattered and loved ones lost, future and past alike destroyed. They were people, like those men and women in the Parents Circle-Families Forum of Israel and Palestine, who, having lost children of their own to the decades of conflict, could look with empathy through the eyes of "the Others" who had faced the same loss. Through great pain, they shared their stories in the hope that others could see and hear and feel the hurt on both sides and, from that understanding, be willing and able to engage in critical thinking to find solutions. Still, despite the many people, Israeli and Palestinian, who devote their lives to listening, thinking, praying, and speaking carefully, with love, into the conflict, the violent emotions of hatred, fear, and rage still hold sway. Yet, always in that darkness, remain those who are determined to bring light.

We are at a watershed moment in this American culture today. Will we continue down this path of labels, tribes, and separate spaces? If so, we risk the explosive conflict of the former Yugoslav Republics, where literal neighbors turned on one another based on ethnic identity, regardless of former points of common ground. A decade after the death of the strongman that had presided over the created nation-state of Yugoslavia, the various ethnic populations found themselves defined by ethnicity alone, locked in combat with "the Other," though just a few years before, they had been friends, family, co-workers. When the people of Yugoslavia stopped seeing themselves as individual members of one nation but as collective members of one ethnic group or another, they became unable to see past the labels—their own, as much as the ones they placed on others. We are growing ever closer to that place, ever closer to being unable to see the person behind the label, behind the religion, behind the color of the political sign in their front yard. Can we stop our slide to the precipice? Can we rebuild bridges instead of building bulwarks?

Creating the space for healthy conflict, reconciliation, problem-solving, and true and lasting peacebuilding requires a renewed understanding of the importance of hospitality and the need for beautiful, restful, and inspiring places. But hospitality alone, time in Creation alone, sharing a meal alone, isn't enough to sustain the dialogue that we are lacking. We must also re-energize our collective moral imagination through a shared cultural foundation on stories, words that fire the imagination of children, spark wonder, and help them develop a firm sense of that old-fashioned word "virtue." Children who grow with curiosity, wonder, and the freedom to wrestle with difficult ideas become teens and adults who are capable of learning and using critical thinking and the value of Socratic questioning. Without that, we are trapped in a cycle of conflict and alienation.

We are a people looking for reconciliation, fumbling for a way forward in a time of fractured, hurried space. We have lost touch with our basic, most fundamental needs and roles as human beings due to our collective angst, politics, climate crises, pandemic panics, wealth, poverty, and even our individual dreams. We have forgotten that we are all created in the Imago Dei, the image of God. With no common sense of identity, even in our shared humanity, there is an increasing distance from the power and virtue of fairy tales and myths in building a shared foundation. Instead, we rely on inflamed emotions with a bewildering loss of a real understanding of the role of emotion in critical thought. With our culture ever more rootless and disconnected, we need to create spaces to hear and to be heard. We do that through hospitality, stories, art, the work of critical thinking, and the vulnerability that comes from sharing time and natural space—and, no less importantly, good food. In the chapters ahead, I lay out the framework for a restored vision for healthy conflict: place, stories, and critical thinking. Let us be the weavers in this new tapestry of restoration.

The Need for Place

"Hospitality, therefore, means primarily the creation of free
space where the stranger can enter and become a
friend instead of an enemy."
— HENRI NOUWEN[5]

"Everybody needs beauty as well as bread, places to play in
and pray in, where Nature may heal and give strength
to body and soul alike."
— JOHN MUIR, *The Yosemite* (1912).[6]

"...[I]f you don't know where you are, you probably
don't know who you are."
— RALPH ELLISON, *Invisible Man*[7]

Place matters. Part of our very identity comes from place: where we were born, where we were raised, went to university, got married, had our first home, our first dog, our first child. We identify as being "from north of Pittsburgh" or say we were "born in New York but grew up in Texas." We sing songs about being a country girl or about the streets of our hometown. Our soul-deep drive to belong leads us to Ancestry.com or inspires us to learn to cook "real" Italian food or wear our family plaid from our Scottish clan. We want to know where we are from so we know who we are. That desire drives much of the fierceness with which we cling to an identity culture today. When we ask people where they are from, we don't want to know where they live now, but *where are they from*?

The Ralph Ellison quote above upends that. If we don't know where we *are*, here and now, in *this* place, can we know *who* we are? Can we put down roots and grow, even if we don't know for sure how long we will stay in our mobile world? Can we come from this new place even while being from the old? If I'm from New England, can I also be from the South if I move to Atlanta? Can I be urbane and sophisticated if I move to a farmhouse on 62 acres? Who am I?

I've lived in myriad settings, seeking to belong, to find community, to become *from* there in most of them. I was born in a small city (or is it a large town?) in Western Pennsylvania. Not Pittsburgh. Or Erie. Or anywhere in particular in between. Not rural or urban. Not true deep Appalachia, but somewhere on the outer fringe. Coal country still, but strip mines, not deep mines. Oil, but not like Texas. When I was eight, we moved 90 minutes northeast from the town where I was born. And I most certainly was not from this new place. Smaller town. More coal. More oil. More small and dying farms. Fewer Italian last names. Forty-odd years on from that move—followed by many more—and I still don't quite know how to answer "Where are you from?" But now, I also struggle with the questions raised by Ellison. Where am I? Who am I? Are the answers to both questions the same? And why does it matter?

Today, I live with my husband, kids, various animals, and the recent addition of my mother on a 62-acre historic farm in central Maryland. We have approximately 35 acres in ongoing crop production managed by my husband and another 25 plus acres of woods and wetland that we are slowly trying to rehabilitate. Slow means glacial in our case, as land stewardship usually takes a backseat to paying work. My husband is proud to claim his title of gentleman farmer, in the time-honored tradition of men like Thomas Jefferson. He is fascinated by gardening ideas and the impact of different farming methods on our small acreage.

Yet when he tells people we live on a farm, I am always quick to jump in to say that we live on a farm, but we are *not* farmers. Where are we? Who are we? Why does it matter?

Even our house has a bit of an identity crisis. I love our house. It is over two hundred years old, a box of a federal-meets-Georgian-meets farmhouse brick house with a fascinating hodgepodge of moldings and trims unique to homes built on the edge of civilization. It was a large, well-built home for the time and place. Clearly, the family was wealthy. Yet, despite a few touches of elegance in the woodwork, the house isn't fancy. Neither rustic farmhouse nor fancy manor, it is simply a large brick family home from 1820. How does one style such a place? It's not a formal or elegant building. But it certainly isn't farmhouse chic either. It's somewhere, again, in between.

We've lived in this house for over five years, and I am slowly (there's that word again) making it my own. Room by room, piece by piece. There are those who can decorate a home before they ever move in. They have a sense of style. They choose paint, curtains, sofas, and art based on a specific look. I need to live in a place first. I need to feel the rooms and the space and how I use them. And I want to be surrounded by my things. No minimalist am I. My entire family was away for a long weekend recently, and I took the opportunity to "move furniture" again. My mind was spinning with a thousand new ways to arrange our things to make the rooms both more functional and more beautiful. I want my eyes to rest on lovely things from every vantage point. I want to glance up from my laptop to see a painting done by a talented friend. Or the cylindrical vase of pinecones and fascinating feathers collected by my youngest son on our walks. Or the little bust of Socrates given to me for Christmas that holds pride of place on my secretary. Why do these things matter to me? Where am I? Who am I?

Writer's forums are filled with aspiring authors asking others, "How do you set up your space for writing? Show me pictures!" They aren't asking only for pragmatic solutions about desk size or comfortable ergonomic chairs. They are seeking models for making their own space beautiful and inspiring. Space matters. Why? I am sure many great words are written from a grey cubicle awash in a sea of fluorescent light. No doubt, many a writer works in such a space. Yet, if polled, I imagine a great number of them would say they take care of business items at that official desk, but their best writing occurs late at night in the comfort of their home or tucked away in a corner of their favorite coffee shop down the street.

Part of what turns a space into a Place is beauty. From medical offices to wedding venues, we instinctively relax in a place of beauty. We all have a need to rest our eyes on things that bring us comfort and rest. One of our favorite family picture books is *Miss Rumphius* by Barbara Cooney. If you don't know the story, a little girl named Alice is tasked by her grandfather with a final, most important life goal: to leave the world more beautiful. Space matters.

When I was in college, decorating your dorm room was an important rite of passage. We all lugged those few extra things from home that made our half (or third) of a shared room our own. My personal space looked like a Valentine's special edition of *Victoria* magazine. My roommates were a bit more traditional. But we all had our little things to make our space feel like home. Today, social media has taken that further than I imagined possible, with young women, in particular, building fancy headboards on their institutional beds, adding fluffy rugs and special light fixtures, vanities, armchairs, and even peel-and-stick wallpaper. It may feel a bit extreme or overdone, but the impulse at heart is the same one that led me to drag an antique porcelain table lamp from western Pennsylvania to Cambridge, Massachusetts, and my daughter after me to carefully package a lampshade I had made for her to transport across the Atlantic to her dorm room in London. We want our space to be beautiful. We want it to be ours, to reflect a little of who we are. Away from home for the first time, we ask, where am I? Who am I? That fluffy rug and framed poster help us to answer those questions.

Today, it's my books, art collected on my travels, tchotchkes gathered from all stages of my life. I have fewer lace doilies but no less affection for teacups, throw pillows, and cozy blankets than I did in that dorm room at MIT. These things help tell the story of me. And I strive to make my home a place of comfort and beauty. A place the stranger and friend alike can find rest for body and soul. The beauty is more than the belongings. It's also my wavy glass windowpanes that frame my fields and my trees and the constant play of light across the ridges that line the valley. I learned along the way that as much as I love the city, I can't be at rest without my trees.

Still, some days, I miss the liveliness and the sense of anonymous belonging to be found in the city. E.B. White wrote, "… Every block or two, in most residential sections of New York, is a little main street. A man starts for work in the morning and before he has gone two hundred yards he has completed half a dozen missions…"[8] The energy, the convenience, the *life* that can be found in those "little main streets" is thrilling. Yet even in the midst of the thrill and the rush and aliveness, I sought green spaces to rest my soul, to let my eyes revel in the beauty of flowers and trees and sky and the smell of earth and green, growing things. What finally drove our young family from the city wasn't the crime or the crowds or the noise, but the lack of green space. Where am I? Who am I? I answered those questions with a set of moves that eventually brought us to our farm in Pleasant Valley.

But it is not only me who seeks trees for rest. Our farm is approximately 30 miles from Camp David, less as the crow flies. Why is one of the most famous peacemaking places on earth here in the ridges and forests of Central Maryland? There are plenty of places that are private, secluded, and secure, close to Washington, D.C. Why here? Space matters. Catoctin Mountain Park is a beautiful place. Even driving through the park, one begins to calm. It's quiet there. A place of strong old trees, moss and lichen-covered rocks, tumbling creeks, and carpets of pine needles and oak leaves. It is a place for letting go of the concerns of the workaday world and to feel the solid ground beneath your feet. A place where every sense is fully engaged. It is a place of fresh ideas, possibility, and new beginnings, yet a place that is rooted deep in the ancient Appalachian Mountains. When we distance ourselves from nature—and from the beauty inspired by nature—we are restless, harsher, less empathetic, less creative. Finding or creating places of welcome and beauty is one of the three strands that form the rope that can haul us out of this chasm of discord.

Working alongside the peacemakers of the Middle East some two decades ago, I observed that the most impactful moments were those held in comfortable settings, with a host who served good coffee and good food, where "the Other" was welcomed as a guest. Camp David aside, government diplomacy often still needs to happen around a conference table in a bureaucratic office building, but the work of peacebuilding must happen around the dinner table or the coffee table, surrounded by beauty and nourished by nature. It is up to us to build (or demand they be built) those places where conversation is fueled by hospitality and not hostility.

Yet, the buildings themselves are still often plain, utilitarian, all right angles and harsh lighting. There is little "scope for the imagination," as L.M. Montgomery's Anne of Green Gables would say. Cultures that prize efficiency over beauty fail to thrive. The Soviet Union celebrated its proliferation of urban workers by developing concrete slab housing panels in the 1950s. For three decades, those ubiquitous concrete blocks represented Soviet design across the Communist world. Albania, a communist country long isolated from most of the world, had its fair share of bleak concrete cities. While Albania opened its doors to the world in the early 1990s, it struggled to form a cohesive government. The economy struggled to recover from decades of stagnation and corruption. Prime Minister Edi Rama, elected mayor of the capital city Tirana in 2000, was an artist as well as a politician, and he wanted to break the twin cycles of crime and despair in his city. What better solution for an artist than paint? Visiting Albania in 2005, I delighted in the brilliant, chaotic surge of color and pattern on all of those grey concrete slabs. And true to Rama's belief in the power of beauty, the rates of crime, including vandalism, dropped. Hope for future prosperity blossomed.

In my own high school, decades ago, we came back to school one fall to find that the classroom windows were covered with insulated wallboard. I'm sure the intentions were good—to lower heating and cooling costs associated with large, outdated, inefficient windows—but the visual and emotional impact was terrible. Already in an uninspiring and insipid institutional building, classes became less pleasant and more sleep-inducing with the lack of sunlight, green trees, and the occasional object of interest outside. When we expect creativity and delight in learning to happen, we should demand those spaces to be ones that inspire such things. All too often, they disappoint. I often wonder how I could have made a positive change in my school. Could we have offered to paint murals on those blank spaces? Could we have raised money for new energy-efficient windows? Kindergarten teachers use rugs and pillows and colorful posters to comfort and inspire our youngest learners. Can we take those lessons to our upper grades? Tenth graders may need to gather on a soft rug for reading time as much as five-year-olds. I know that my high school sons most enjoyed the times their classes were allowed to meet in the room with the piano, carpet, and sofas. I often take my students outside. Ask your children, your students. I can guarantee they have a thousand suggestions ready for how to make their learning environments beautiful and inspiring.

We've all heard things like "home is a person, not a place" and other sweet sayings that remind us that true contentment and joy come from relationships and not material objects. But that is not incompatible with our need for beautiful, restorative spaces. Laura Ingalls may have grown up in a series of log cabins and soddies on the Midwestern prairies, but over and over again in her books, she describes Ma Ingalls' attempts to make those rustic spaces into places of beauty and comfort. Home was Pa and Ma and the family, but home was also soft homespun blankets, colorful quilts, fresh flowers, an exquisitely carved wooden shelf, and a porcelain shepherdess. Each new cabin became home when Ma brought out their precious things to add color, beauty, and art.

We seek the same today—whether in a new suburban subdivision, an inner city rowhouse, or a hundred-year-old farmhouse. The popularity of design and home buying shows on HGTV is enough to make it clear even if the endless array of candles, throw pillows, and decorative baskets at Target or Walmart do not. Whenever we move into a new apartment or house, or even a tiny bedroom in a shared space, we immediately begin to decorate. Even college boys, mocked in movies and TV for decorating with beer bottles and posters of women, add their own touches—bedding in a favorite color, a special mug from home, or a cool lamp. We all want to put our own stamp on our space, make it feel *right* to us. And when we welcome people in, we want them to feel *at home*. Whether seeking to impress a date or a business associate, we want them to like our space and feel comfortable there, to feel like they know us a little bit better.

My parents bought their first house together when I was thirteen. The house was nearly a hundred years old, with shoddy, dated renovations over the years. Every room needed both cosmetic and structural updates. Our kitchen was the first project undertaken by my dad because we all needed a functional kitchen. He worked hard by himself to do more than the necessary work of updates and repairs to give my mom a pretty kitchen where she could happily host large family gatherings. A kitchen that not only met her needs but one in which she could take pride. He opened the attic space to make a vaulted ceiling with tongue and groove boards that he painstakingly stained and finished. We have photographs of high school me sitting on top of the temporarily relocated refrigerator, holding up one end of a board while doing my homework with the other hand. When he was finished, he had created a lovely space with a hexagon window high in the peak of the roof, glass-doored cabinets, and a handmade shelf for my mom to display her prettiest things. Many a holiday or celebration occurred there, the counters crowded with food, the table crowded with family or friends.

After the kitchen, I assumed he would move on to the bathroom or continue making the downstairs into the forever home they wanted. Instead, my dad began the renovations to my room. I was in high school then, graduating a year early, and he wanted to make sure I had the most beautiful, restful, perfect room of my dreams to enjoy those last years at home. Once again, he went far beyond mere practical upgrades and repairs. He handmade a fairytale casement window above my bed, stained a gorgeous cherry color with a dainty porcelain knob to open it. He cut a million pieces of wood by hand to make faux wainscoting and crown molding, built a bench with an old car seat for under my window, painstakingly measured and measured again to build shelves for my many books into the wall between the studs, framed by leftover tongue and groove boards from the kitchen. He let me choose the pricier ceiling tile because it was *prettier*, and he made sure the carpet was fluffy enough that I could sprawl on the floor to read. Uncovering an old iron floor grate, he sanded it, painted it gold, and found a way to connect the modern heating ductwork to the much larger antique grate. In the end, my room was a work of art, a pastel, rose, and lace-covered ode to my beloved *Victoria* magazine. I loved to have friends over to a room that was comfortable and cozy and so very particularly me. My dad understood the importance of space.

But then, of course he did. My father, until retirement, was a park ranger with the U.S. Army Corps of Engineers. He was tasked with overseeing the recreational and environmental stewardship aspects of a park, including both lake and creek, surrounding a 164-foot concrete flood control dam on a tributary of the Allegheny River. His job was to create and maintain outdoor spaces that people would want to visit, whether that be playgrounds, fishing spots, or hiking trails. My dad understood that people need outdoor places that are easy to get to and easy to access onsite. He knew the importance of access to nature and how low the barriers to access need to be for some people to fully enjoy it. For all that he was (and is) not a "people person," my dad knew what people needed, and he worked hard to create it. He still does.

Last year, my dad, a Vietnam-era veteran of the Air Force, worked with his local American Legion post to obtain the property for a veterans' memorial park in my hometown. He and the other vets spent countless hours in the sun one summer preparing the ground, laying stonework, and creating a lovely, welcoming space for people to come and remember those who served. Place is important.

Not only is the park a place for remembering and honoring, with flags and memorials, it is also a place of beauty for quiet reflection. It is a work in progress, and the plants will take a while to come into their full loveliness, but it is a small oasis of nature in the midst of town. Most memorials are such places.

Whether we are setting the table for a hurried dinner with our family of young children, preparing to welcome the neighbors for a holiday open house, or walking a trail in a local park with others from our town, we are establishing our place. We are creating space for communication, space for connection, space for reflection, contemplation, and vulnerability. When we lock ourselves, either metaphorically or physically, inside our houses and offices, we miss out on the needed connection with both our natural world and the various communities in which we exist. If we want to be part of changing our culture of division to one of community, we must be part of creating those places, personal and public, inside and out, that welcome "the Other" with genuine care, respect, vulnerability—and hope.

The Need for Stories

I don't remember a life without stories. My world was always full of words—whether loud family gatherings where everyone talked over each other, bedtime stories, or a young single mom or early widowed grandmother who talked to toddler me to fill a little of the silence around them. My earliest memories come more from the stories told to me than the events themselves. Do I *really* remember dancing around the living room being a queen with the gold ring from the metal lampshade on my head for a crown? Or is that a story told to me by an older cousin? Are my memories of my gigantic orange tabby cat Dusty Allen real, or do they come from the many stories shared by my mom through the years? Does it matter? Those stories kept the memories alive—and attached them to people and places from the past and the present. They gave me a sense of self and a sense of place and time. Because of their stories, I know I was a mouthy, precocious, and very independent toddler who liked to dance and sing and watch *Captain Kangaroo* and help Mama clean and boss around my teenage uncle when he lived with us. I was tiny and cute and "too smart for my own good." I know I was fussy and particular. My grandmother called me "Prudence" and "Granny Gert" because she said I was like a 75-year-old woman in a toddler body.

And I pass those stories on to my kids. My oldest son is a lot like me and my grandmother, and I have always told him that he, too, was like a little old lady in a little kid body. My mom and I have shared with my daughter all the funny stories about the wildly unexpected things I would say to people as a toddler because she, too, has a sassy, spunky, mouthy streak. When she told her father, at slightly under three years old, that she was negotiating with him, I just had to laugh. Then I shared how everyone always told my mother I was going to grow up to be a lawyer with the way I could argue. Then, when we tell that story about my daughter "negotiating" at three, we often share my stories as well, linking her to my family and my past. The stories help my daughter feel seen and understood and connected. We've told our middle son stories about me talking to elves and trees in the woods of the park where I grew up—while sharing our family stories about him talking to himself as he wandered the yard in costume, making up stories and living them in his head. Stories help us see who we are and from where we come—and from whom we come. They root us, give us identity, and ground us in a past that allows us to grow into the future.

Some of my favorite memories as a child and young adult are from family gatherings: family reunion picnics, holidays, birthdays. My mom's family was loud. Nearly all of them were happy to speak at any time, no matter who else might already be talking. They bickered and blamed and bullied but also laughed and loved hard. I was part of a tangle of second and third and x-removed sort of cousins on my mother's mother's side of the family. As far as I was concerned, we were all just cousins of some sort; I didn't bother much with the details. My mom and her mom, however, knew how everyone was related and could sit for hours detailing each family history (and scandal!) while I listened in fascination and tried to keep the threads untangled.

But they didn't just clarify relationships; they spent hours rehashing family lore. Some of the stories were simply informative—the who, what, where of family history. Some were funny, like my grandmother's stories about going to work in Atlantic City with her big sister after graduation in 1945. Some were tragic, such as the death of her baby brother Richard when he was only four from stepping on a rusty nail. Even sixty years later, my grandmother would get quiet and sad after mentioning Richard. I never learned much about him, but I learned empathy from seeing my usually gregarious grandmother so sorrowful. I learned that little kids die in real life, not just in sad stories.

My grandmother passed away suddenly two weeks after my wedding, and I often find myself unexpectedly missing her in some new way. I wish my children had been able to hear her stories. To hear them all talk together, telling stories—my grandmother, my mom, and my aunt, her sister, who passed away when my youngest was a baby. I try to tell their stories myself, as best I can. My mother moved in with us last summer, and I try to talk to her like they used to, letting my children hear the jumbled, tangled tales of kith and kin. To connect them to that history—*their* history.

Stories matter. We all have them. Our personal history, like that tangled tale of our national history, has shaped and formed us in ways we probably can't fully grasp. A 2010 study at Emory University concluded that "Children understand who they are in the world not only through their individual experience, but through the filters of family stories that provide a sense of identity through historical time."[12] I know for myself that there is always a bit of a pang of emptiness when I consider my paternal history. My biological father left when I was two, and when I was six, he signed and mailed back the papers allowing my stepfather to adopt me without even appearing in court. My mother, wise woman that she is, kept his family stories alive as best she could. She tried to keep the actual relationships alive as well, but failing that, she told me stories. I don't know my "bio-dad's" family, but I know stories of my great-aunt Bonnie, who was a professional wrestler. I know my Uncle Charlie doted on me, and my grand-mother was very young when she married my grandfather in West Virginia. I know I look a lot like my Aunt Jane—but also that I didn't like her when I was a baby. I know my grandfather hated being mistaken for Italian and always insisted he was Irish (partly right). All of this helps me create a richer sense of self.

I love my Dad, my adopted father. I was always told I looked more like him than I do my mom, and I copied many of his mannerisms. We link my children to him as we tell our oldest son that not only does he look like his Papa Mike, but he acts just like him, too. We share as many stories of my father's childhood that I was able to pull from him. But my father, too, was adopted by his stepfather and never knew his biological father's family, nor much of his mother's family. His adopted father's family was a large, boisterous, Italian-American family that overwhelmed my quieter, introverted father, and he never felt that he quite fit in. I feel the lack of rootedness there, as though I am a tiny bit lopsided. The Emory study, along with their Family Narratives Lab, is a powerful reminder that our stories matter—that the passing down of our stories matters.

Our children need to know who they are. They need to un-derstand their place in the web of humanity. At first, it's just that connection to their immediate family around the dinner table, sharing stories about what everyone did that day, remem-ber-whens about how the youngest couldn't say "yellow" until he was nearly twelve, and mom telling everyone how the oldest child thought her younger brother was a special gift for her because she got to dress him up like a doll—but she had to stop teasing him when he ended up half a foot taller than her by the ninth grade. Those stories forge the bonds between family members that help adolescents weather the storms of growing up. They can better lean on their parents, being more emotionally tied to them, feeling understood. While we have long understood that anecdotally, science is beginning to catch up with studies like that at Emory, demonstrating that children who grow up hearing family stories around the dinner table become adolescents and young adults who are more resilient, more empathetic, and with a stronger and more positive sense of self.[13]

We can't sit around a dinner table swapping stories and remembrances with everyone. Even holiday gatherings, dinner parties, and receptions are limited in reach. Yet, those are the places where stories flourish and bind us in ways that allow for vulnerability and growth. Fueled by beauty, food, and drink, around a table or around a fire, stories weave a web of connection that fosters ever deeper and more meaningful discussions. In these moments, whether at a family reunion picnic on the farm or when I found myself at a banqueting table in a Bedouin tent restaurant near Bethlehem, we *see* "the Other," and we *hear* them through the medium of story. How do we learn from each other's stories and cultivate those connections in a far-flung world? In order for everyone to thrive, we must somehow learn to see, hear, and understand people who are distant from us in space, culture, and beliefs.

Our first step must be to cultivate a culture of stories at home. From the first bedtime stories, fairytales, and myths to dinner table conversations with our teens, spouses, and friends, we must share our stories. Good stories challenge us, awaken our imaginations, stoke wonder, and build a moral imagination that teaches the power of shared virtues and how to see past differences of presentation.

Fairytales and mythologies from cultures around the world tell similar tales of courage, loyalty, patience, temperance, justice, mercy, kindness, and love. Many people don't realize that Cinderella stories have arisen in nearly every time and place, from China to Persia to France to the Algonquin people of North America. The tales differ in details—in the agency of the protagonist and the identity of the prince—but all are tales of courage, kindness, and faithfulness. My daughter loved a French version and *The Persian Cinderella* by Shirley Climo, an adaptation from an Arabian Nights tale. That story led her to the rest of the *One Thousand and One Nights* and to dressing up as Scheherazade one Halloween. How does an American six-year-old learn to identify with the heroine of a thousand-year-old collection of tales from the Middle East? Through the power of fairytales and their shared foundation in the virtues in our very humanity. Stories are powerful.

And we all have one. The key is first to learn our own and then to learn to listen and understand the stories of others. Their stories formed the same as ours have—in the shared family stories around a dinner table or through the books they read or the conversations they had with friends and family. Or perhaps they have no early stories and are only now crafting the story of their life. Maybe our stories are ones with more tragedy than sunshine, more despair than hope. Maybe our stories formed from a lack of family connectedness. Perhaps our stories arose out of war or illness, abuse or poverty, shame, fear, or abandonment. But if we can find common ground through ideas like loyalty, patience, or courage, we can find a way to listen and weave our threads together. It is easier to do so when we speak a common dialect of imagination.

My first trip to the Middle East was as a policy advocate with World Vision. I went with very little background on the Israel-Palestine conflict. I knew the basic history, the basic geography, but I knew little of the people, their hopes and dreams, their fears, their worries, or their anger. I knew little of the complexity of their tangled roots in that small slice of land. But I did know Anne Frank, Corrie Ten Boom, and Dietrich Bonhoeffer. I knew the stories of Jesus walking the roads and fields in Galilee. I knew stories of Bedouins and their slow move into modernization. I had read Elias Chacour and wept with a young boy watching people die as they were forced to leave their homes. I also knew the sting of not belonging. Of being called a *damn dago* (a slur against Italian-Americans), of being asked if my family was in the mafia, if my mom was sleeping with her boss, and were they running drugs in those oil trucks? I knew the sorrow of leaving my hometown. How could I draw on that to help understand the people I was there to help?

I could have empathy for each group. I could feel sorrow for their pain and anger at the injustices against them. I could remember the stories of the Holocaust and the Nakba both. And I could understand the need for family and a desire to remain connected to their land, their place, and their roots—and a desire to find those connections that had been severed generations before. I was there merely to observe and to learn, so my visit was one of meetings in hotel conference rooms, our local office, a military checkpoint, a college, restaurants, and homes. I learned over Turkish coffee, hummus, and platters of roasted vegetables and meat. I learned while stories were shared. I could hold my own in those gatherings of loud fast-talkers. I was quiet, young, new to the work, but I was able to join in because of *my* story in my loud and overwhelming extended family. I knew the story-telling rhythms of such meal-time gatherings, and I knew that laughter is sometimes shared with pain or with anger and that sometimes the laughter shows forgiveness—but not always. Daniel Nayeri writes in his brilliant book *Everything Sad is Untrue* that "memories are always partly untrue."[14] These stories they shared were both true and untrue, as all stories are. Yet in their telling, the storytellers became human, known, impossible to hate, and worthy of peace.

That first trip to Jerusalem illustrated vividly the invaluable lesson that "[s]tories are memory aides, instruction manuals, and moral compasses."[15] Everyone had a story they were eager to tell. Stories of displacement or sorrow or hate or fear, as well as stories of triumph, courage, loyalty, determination, and great love. I was shown keys worn to help remember a home left in a hurry with the unfulfilled promise of return. I was told stories of how the world once overlooked atrocities that could never happen again. And I was introduced to women writing new stories of standing firm against injustice, no matter which side of a wall they were on. Stories are powerful, and they allow us to see beyond headlines, soundbites, and our own fears and prejudices.

Nayeri writes that the point of the stories in *Arabian Nights* is that:

> ...if you spend time with each other—if we really listen in the parlors of our minds and look at each other as we were meant to be seen—then we would fall in love. We would marvel at how beautifully we were made. We would never think to be villain kings, and we would never kill each other. Just the opposite. The stories aren't the thing. The thing is the story of the story. The spending of the time. The falling in love.[16]

Stories allow us to spend the time getting to know one

another as fellow creatures made in the image of our Creator, all valuable, all worth our care. Scheherazade, the storyteller of Arabian Nights, didn't tell stories to entertain the king, Nayeri explains. Rather, she told him stories to "make him love life." He learned to feel again, to be human again, to love others again through her stories. I may not have agreed with every storyteller in Jerusalem, felt their cause was the most just, or their actions particularly justifiable, but I could hear them, feel with them, and love them, just like my crazy family around the Christmas table.

I see this empathy missing in the noise of today. Children's reading education focuses on comprehension, not wonder. We are encouraged to tell *our* stories but less encouraged to *listen* to the stories of others. Everyone has a story, but how do we hear them when it's the fourth TikTok we've mindlessly scrolled past while waiting in line at the coffee shop? Do content creators feel heard? Seen? Do those endless reels of soundbites help us fall in love with each other? Are we still listening to family stories around the holiday table when crazy Uncle Bob is no longer invited because "all he does is rant about conspiracy theories, and we don't have to listen to hate?" Are we still able to listen when our family stories include the ones about Great-Great-Great-Aunt Eliza, who was a "gypsy" fortune teller with the circus? (True story, by the way, and yes, I tell the tale as I've always heard it with a smile.) Fearing to offend, we stifle ourselves, muffling our family stories, staying in the safe lane.

But telling my kids about Great-Great-Great-Aunt Eliza is important. It's a funny, silly story at first glance. I used to love imagining some long-dead aunt dressed in bright, flowing skirts and scarves, traipsing around the country with the circus. I could picture the family's horror when she came for dinner and regaled them with her tales of circus life. I could imagine it because I heard it and saw it. I heard my Great-Aunt Ida sigh and try to find a way to explain away her Great-Aunt's eccentricities. I also heard, quite plainly, that despite her somewhat scandalous lifestyle, Great-Great-Great-Aunt Eliza *came to dinner anyway*. I also learned that sometimes things aren't as they seem. In describing their aunt, decades later, my family wondered if perhaps she had an illness, perhaps even a form of epilepsy. Perhaps, the family of the 1980s and 90s wondered, she suffered a form of seizures that weren't identified and understood. Perhaps she chose the path she did because she wasn't accepted anywhere else. In hearing those stories over and over again, I absorbed invaluable lessons about my family, about loving others, about acceptance, about compassion, about understanding, about being wrong.

I don't actually know much at all about my Great-Great-Great-Aunt Eliza, who died long before I was born. It's entirely possible that none of the stories I heard about her are true. That's the funny thing about stories: The specific truth gets bent and stretched and rearranged until it reveals some greater truth about the world at large. I don't know if Great-Great-Great-Aunt Eliza was a "gypsy" fortune teller with the circus. But how much richer is my understanding of my family and of people for the stories that were told!

Stories, particularly myths, fairytales, and family lore, encourage critical thinking in children. Most of these stories are intricate narratives that require children to question their ideas, make new connections, and think deeply about the characters and events described. Not only do they learn empathy and virtue, but also how to look beyond their own daily life and cultural understanding and to use their imaginations to problem solve outside their own experience. Stories are the way we learn to make sense of the world around us, to put our feelings and experiences into a larger contextual framework of our families, our communities, and our world at large. It's how we are created as human beings. As Professor Gregory Cajete of the University of New Mexico writes, "[W]e make stories, tell stories, and live stories because it is such an integral part of the way of being human."[17] We are created to be storytellers, as much we are created to be part of the story. When we forget that, we lose not only a connection to our deepest selves but also our ability to connect most deeply with others.

We forge those connections out of shared stories, myths, and virtues that teach us to empathize with those unlike ourselves, to think deeply and critically about who we are, and to solve problems creatively together. It begins with parents marveling over their new infant, exclaiming that they have their grandmother's eyes or their uncle's nose. They tell their baby and each other stories about the world and their own childhood. Haven't we all heard some variation, spoken to an infant barely able to hold up their head, of "Look at the pretty flowers! Your mama's favorite flower is violets. Let's pick Mama some violets!" Or maybe, "This is perfect soccer weather. I can't wait to teach you to play. Look at those legs kick! When I was little, I had a black and yellow uniform, and we looked like little bumblebees on the field. You are going to be the best soccer player just like Daddy!" Those are stories, connections we make with our littlest people. Later, those stories turn to nursery rhymes and songs such as "The Itsy-bitsy Spider." We help our little ones mold their fingers to climb the waterspout, and we shout with glee along with them as we all throw our hands in the air when "out comes the sun." It's a story. One that we share with our children, making eye contact, touching them, experiencing the excitement and wonder with them—and teaching them determination, perseverance, and hope. Big concepts for a nursery rhyme, but it's a story that even our toddlers can hear and understand.

And then, we move on to laughter and stories around the

dinner table. Stories about our day, family stories remembered from last year or last century. We share our broader family history, and we share our current stories, strengthening those family connections. When we laugh and remember and tease our oldest son about the year he only ate a roll with ketchup for his Thanksgiving dinner, we are also strengthening his sister's sense of protectiveness. We are letting the little brothers laugh at their big brother, feeling better about some of their own quirkiness. Importantly, we also remind them all in that story of times when we got together with extended family and their grandmother hosted a big traditional holiday meal. It is good for the older ones to remember and the younger ones to know that they have a wider web of family and a deeper level of traditions than appears to them now. It's a funny little story, but it connects the siblings to each other, their grandmother, and other family members.

Stories connect us to communities beyond the family. I grew up in rural western Pennsylvania in small towns that used to be coal, steel, or natural gas towns. Like the rest of true Appalachia and the Rust Belt, those little towns and cities have struggled to survive as industry changed and the coal was gone. My children have grown up in Washington, D.C., Northern Virginia, and now on a historic farm property in Maryland. They've seen wealth and privilege around them that far exceeds anything I experienced as a child. When they spend time with my family in that part of Pennsylvania, they see a world that is very different from the suburbs of the capital. When they jumped on the neighbor's trampoline with the kids next door or went to the county fair, they got to see and know kids growing up very differently than their neighbors back home. To a seven-year-old, someone with a trampoline is RICH. And a big yard! And dogs! They loved going to Pennsylvania and said it felt like summer camp! Now that they are older, when we tell stories of those summer adventures, they understand more about the struggles of that community. They recognize some of the cultural gaps they didn't grasp back then. And they see past those to the friends they made and the fun they had. It's not urban vs. rural to them. It's not Trump vs. Harris or rich vs. poor or college-educated vs. high school. It's a real place with real people who are intimately linked to their happy memories of their Nonna's house. Every single story we tell of those summers reinforces that connection to a place that their friends in the D.C. Metro may understand only from the news. Those stories matter.

All of my children are growing up to be storytellers. Correction—they are growing up *aware* of themselves as storytellers, for we are ALL storytellers if we remember we are. A couple of them write stories. One of my sons is an observer, commenting on the stories he notices of those he encounters. He then weaves those into stories about the things he creates. My oldest son would probably refute any role as a storyteller, but he is the family memory. He, most of all my children, hates children's books that teach. He wants the story. He wants to feel the emotions and figure out what is important. He hates books that tell him what to think and how to feel. Storytellers are important. They are our cultural memory and our creators. We must grow the next generation of storytellers. Tell them stories, listen to their stories. Encourage your children to tell stories by telling your own.

Stories define us, shape us, and help us understand the people and world around us. When we grow up surrounded by stories, good stories, we learn to listen. We listen for the intent of the story, the meaning, and purpose. We learn about the storyteller as we listen. We empathize. We hear. And we connect. Stories matter.

The Need for Critical Thinking

"I found that I was fitted for nothing so well as for the study of Truth... with a desire to seek, patience to doubt, fondness to meditate, slowness to assert, readiness to consider, carefulness to dispose and set in order... being a man that neither affects what is new nor admires what is old, and that hates every kind of imposture."
— SIR FRANCIS BACON[18]

"Critical Thinking: [T]he process of analysing information in order to make a logical decision about the extent to which you believe something to be true or false."
— *The Oxford Learner's Dictionary*[19]

I have long had a homemade sign hanging somewhere in my house that reminds us to "THINK" before we speak: Is it True, is it Helpful, is it Inspiring (encouraging), is it Necessary, and is it Kind? The sign has been as much for me as for my children. My pride in my bluntness takes a hit when I wield my words unthinkingly. Do I, as the parent, peacebuilder, and voice of logic in the home, always THINK before I speak? When I engage my mind before my mouth, I can be blunt with effectiveness and grace. The little anagram is always a helpful visual, but if you look deeper, it reflects a need for critical thinking. Place matters, and through beauty, warmth, and vulnerability, we set the stage for community. Through stories, we fashion connections to others, building the bridges of relationship with empathy and wonder. We begin to truly see them through the perspective shaping of restoration glass, bending the light towards grace and understanding. What then? What final strand do we need to weave a rope strong enough to be a lifeline in a storm of unhealthy conflict? We must learn to be thoughtful questioners of fact and belief, starting with ourselves.

Critical thinking was once a term of art that described a very particular way of absorbing and processing information. Today, however, the meaning of critical thinking is watered-down and does more to confuse than illuminate. John Dewey may be credited with the term *critical thinking* from his 1910 book *How We Think,* but the concept existed long before the American progressive education movement and the resurgence of the term beginning in the 1980s. Socrates, Plato, and Aristotle valued critical thinking, defining it as the ability to ask questions and to test the answers against their own thoughts, beliefs, and values. They were followed by Thomas Aquinas, Erasmus, Sir Francis Bacon, Descartes, and even Machiavelli. All of these thinkers and philosophers emphasized the importance of questioning deeply held beliefs, scrutinizing new information, and then testing new information and insights against those beliefs. This classical understanding of critical thinking is more or less synonymous with our modern scientific method that constantly subjects theories to new data.

Unfortunately, despite the plethora of articles, books, and classes on the topic of critical thinking, we are more and more removed from a solid understanding of critical thinking and even further removed culturally from the ready practice of it. In 2022, the U.S. Department of Education's National Assessment of Educational Progress (NAEP) found that by eighth grade, less than 40% of teachers were emphasizing the teaching of critical thinking skills.[20] Why do we fail our students just at the age when their brains begin to develop a greater capacity for logical reasoning and crave debate? This begs the question: Does the Department of Education or our teachers have a clear understanding of critical thinking themselves?

Critical thinking isn't a skill set to be learned. Rather, it is a *way of thinking* and knowing when and how to use that thinking. It is the ability to not only pull information from multiple sources and analyze it but it is also the ability to recognize the need to do so and access the right sources. It is knowing which beliefs of our own relate to the new information in front of us and knowing how to compare these beliefs, what questions to ask of each source. Even a Carnegie Mellon University website aimed at helping teachers teach critical thinking feels the need to tell teachers to "define critical thinking for your context."[21] But critical thinking is not context dependent. Critical thinking is a way of approaching information—any information. The website itself has good suggestions for helping students understand teacher requirements or how to use critical thinking in different types of situations, but to start off by suggesting that critical thinking itself can be *defined* differently depending on contexts is misleading at best and completely false at worst. If even a top-tier college such as CMU fails to adequately describe the nature of critical thinking, how can we ask teachers to do so? Or journalists or politicians, for that matter?

Critical thinking goes beyond mere thinking on a topic to an intentional use of logical inquiry and reasoning, the examination of beliefs and biases that may impact ideas, and a studied appraisal of arguments and conclusions. We start our critical thinking process by questioning *our own* beliefs and biases. We explore our knowledge and understanding and seek to gather more information for further clarity. Working from our experiences and knowledge, we attempt to draw logical conclusions that align with other things we know about the world around us. When we encounter information that is inconsistent with what we already know or believe to be true, we can test both the new information as well as our own understanding. That particular process will look different when part of a scientific inquiry versus one's response to daily news sources, but the defining process is the same.

Being a parent is a daily exercise in critical thinking. We start out anticipating the birth of our first child with, usually, some mix of fear, excitement, anxiety, and hope. Picture your local bookstore and the shelves upon shelves of parenting books covering everything from birth to adulthood. Whether you are one who reads those books or not, we tend to enter into parenthood with a certain set of beliefs about how it will go, how we will parent. And then our child is born. Maybe you won the sleep lottery and were blessed with a firstborn who happily settled into a sleep pattern within a couple of weeks. Regardless of your chosen sleep philosophy, you probably felt pretty good about that method. That was most assuredly not my experience. For many reasons, my firstborn seemed downright allergic to sleep. I was forced again and again to reevaluate my beliefs about infant sleep. I researched, I prayed, and I cried a lot. Well-meaning friends offered loads of advice from their own "tried and true" sleep methods. Clearly, they thought I was "doing it wrong." Or was I? My second child loved to sleep. We pretty quickly settled into a nap and bedtime routine that suited him. Had the birth order been reversed, what would I have done? I saw that play out with friends. A firstborn child slept easily through the night as the parents implemented their chosen sleep method. The second child did not. In some cases, the parents reevaluated. They turned back to research, studied their children, adapted their understanding. A few parents dug in. Their method, they determined, was fine. After all, it worked on their first child. In this case, they decided the second child was the problem, not the method. I watched them struggle for months (or years) to get their child to sleep, with many tears from both parents and child, much frustration, and growing resentment. How might things have been different if these parents had been able to consider the sleep challenges critically—to examine their belief in the rightness of one method and, looking at the inconsistent results and what they knew of their two children, to research different solutions?

We all have a knowledge base formed from things we have been explicitly taught, whether in school, at home, at work, or a play, as well as from those things we've learned by observation and experience along the way. From the knowledge base, marinating in the values of our culture—familial, community, ethnic, religious—we develop a set of beliefs about the world. When we encounter new information, we have a choice: Do we accept the new information as true and add it to our pool of knowledge, or do we dismiss it as false or irrelevant? The easiest course is to check it against what we already know and believe. If it matches, we keep it. If it is inconsistent with our prior conclusions, we are free to disregard it. Right? Shouldn't we simply discard that which doesn't align with our existing understanding? Of course not! Rather, when we encounter new information, we must test it against what we already know, and when we find an inconsistency, question again what is causing that inconsistency. Is it that our own beliefs need to change to account for new facts? Perhaps. Critical thinking requires the flexibility to absorb new knowledge and to change our beliefs if new information requires it.

In a world of a 24/7 news cycle, the haranguing of talk show hosts, and omnipresent social media, it is easy to find oneself clinging to a set of beliefs—or facts—that are known to us. It is all too easy to find confirmation of our beliefs in reputable—and not so reputable—sources. Confirmation bias grows and further solidifies our beliefs into absolute fact. It becomes easier and easier to dismiss that information which doesn't align with what we already know because we can so readily find sources that support us with arguments all neatly made for us. Why should we trust this new information when it is so clearly false? How do we push through the noise, the bombardment of "facts" to find what is good and right and true? What incentive do we have to do so? Journalism schools used to teach the importance of not just "getting the facts right" but getting the right facts that give readers a more honest portrait of reality, always open to examination and review.

One relatively straightforward method for pushing through the noise is the SIFT[22] method. As developed, it is not a bad approach to quickly analyzing information that passes across your screen. A 2021 article in the New York Times by Charlie Warzel[23], however, does not itself stand up to the test the article purports to describe. It's "designed for casual consumers," Warzal writes, "not experts or those doing deeper research." He suggests using Google to help you understand what you are examining and that the first results are usually good, that you might see a pattern in those first links, a consensus. That, he tells you, is when you should stop. If you already believe in the common consensus, you are now merely confirming your own bias. If Galileo had accepted the consensus opinion that the sun revolved around the Earth, how much time would have passed before someone else came along to challenge it? Warzal's arrogance assumes that the average media consumer is unable to adequately assess the validity and value of a source without resorting to the top five Google results to find "consensus," but journalists doing "deeper research" are able to do so. The venerable *New York Times* apparently endorses this belief that its readers are incapable of critical thinking. I insist that we all must be capable of doing so if we want to be truly thoughtful in our understanding.

It is easy to collect a custom set of sources on which we depend for information. It is natural to return again and again to those sources that have been trustworthy in the past. With so much information flooding our senses—news channels, podcasts, social media—we crave some measure of order, a way to make sense of the deluge. I have worked purposefully to curate a diverse set of news sites that I can browse every day. I want to feel that I am being wise in my media consumption, avoiding confirmation bias, and reading opposing viewpoints. Over time, however, as life has gotten busy and the news seems ever more dire, more catastrophic, depressing, and angry, I have realized I am dipping into some sites far less often than others. And the most disheartening part of that was the realization that *the more I did that, the more lopsided, angry, and disillusioned I have become.* I have relied more and more on news that confirms what I already think I know. My husband's job requires him to be more deliberate in his news consumption, and he is known as a trusted source of relatively rational and level-headed analysis. When I start sending him news clips that increasingly confirm one perspective or another, he eventually challenges my bias.

I'm lucky to have a partner who acts as a check on my biases (and I on his), but how do we police ourselves? The frustrating reality is no one is immune from this comfortable bias. We see reports about how search engines manipulate our findings, and we hear about *algorithms* and optimization, but somehow, we feel that we aren't the ones affected. And the ever-helpful internet happily confirms for us it's the *other side* that is falling for such misinformation. *We* are the careful ones, the thoughtful ones, the ones justly searching for unbiased sources. Only, it's not Them; it's Us. We are the ones circling the wagons, chasing our tails, and patting ourselves on the back about our ability to "cut through the noise" to know the Truth. While I do think we can and should do better, I know it isn't that simple. If I did not have other opinionated news consumers in my family who like to challenge me, would I manage it on my own?

It's insidious. And it's normal. Even back in those pre-CNN and cable news days, and way before the internet, we had our favorite newscasters and our favorite evening news channel. We liked the familiarity. It's comforting to have the same face or the same voice entering our homes each day to report the news, especially when the news is hard to hear. Everyone had a favorite newspaper. Sure, the most enlightened might read both the *Washington Post* and the *Washington Times*, but you still had a favorite. Or maybe you read the *Wall Street Journal* and stayed above the sordid fray of party politics—or so you thought. We want the familiar. We like routine. We like the expected. There is nothing wrong with that. People have been arguing the point of view of their personal news source since the printing press began churning out daily broadsheets.

What we must guard against today is getting mired in the quicksand of one perspective so thoroughly that we can no longer even hold a rational—and thoughtful—discussion with someone who disagrees with us. To do that, we must be increasingly wary consumers of all types of media. Francis Bacon wrote at length about our very human tendencies to fall prey to this quicksand.[24] He described these pitfalls as *idols*, transient images of things, rather than the things—or thoughts—themselves. Bacon's idols of tribe, our predilection to over-generalization and reliance on our senses, and the idols of the den, our tendency to latch onto our own ideas and perceptions as true and right, are compounded today by the ease with which we can find information to bolster our own beliefs. Bacon's idols of the marketplace are then reflected in our consumption of public media. According to Bacon, not only do we use words to communicate logic and reason, but the meaning of that communication is filtered through a lens made of our own understanding. We cannot escape our own prior beliefs as we absorb new information. Oliver Wendell Holmes, Jr. wrote in *Path of the Law*, "Behind the logical form… often an inarticulate and unconscious judgment…the very root and nerve of the whole proceeding."[25]

While it is true that information is distorted as we process, it is also true that being aware of that distortion allows us to overcome it. How? Through conscious, deliberate questioning and testing of our beliefs. This is called Socratic questioning; it isn't to be aimed at our opposition but at ourselves. We examine ourselves, probing and testing our inconsistencies, which result from those innate distortions. When we come to the table, we bring with us our stated beliefs and assumptions, as well as our unstated assumptions and thought distortions. When we are willing to lay those on the table honestly, forthrightly, we can begin to communicate clearly and overcome idols of the marketplace.

It is hard to be honest about our most deeply held beliefs, those things that might be most dear to us, part of our very identity. We might worry about how we'll be heard, what people will think of us. I have had to learn to approach difficult conversations carefully, knowing certain assumptions I hold close might impact my ability to see clearly. Growing up as newcomers to a small town, I remain deeply suspicious of the motives and true friendliness of small-town folks. Is that fair? Of course not. I know this. I recognize a bias I don't always realize I am experiencing. Is there some truth to my assumptions? Yes. Just enough to let me hold onto that distrust honestly. The problem is that assumption, that belief, hangs out in the background in all sorts of situations where it might cause me to think less clearly, creating an internal inconsistency in my beliefs. It's a distortion I can't overcome until I bring it out into the open and wrestle with it. Sometimes, I can do that on my own, but sometimes, it probably needs to be on the table for everyone to see. That is deeply uncomfortable. It lays bare insecurities that go back to elementary school, hardened into permanence by high school. It sends up a notice to everyone at the table that I felt like an outsider, that maybe I *was* an outsider. No one wants that label or wants to broadcast their insecurities and weaknesses. We've been trained to hide our weaknesses, particularly in conflict. So why would I make myself an easy target? Because by admitting my underlying assumptions, we can address them head-on.

Importantly, acknowledging my beliefs gives me credibility and an opportunity to build connections with people I instinctively distrust *and* with people from other backgrounds. I become a trustworthy bridge when I share the basis for my conclusions, good and bad. I allow those whose sincerity I struggle to accept to show me who they really are, and I allow those coming from the true "outside" a safe place to share their concerns. I can't do that if I never allow the reasons for my seemingly inconsistent beliefs and reasoning to come to light. That honesty and vulnerability allows space for others to be heard. It gives others the opportunity to share similar thoughts and beliefs and to realize that maybe there is common ground. I know I risk offense when I reveal my hidden assumptions—and that risk is what often holds us back. I don't want to risk either the recoil from my revelation or the hurt to others, but if all sides are approaching a conflict with honesty and a mature commitment to reconciliation and keeping the personal from the debate, then I can find the courage to speak up. In return, I earn respect and, hopefully, vulnerability and openness back.

We also need to be wrong sometimes. We need to be told that we are wrong, that our thinking is distorted, that maybe we don't know as much as we thought we knew. I would rather know that I am incorrect or that my understanding is incomplete and work to better my understanding and knowledge, than to believe, falsely, that I am right and have all of the information that I need. Socrates called a state of confusion and impasse *aporia*: "without a way."[26] When we reach a point of knowing how much we do not understand, when we find ourselves confronting directly the confusion and uncertainty of a point of conflict, that is when we are ready to make the breakthrough needed for either a solution to a problem or reconciliation of a relationship. That is when our own egos and thought distortions are out of the way, and we have finally reached that space of really hearing and being heard.

Critical thinking is often mischaracterized as a focus on logic and reason to the exclusion of emotion, but our emotions underpin our reasoning. Whether we recognize them or not, our feelings influence our understanding of arguments for better or for worse. Our logic is informed by our emotions and our reactions, too. Our emotions arise from the beliefs that we bring to a situation. If I come to the table with an unacknowledged skepticism of the motives of someone from a small town, I also bring possible resentment, fear of rejection, sadness, loneliness, and maybe even guilt over my reactions. I "hear" their perspective through that distorted lens, and I make my own arguments from that quicksand of negative emotion. My emotions may have been born of legitimate grievance, but my failure to bring them to the table prevents anyone from addressing them. My feelings are not wrong—but the consequences of harboring them unexamined lead to the prevention of true and lasting resolution and reconciliation.

Emotions are not signs of weakness, and they have a necessary role in resolving conflict. Our feelings inform us and guide us as much as they can obscure and distort. In *The Irrational Season*, Madeleine L'Engle wrote, "I pray for courage to mourn so that I may be strengthened."[27] Grief, mourning—those emotions can shape our thoughts and cloud our judgment, but acknowledging them is also a way to give strength to our arguments, helping us to understand ourselves and others. It is when we refuse to heed our emotions or else give rein to them unchecked that we find ourselves mired in conflict we cannot control. It is then that our emotions may be spinning us beyond conflict into a state of *high conflict*, in which the conflict itself is in control.

The book *High Conflict* by Amanda Ripley explores the nature of high conflict and how we arrive there. Healthy conflict, she says, is defined by curiosity and questions and, as Socrates desired, leads somewhere. High conflict, in contrast, has only the conflict itself as the destination. The conflict creates a new reality in which it can flourish, and winning becomes the goal rather than understanding and truth. Winning, however, remains a mirage always just out of reach.[28] In true conflict, we seek solutions, we seek truth, we seek to understand and to be understood. Those things are not always found in agreement. When we allow conflict, we create the conditions in which we can question our way to deeper knowledge and real resolution. Conflict can be good and healthy—indeed, it might be absolutely necessary in order for us to move beyond the limits of our beliefs and biases, the idols of Francis Bacon.

When we sit in agreement, we can stagnate and draw around ourselves a wall made of our convictions and our beliefs, regardless of the thought distortions that may underlie them. We are free to move more deeply into the caves of our beliefs, decorating them with all manner of ideas and thoughts and facts, paying no heed to whether or not they fit together well or if they are careful and accurate representations of truth. We invite in others who admire the décor and add suggestions that seem pleasing in the light as it is filtered through the doorway. We become comfortable there and come to believe ourselves quite well-informed and cultured. We may even be proud to proclaim the wide variety of media we consume, showing how open-minded and wise we are. Yet, all the time, we are holding things up to the crooked mirror of our own minds, comparing them to the wonderful array of beliefs with which we have surrounded ourselves. Is it any wonder that we find it difficult to engage in good and healthy conflict with others?

We humans, for all our fierce independence, are communal creatures—herd animals, if you like. Whether or not we truly create a village around us as we go through life and raise our children, we certainly try to surround ourselves with the familiar and the comfortable. No longer tethered to our hometowns, we seek neighborhoods that represent the vision we have for our lives, the things we value. We look for the "right" schools for our children, we "shop" for a church that is a good fit. Businesses increasingly seek to hire people who share their "vibe." And social media gorges itself on our preferences, spitting back out at us recommendations for friends, pages we might like, and groups to join. The more we accept, the more data feeds the algorithms that churn out those recommendations, narrowing the parameters, helping us decorate our caves. It's so easy to follow their lead. Our lives are noisier than ever, and we crave order in the chaos. If Facebook will recommend a local group I might like to join, that simplifies my search. Out of seven potential mommy and me groups in a town, how could I ever choose? But Facebook has analyzed my friends, my posts, the news I consume, the recipes I peruse, and the books I read, coming up with just the right group to suggest. One click and I can read all about them—are they vegan or crunchy or traditional or progressive or all about music or technology or nature play? The suggested group most likely appeals to me because it's been carefully curated to match my tastes. And maybe I make an attempt to search out some of the others, but if this seems like a good fit, why bother? I can find my herd right there.

To some extent, that is absolutely wonderful. The toddlerhood of my oldest child was made much more smooth because I could check out the suggestions made in my searches. Playgroup? Mommy and Me dance? Music time? All right at my fingertips. But that was twenty years ago, and social media was in its infancy. As my children grew and my own online presence developed with them, I noticed more and more suggestions tailored to the interests I had already expressed. I joined the Facebook group for the local Little League organization when my oldest son was five. He's nearly done with high school now, and after years of him playing ball, my social media feeds are full of baseball memes, baseball camps, baseball mom paraphernalia, heartstring-tugging posts about mothers and sons. When we moved, and I tried to find other sports for him to try, I was frustrated at every turn as my social media accounts simply updated to show me baseball options in our state. On the plus side, they also started to overflow with suggestions for homeschool organizations in our new home. Social media made it all so easy. Insidiously so.

The Socratic method, as described by Plato, still remains an effective way to examine one's beliefs and do a little housecleaning now and then. We choose our neighborhoods, our churches, our gyms, parks, and social networks, and we choose them because we are comfortable in them. But that comfort lulls us into thinking we are using critical thinking when, too often, we most decidedly are not. If we want to be reconcilers and restorers, community builders and peacebuilders, we absolutely must do the work of challenging ourselves, being wise with our emotions, and intentionally seeking out "the Other" to better understand both them *and* ourselves. If we make this the norm, if we demand this of ourselves and our children and of the media we consume, we can turn this moment of cultural high conflict back to healthy conflict that solves problems and builds community.

PART ONE:

THE POWER
OF PLACE

CHAPTER 1
Hospitality All Around

"That boy's yo' comp'ny and if he wants to eat up that table cloth you let him, you hear?"
— HARPER LEE, *To Kill a Mockingbird*[29]

"True hospitality consists of giving the best of yourself to your guests."
— ELEANOR ROOSEVELT, *Book of Common Sense Etiquette*[30]

My first visit to Haiti was with a dear friend who was visiting his family for a wedding. I had only briefly met his mother at our college graduation and none of his vast extended family. It was my first trip out of the country and my first foray into a wildly different culture. I obviously spoke no Haitian Creole, and my high school French was just barely adequate to read a few roadside signs. I found myself ensconced in an echoing room on the second floor of his mother's home, behind a high wall and locked gate. I had my suitcase, a small bed, and a little bathroom next to my room. My friend gave me little advice on what to expect in the morning, only that he would see me then. He was not staying there. I awoke in the morning, hot and disoriented, with the sounds and smells of Port-au-Prince coming through the louvered windows. Should I get dressed? Go downstairs in the shorts and t-shirt in which I had slept? Should I shower first? But I wasn't sure how the shower worked or if water was available all day. Hesitantly, I decided to dress, brush my teeth, and make my way downstairs. I remember standing in the center of the room, working up the nerve to open the door, when I heard a soft knock. A little girl slipped shyly in, carrying a small tray. She was, I learned later, the daughter of my hostess's helper and friend. She spoke very little English, but she smiled brightly and handed me the tiniest of espresso cups and a little bun. Coffee, she told me, beaming.

I didn't drink coffee. At all. And I certainly didn't think I wanted *that*. It was thick and dark and strong. And, when I took a polite sip—because how could anyone refuse the invitation in those bright eyes—I discovered it was also very sweet. I must have said as much, for she nodded emphatically and said one of her few English words, "sugar!" Of course. Unfortunately, my palate did not yet have a taste for coffee in any form, and I was never going to be able to drink even that tiny cup. But what else could I do but thank her profusely, with a big smile of my own. She left then, confident I was enjoying my treat and would be downstairs with everyone soon enough. I spent nearly a week there, and several tiny cups of strong, sweet coffee went down the drain in my little white bathroom.

But, oh! I felt so very welcomed. The Cambridge Dictionary defines *hospitality* as "the act of being friendly and welcoming to guests and visitors."[31] Biblical hospitality goes further in admonishing us to treat guests and visitors as we would our family. Merriam-Webster defines *hospitable* as "given to cordial and generous reception of guests," "promising or suggesting generous and friendly welcome," "offering a pleasant or sustaining environment," and "readily receptive: OPEN." All of these encompass the nature of hospitality. To be hospitable is to open our spaces to others, strangers and friends alike, to do so with generosity, and to create a space that goes beyond mere sustenance to something that brings pleasure and sustains us.

It's been 25 years since I last traveled to Haiti, but I can still feel the heaviness that descended upon me each time I exited the plane. Visiting Port-au-Prince remains one of my favorite travel memories, but it is also one of my saddest. The violence, poverty, and "forgottenness" that hovers over the city leave it far from a typical tourist destination. Yet, the "generous and friendly welcome" I received there, not only from my friend's family and later from work colleagues but also from the people casually encountered on the street, still brings warmth to my soul so many years later. That is the nature of hospitality: to take a stranger and treat them with such welcome care that they feel the warmth of friendship linger long after the encounter.

The welcome offered by my friend's mother and her little helper eased my anxious heart on my first international adventure. While surrounded by the unfamiliar lilting melody of Haitian Creole, I felt comfortable and accepted. I, a naïve and nerdy white girl who grew up (mostly) an only child on the underside of the lower middle class in rural western Pennsylvania, who never did master her high school French, and knew virtually nothing of Haiti's rich and colorful past, was made to feel like I belonged and I mattered in the midst of a large, boisterous, chaotic, relatively wealthy Haitian family. That is the power and miracle of hospitality.

I held that lesson close to my heart as I moved out into the bigger world beyond college. What does it mean to show hospitality? Though I had encountered plenty of it over the years, that trip to Haiti created a desire in me to explore what it really is. Fresh out of college, I was then what my friends called a "baby Christian," someone whose faith was new and growing. Campus ministry, and to be honest, most of the adults in our lives, talked to us more than a bit about "spiritual gifts." We read Romans 12 and debated what our gifts might be. I was as sure then as now that I do not have a spiritual gift for teaching or for exhortation. I thought maybe my gift might wait for some grand reveal.

In the meantime, I pondered the rest of that chapter in Romans. I wholeheartedly embraced the idea of being individual members of one body, all with different functions—or, as I felt relieved to think, different quirks. I didn't have to fit into a mold to be a good Christian. I just had to be me. And surely, along the way, I'd figure out who that was and what I should be doing. But what touched me most deeply in Romans 12 were the verses following that list of gifts: "Let love *be* without hypocrisy. Abhor what is evil... *Be* kindly affectionate to one another... in honor giving preference to one another... distributing to the needs of the saints, given to hospitality." (Romans 12:9-13) It seemed to me that those spiritual gifts had to be used well—that they had a purpose and a process. And how was I supposed to do those things? I kept reading. "Bless those who persecute you... Rejoice with those who rejoice, and weep with those who weep... Therefore 'If your enemy is hungry, feed him; If he is thirsty, give him a drink...'" (Romans 14-21)

So, if I was going to be a Christian, someone following Christ and living what I said I believed, then, regardless of those mysterious gifts I didn't quite understand, I would need to show love. I needed to welcome everyone with affection and kindness, even my enemies. I should feel joy and pain alongside others, give where needed and, to make those grandmothers and great-aunts proud, feed people. I may not have always known what to say to people. I may have been a little shy and awkward. But man, I could feed people. I already did that!

For me, the seeds for hospitality were planted as a child, with family gatherings on the holidays and a great-grandmother who never failed to have chocolate chip cookies, Charlie Chip potato chips, and teaberry gum. And my mom took care of everyone. When my widowed grandmother moved out of state, my mom's younger brother, still a teenager, moved in with my single mom and me. A couple of years later, my mom and I moved in with her grandmother to help care for her after a stroke. It wasn't much of a debate—that's just what family did.

As a teenager, my friends were always welcome in our home. Sometimes to the point of irritation on my part. I had to get used to coming downstairs to unexpectedly find a friend for whom I'd been waiting, sitting at the kitchen table, having a snack, and chatting with my parents. My mother and her second husband, my adopted dad, took hospitality even further, adopting my brothers out of the foster care system at ages 16 and 10. When the older one was a senior in high school, his biological brother, then over 18, moved in as well. Later, a friend of my brother moved in temporarily when he needed a safe space to land. While I was away at college, my parents had a steady stream of foster kids for whom they provided respite care. My dad also acquired a tiny, chatty shadow in the form of a neighbor boy who followed at his introverted heels as he puttered about our property fixing and planting and building. He became so much a part of my family that his bewildered kindergarten teacher found that he added me, my dog, and my cat to his drawing of his family. In my parents' home, people came, were fed, were listened to, and made to feel that they mattered. Hospitality.

My parents gave generously of their time and resources to welcome anyone into our home. We weren't rich, but my parents created a comfortable space and were quick to offer a drink— water, coffee, tea—and any snacks we had on hand. My dad put aside his love of alone time when he allowed his young neighbor, Shawn Michael, to trail him around the yard, patiently answering question after question, asked with all the relentlessness a 4-year-old can muster. He could have sent him home, but instead, he let him tag along, always listening, always seeing the small person with him. My mom had an open-door policy for every friend, and they knew it and appreciated it. One friend who was often found at the table, chatting away with my mom about his day, had first found welcome with her as an anxious, hyper, mischievous 7-year-old that other parents avoided on field trips. My mom, however, made him feel special, loved, seen. He didn't have to curb his energy with her, his curiosity, or his enthusiasm. She welcomed all of him—and because of that, he was calmer and quicker to listen and obey. That sense of safety and comfort became a hallmark of hospitality for me.

I wanted to practice that hospitality myself. Sharing a dorm room with two other girls wasn't necessarily the place to begin, but I specifically applied for the dorm consisting of suites with shared kitchens and living spaces. I ate a lot of ramen and peanut butter in college on my very limited budget, but I always had baking supplies in my kitchen. My aunt had given me a set of pink stoneware dishes for graduation, and I had gotten a mixer, measuring cups and spoons, and baking pans, as well. I never failed to have my little hotpot boiling water for tea on cool New England nights, and I began to build my recipe box with treats I could share with my floormates. I wasn't always great with interpersonal relations, but I was a listening ear, a plate of cookies, and a safe place for anyone who needed a spot to land for a minute or two. I wanted to live up to the image of my great-grandmother—cookies and comfort for all, no matter when or who or why.

But I also needed that friendly, generous welcome, and I found it in an unexpected place. Not many people from my neck of the woods ever applied to (or necessarily heard of) MIT. (I was asked more than once by a puzzled acquaintance why I was going to "that trucking school," otherwise known as MTI.) A teacher in my school, however, had a son-in-law who had gone to MIT for grad school and still lived outside Boston. Her daughter and her family were visiting for the holidays, and she arranged for them to meet me at the high school so I could ask questions about MIT. I met Debbie and Chris and their toddler son, Nicky, and asked a few awkward questions in the school office. I wasn't sure what to ask or how helpful they could be, but I appreciated the thought. Debbie wouldn't leave without giving me a slip of paper with her address and phone number. "Just let us know when you get to Massachusetts. We'd love to see you." I dutifully took the information and entered it into my address book. A month or so after arriving on campus, I got around to mailing them a short note that I had arrived and was settled on campus. It didn't take long for Debbie to call—and to insist I come to visit. Over the next several years, they became my home away from home, more family than friends. I knew I always had a place of respite in their cozy home, a yummy meal, a soft bed with extra fluffy blankets, a funny little boy to play with and entertain me, and a couple of big, goofy dogs to cuddle. Sometimes, I think it was their generous hospitality and warmth that got me through college.

The meals and the weekends I spent with their family showed how little we need in order to show hospitality. I am sure they did nothing "extra" for my visits. From the first evening I walked into their kitchen, I was handed dishes and instructed to set the table. I cleared tables, learned how to make gravy and hot fudge, and found out how amazing a down comforter feels on a winter night. I learned it's okay to use the good dishes sometimes and that somehow it's easier to talk about hard subjects while eating dessert or with your arms buried in sudsy dishwater. But all Debbie did was welcome me into her home, a "pleasant and sustaining environment," and treat me as she treated her own family. She didn't cook a fancy dinner, decorate her table, or plan a special event. She simply offered welcome.

I've realized over the years that that is really the heart of hospitality: welcome. "Well come." It is well that you are here, that you have come, a desired guest. And I learned that absolutely anyone can be welcomed; anyone can be a desired guest. Hospitality shares the Latin root *hospe* (derived from *hostis* and *potis)* with host and hospital. In its original use, it could mean host or guest—or stranger. Over time, the meanings diverged and hospitable shares its root with hostile, suggesting that hospitality isn't about feeling hospitable but rather the action of extending a welcome. The definition and etymology do not suggest a guest that is known before, a guest that is family or close friend, or even one that is *liked.* The origins of the word do not require the guest to be of like mind to be desired. The heart of hospitality is to give to anyone the welcome of a desired guest (*with, of course, the caveat that one isn't welcoming someone intending actual harm!).* The Bible translates the Greek *philoxenia,* meaning *love* and *stranger,* as hospitality. To love the stranger—do we truly find ways to do that in our culture today? Or do we see our hospitality as something we extend to our friends and family alone? What would it look like to "love the stranger?"

That is where hospitality teeters between our visions of décor and food, laughter with friends and family, and our call to welcome the stranger. In 2018, an art exhibit at the Highlanes Gallery in Drogheda, Ireland, explored the tension inherent in the history of the word hospitality for host and stranger alike. Described in *The Irish Times,* the exhibit drew from French philosopher Jacques Derrida's work on hospitality and the ways in which we draw boundaries around our hospitality, protecting our identity, our homes, our *space.* The article draws the conclusion that "emotions are at the heart of the hospitality dilemma. They include not only the joy of welcome, but a keen sense of fear."[32] Whom do we welcome and how? Do we care for them, protect them? What is our role in the invitation? Or is an invitation even needed for true hospitality to thrive? We struggle with being vulnerable in front of those who might exploit our vulnerability. And that's okay. Hospitality doesn't ask us to abandon wisdom or to be incautious of either our reputations or our safety. Welcome is needed in our fractured culture today, but to do so, we must embrace not only the joy but also the fear.

I John 4:18 says that "perfect love casts out fear," but how does that apply to opening our homes—and our hearts—to others? That "perfect love" comes from surrendering our own will and desires to the desire and will of God and living boldly as we practice hospitality, the very act of loving. Our human hearts fear lots of things: rejection, isolation, mockery, anger. Beyond emotional wounds, we fear physical danger, the destruction of our homes or belongings, and injury or pain to our loved ones. We risk much when we open our doors to "the Other." We also risk change. We risk our beliefs and assumptions about ourselves and the world being challenged. It is easier to tell ourselves that it is okay to want to protect our home or our family. We are just being wise. Careful. Safe. But the God who called Peter to walk on the stormy waves doesn't call us to be *safe*. His open hand to Peter, His command to "come," is our example. We open our door to our family, our friend, our neighbor—a stranger—and we invite them to come.

I was the stranger the summer after my junior year of college when I warily accepted the invitation to room with Alissa, a sorority sister who was just becoming a friend. She wholeheartedly lived her commitment as a follower of Jesus to love others—even agnostic, sometimes antagonistic me. Living with my new friend was a daily exercise in the practice of hospitality, one in which I got to play the dual roles of host and guest. Everyone was welcome in our little apartment. We fed everyone who came to the door. Mothered, bossed, and chastised all indiscriminately. My friend could be brutally honest with everyone because she was unapologetically authentic and generously loved every person who walked through her door. Her vulnerability in opening her home to friend and stranger alike created space for challenging and provocative conversations and honest discussions of both personal struggles and world events. The summer I spent with her was healing, life-changing, full of growth, and some of the most fun I've ever had before or since. That kind of "readily receptive" welcome and "generous reception" of everyone, if practiced in every household, church, and community, would change the world. It certainly changed me and started me on my own journey of faith.

That sort of welcome was found in the church she introduced me to that summer. The members, mostly wealthy members of a Boston suburb, took in our ragtag group of students wholeheartedly. They drove to campus to pick us up, brought us home for meals, mentored us, encouraged us, and shared their lives with us. As a young adult who was exploring her future options, figuring out what "loving your neighbor" meant in real life in real time, and taking part in her first national election in the midst of the political turmoil of the early 90s, I felt free to discuss absolutely anything. I never felt that my views weren't welcome or valid. My perspective did not always align with the thoughts of this suburban church, and my interpretation of Scripture was often different. I argued human rights, freedom of speech, poverty and hunger, the education system, and the meaning of verses about divorce with impunity. My thoughts were welcomed. Perhaps they felt they could better guide me to agreement if they let me talk, but regardless of motive, they were always open and welcoming.

Living in the Boston area after graduation, my friends and I had a habit of somehow just "ending up" in the neighborhood of one church family around dinner time on an extraordinary number of Sunday evenings. Whether it was one of us or four, we were invited to stay and to eat. Plates were added to the table, our hands were put to work, and we laughed and teased and argued as if we were honored—and expected—guests rather than poor young singles hoping to score a free meal. There was always room for us, and we were always encouraged to join in. The welcome was abundant. The families in that church went out of their way to show us hospitality in all its richness despite vast gaps in our socio-economic status and differences in ethnicity, culture, or race. We babysat and mentored their children, drove their cars, house-sat for them, and learned much of how to engage and love people very different from ourselves. We were part of the family, and we loved it. Their ability to embrace us with a Christ-like love drove out fear—the fear of not enough time, not enough resources, not enough energy, not enough boundaries.

My church then wasn't perfect. Not everyone was open and welcoming all the time. I've often found myself disagreeing with some of the theology believed and taught. People made mistakes. But it was a place that overall practiced the "Christian behavior" of Romans 12. They loved (as best humans are able) without hypocrisy. They clung to the good and were "kindly affectionate," treating us with brotherly love. They did not place themselves above us, though we were poor students and recent graduates with little in the way of material goods to offer and little life wisdom to impart. They served the Lord by serving others and were certainly "given to hospitality." They had trials and troubles and were vulnerable in those, allowing us to help as we could and letting us see that no one is immune to hurt and everyone has something to offer. They showed humility in letting us minister to them in times of need and admitted to us when they learned from us. As much as the actual invitation to join them for dinner, their attitude of humility welcomed us in and showed true hospitality. We sometimes saw them as benefactors, graciously bestowing gifts on us out of their abundance, but we also got to see them as flawed, hurting, imperfect human beings who could be gifted by us, as well. Hospitality falters when one sees oneself as only the giver and the other as only receiver. Hospitality requires humility and grace to extend in both directions. And it can be found anywhere.

Pinterest and Instagram show us hospitality of the kind I found in that well-heeled New England suburb of stately homes and crisp table linens, but the vulnerability and openness of welcome can also be found in places like the slums of Manila, the sprawling capital of the Philippines. Before I started law school, I spent a summer serving with International Teams (known now as OneCollective), a Christian ministry that sent short-term teams to serve with longer term missionaries around the world. I spent most of a summer in Manila, my second international adventure. Our team was split into pairs, staying with different families that were part of the local ministry team. I was privileged to live with Pastor Neil and *Ate* Heidi and their two children for the summer. Pastor Neil lived in a nice home that was close to the palace. Because of that proximity, they had electricity nearly all day and running water for several hours. Yet their home backed up to the slum where Pastor Neil ministered. Our bedroom window opened into the alley, and to this day, I can smell the frying chicken feet below. I was far from rich growing up and had many years of hand-me-downs and free school lunches, but I also knew I was wealthy compared to others, even in my northern end of Appalachia—people without running water or without access to medical care or food security. But I had never seen poverty like I experienced that summer.

Pastor Neil and *Ate* Heidi welcomed us into their home and family with great love, but the hospitality that was truly humbling was bottles of orange pop purchased by slum children with precious coins their parents pressed into their hands so their guests could have something to drink. It was the unidentifiable meat in savory brown gravy with noodles that we knew they could hardly spare, and it was the rickety wooden crate offered for me to sit on while our hosts stood in their shanty made of sheets of tin and cardboard. What I was eating didn't matter. I knew that to refuse the offer of a meal would cause offense. These families welcomed me for no reason other than that they loved Pastor Neil and felt loved by him, and they wanted to honor the guests he brought to their homes. To refuse what they offered would suggest I didn't need it and didn't appreciate it. But I did need and appreciate it. Far from my own home, a stranger, I basked in their kindness and generosity. But also, I needed them to know they had worth, that I valued my time visiting them. They had little wealth or possessions, yet still they welcomed me in a way that offered a "pleasant and sustaining environment." I spoke nearly no Tagalog, and many of the families spoke hesitant English at best, but we laughed and sometimes cried as we shared stories and warm soda pop. Not just laughter and tears were shared, but real learning and insight as well. I learned much of strength and resilience, certainly, and the love of parents for their children. I learned that some people truly do learn, as Paul did in the Bible, "in whatever state I am, to be content." (Philippians 4:11) But I would dishonor the memory of those meals if I didn't also acknowledge the debt I owe to my hosts for teaching me much of politics, economics, history, and sociology. Imagine the difference in our world if the stranger was welcomed in and their wisdom freely shared and heard. This is one of the most important reasons for hospitality and one that has been lost as we have redefined it to focus more on luxurious bed linens and the perfect wine than on genuine reception and rest.

It's been over twenty-five years since I lay in bed praying for the families on the other side of the cinder block wall in the slum of San Miguel, charcoal and chicken feet filling my nose. I've traveled to twenty countries, eaten at tables of everyone from teachers and missionaries and office administrators to pastors, peace activists, members of Parliament, and revolutionaries. I've enjoyed countless kinds of food and learned to love Turkish coffee (and enjoy the debates over the best way to make it). I've argued with Christians, Muslims, and Jews over what non-violence looks like in the context of Israel-Palestine, and I've celebrated engagements, birthdays, and anniversaries with friends new and old. I've been a student, welcomed students into my home, and raised students of my own. I've experienced years where hospitality was easy and periods where hospitality has felt unattainable. Yet, it is always an aspiration.

How many of us wait to extend hospitality until our homes, or our lives, are "better?" We fuss and worry about our furniture, our ability to cook, or our inadequate space. Hospitality, however, doesn't depend on a magazine-worthy kitchen or Martha Stewart meal. When my children were young, I was part of a message board and online community of moms who were attempting to navigate parenting with grace and love. For a while, we celebrated the "Ministry of the Real" and would post pictures of very real and unfiltered "days in the life of." Sink full of dishes and screaming toddler on your leg? Yep. Storytime on the couch, tottering laundry pile simply pushed aside? You bet. We were separated by miles—and even oceans—but we welcomed each other into our lives. We wanted to grow in hospitality. If we couldn't even bear to show a picture of one piece of our messy homes and messy lives to our online friends, how could we welcome our real-life friends or, heaven forbid, a stranger? It was openness and vulnerability in a very raw way. If we hold back and only present an image of perfection that we don't actually achieve, we are not encouraging our guests to reveal themselves either. We aren't truly receptive.

Hosting others can be a position of power. We define the terms of the encounter—where it will be, how it will look, who is invited to partake, and how we will engage. It is hard—and frightening—to loose our hold on that power by revealing too much of ourselves and our weaknesses. How I agonized over which pictures to share! But, share them I did. And it grew me tremendously and allowed deep friendship to flourish both within that group and with others in my day-to-day life.

Hospitality requires openness. There is vulnerability in opening my space to others. From the first footstep in my yard, which is somehow never free of the detritus of boyhood and is often green by dint of ground ivy and clover rather than grass, to the glass in which I offer water—and, for that matter, the water I offer, whether bottled or filtered or tap—tells you something about me. Our identities are often bound to our space, from our homes to our nation-states. I know I am not alone in casting a critical eye over my porch when expecting guests. "Curb appeal," after all, is a significant part of the real estate market. Inside my home, my books and my art, my rugs, my hand soap, all speak to what I value and where I'm coming from. Whether I am hosting a friend and her children for an afternoon of play, my mother-in-law for a visit, or a reception for the Fairlight Forum, I must choose to reveal something of myself. Putting guests truly at ease requires more openness than merely inviting them inside the door. So how do we do that?

For casual situations, we probably choose to let people meet us where we are. While many friends have seen my home in varying states of disarray as my kids have grown, my closest of friends have seen sticky counters, a refrigerator that begs to be cleaned out, and a dining room table buried under days of homeschooling, art projects, mail, and unpaired mittens. They've been offered a drink, a snack, and conversation snuggled into sofa cushions. It takes little to open my home to these friends. Those closest to me are happy to have the freedom to just walk in and know that I am welcoming them.

Other times, I take the time to present my home and myself in slightly better form. We nearly always host a holiday open house of some kind and are blessed to welcome a wide circle of friends, neighbors, and acquaintances into our home. My goal for these parties is to make everyone feel like a *welcomed* and *honored* guest. We fill the dining room tables with food of different kinds for kids, adventurous palates, or traditional ones. We have several beverages and desserts, and we replenish them often. I like to host during the Christmas holidays because decorating is easy—we have a Christmas tree, garland, lights, and candles. The house smells yummy and looks beautiful. Beyond the food and the setting, I take time to introduce people to new friends they might not otherwise get to know. I think about what I know of them and try to introduce them with tidbits that give them a way to get to know one another more. I sometimes reach the end of the night and realize I have had hardly any time to really talk to anyone—but I look around the rooms and see myriad deep discussions among people who had never met before that day. I've given out phone numbers and passed on emails every year—not between potential business partners, but between new friends. No one leaves feeling like they mingled at a corporate meet and greet. They leave feeling comfortably seen and heard. My kids have grown up helping to host these events (some enjoy this more than others), and they all know how to ensure that everyone finds the food, drinks, and the bathrooms. (Oh, the bathrooms! They know to make sure they have toilet paper, clean towels, and soap. My daughter insists on room freshening spray and candles. It's the little things!) They've each grown to introduce their own friends to others and have had the fun of seeing their own new connections made.

Personally, I happen to love the preparations of hosting. I enjoy the process, but I try not to be beholden to the process. I have learned over the years to find foods that are easy for me to prepare, that I enjoy preparing, and that I know my guests will like. I (mostly) do not stress if something doesn't go as planned because I am not trying to impress my guests but to welcome them. If I forget to pull a tray of roasted potatoes from the oven until I get a whiff of scorched garlic, I have no reason to feel an occasion is ruined. It's just a pan of potatoes. The occasion isn't about the potatoes. It's about the people. If we become overwrought about a ruined dish, are we still focused on offering our guests a generous welcome? If our focus and our energy is on the food—or the napkins or the place settings or the décor—our focus and energy is really on ourselves and not our guests.

To offer hospitality, we must learn to hold in tension the desire to create a beautiful, relaxing, and welcoming setting, to offer delicious food and plentiful beverages, with the openhearted vulnerability that creates true hospitality. Guests do need a comfortable place to be. They do appreciate good smells, pleasing sights, and delicious food. It's not wrong to desire those things and to be concerned about them. We are created to enjoy beauty and delight our senses. Those things put us at ease and create the space for us to be vulnerable. But the specifics must never become more important than the guests themselves. Why do we open our homes to others? Why do we welcome in the friend or stranger? True, hospitality does suggest a "pleasant environment," but pleasant doesn't have to mean Pinterest or *House and*

Garden. I've forgotten the bread I intended to make for soup and provided crackers instead. I've realized belatedly that my drink offerings are water, milk, tea, or coffee—and when it comes to that, the milk may be iffy. I've offered up bowls of Halloween candy as dessert and dusted a summer's worth of leaves and debris from porch cushions when offering a seat. But I've done it with a smile (and sometimes a grimace) and shared freely what I've had. Where is my heart and my attention? If it's on the napkins, how can it be on my guest?

Most of us have spent the night away from home as either a guest of a public hotel or with friends or family. Our experiences often determine what we need to be satisfied with our stay. Did we find ourselves having to pull off the interstate at the first available exit due to a blizzard? We may be thankful for a warm room and clean bed. On an expensive honeymoon to the Caribbean we may be expecting more lush accommodations. Or perhaps we are visiting our grandparent in her assisted living apartment, and we are happy to fold our legs to fit on the lumpy couch in order to spend time with her. The specifics of the environment are not what create hospitality. Have you ever slept on a collapsing air mattress yet barely gave it a thought because you were so glad to spend time with your hosts and knew they gave of what they had? Or perhaps you have met the parents of a significant other for the first time and, though staying in a luxurious guest room, have felt the chill of a reserved reception.

I've shared from times of little, and I've been grateful to be able to share from relative abundance. I've taken to heart the lessons from years and miles and continents that the hospitality, the gift, is in the sharing—of my home, my food and drink, and of my heart. "[F]or I was hungry and you gave Me food; I was thirsty and you gave Me drink; I was a stranger and you took Me in" (Matthew 25:35).

CHAPTER 2
The Nurturing of Nature

I love the city. Truly. But when I need to clear my head, refresh my heart, and restore my soul, I head to the country. I find trees, grass, water and sky. Whether to the mountains or seashore, I seek the peace and beauty of nature. John Muir's words on the hope of the world being found in the wilderness— those ring true. My first understanding that a God might really exist, one responsible for the creation of the world, came from the inexpressible ache I felt when standing before some great work of nature's art. I felt seen and healed and whole in the wild places far more than I ever did in the midst of city crowds. And the more I learned of biology and astronomy at MIT, the more I couldn't deny His existence. Something in nature fills us up and reminds us of both our great worth and our great smallness in the web of humanity. I may feel alone in the woods, but I feel more alive and more aware of my relationship to all of mankind when I am there.

When our first three children were born, we lived in Washington, D.C. I loved living there. I loved our little yellow house, our neighbors, the coffee shop, and the corner market. I loved the familiar faces I saw week after week at the farmer's market and the library and on the street as we raced to dance class. The energy of the city was inspiring. I could imagine a million ways to serve others and be engaged in my community. I could eat food from a million cultures. I could visit museums and ride the bus and people watch to my heart's content. But after spending nearly half of my life in a busy urban environment, from Boston to New York to D.C., I was becoming tired and overwhelmed. Overstimulated. I desperately needed more time in the sunshine when the air wasn't heavy with exhaust and waste and the radiant heat from asphalt. I needed *trees*. And I needed to look up at a night sky that wasn't orange from pollution and streetlights but velvety midnight blue and speckled with stars. Perhaps if we had been able to leave the city more frequently for escapes to the mountains or the sea or even the parks outside of the city, I may have been content. I did so very much love the city. But we were not able to run away to the country very often, and I began to wilt.

So we left the city and moved to an outer suburb, an older suburb with a backyard full of mature oak trees, a tiny creek, and overflowing stands of azaleas. The biggest selling point? The many, many acres of empty cemetery behind the cul-de-sac. I could have my trees and my sky and my quiet contemplation. I did not love our suburban neighborhood or fall in love with our perfectly fine house. I did love our trees. I could look out the windows and see nothing but waving branches. Some days, all I could hear for hours was birdsong and rustling wind. I had muddy shoes and dirty socks by the front door, a pile of acorns by the kitchen door, and binoculars and bird books on the windowsills. I missed the liveliness of the city and the way I was known to my neighbors there, but I felt the restoration I needed every time I looked up into the twisting branches of the magnolia tree outside my bedroom window.

And then we moved again. To sixty-two acres of farmland, woods, and wetland. A property that size must have a name, and we diligently searched for just the right one. We settled at last on Fairlight Farm. In every direction, in every season, and sometimes every hour, we are faced with the play of light across our fields and the ridges that border our narrow valley to the east and west. Life is no less complicated or busy or stressful here than any other place I've lived. There are things about it that are much harder than in the city and things I desperately miss. But there is a peace here that is unlike anywhere else. It's a peace that every visitor notices. We watch friends from more urban areas stop and take a deep breath on the old brick sidewalk leading to the kitchen porch. We see them pause and stare at the sky across our southern field as they get into their cars to leave. That breath and that pause—that's where you find the need for natural places.

Not everyone will want to live in a rural area; not everyone is happy going to sleep in the deep, quiet dark of a country night. Not everyone will want to face the surprisingly disconcerting reality that they are too far from town for pizza delivery. We don't all need to flee permanently to the woods to find contentment. We do all need to find some time in nature, however. As much as we seem to know this instinctively, science agrees. Even the federal agency charged with overseeing the development of Washington, D.C., the National Capital Planning Commission, declares that "[n]atural landscapes can help mitigate the stress and fatigue of everyday life."[36]

Anyone planning a visit to D.C. is well aware of the miles of green space running from the Capitol to the Lincoln Memorial. The National Mall, however, isn't the only wonderful natural space preserved in D.C. Rock Creek Park is a national park running through Northwest D.C.—nearly two thousand acres of wilderness with tree-shaded trails, a classic burbling creek, and even wildlife beyond the ubiquitous squirrels of city life. Kenilworth Aquatic Gardens, the National Arboretum, and Kingman Island Park link along the eastern side of the city, and countless parks, large and small, dot the urban landscape. An ongoing development tension between housing density and green space is too often resolved in favor of high-rise condos at the expense of wide-open park space, but the planners recognize the trade-off. The research is clear that urban green spaces foster mental well-being and community connectedness.

Hospitality typically conjures up images of beautifully set tables, fluffy bed linens, and perfectly poured drinks. Yet sometimes, the welcome of Creation is the best taste of hospitality one can find. There is something naturally restorative about time in nature, something that touches us in places nothing else can reach. The University of Washington program Green Cities: Good Health summarizes much of the research on the immensity of the social and community benefits of shared natural space.[37] Social interaction, cohesion, and social capital increase greatly as access to nature increases and this, in turn, leads to lower mortality rates, lower crime, and more positive impacts on children's well-being. Neighborhoods—people—function better together when they share time in nature. In fact, they conclude that "[w]ell-managed vegetation may be one of the most important features that promote the development of social ties." And isn't that the point of hospitality?

We let our guard down more in nature. We relax and allow ourselves to breathe more deeply, think more creatively. Even those of us who thrive in the city among high-rise offices and close-set brownstone homes feel ourselves uncurl a bit when we set our feet on grass or cast our eyes upward through the lace of tree branches against a sky that is somehow bluer than usual. There is a deeper sense of rootedness, of the interconnectedness with "the Other" that we find in nature and nowhere else. Business deals may be conducted in the conference room and high-level diplomacy under fluorescent lights, but true peacebuilding comes when people connect and relate to one another. That happens much easier when we step outside and remind ourselves of our place in the created world. It is not an accident that Camp David is ever linked to peace accords.

American Forests, an organization dedicated to creating healthy forests since 1875, devotes a significant amount of money and time to promoting urban green space for community health and social well-being, as much as for mitigating the environmental damage of dense human activity. They report that people with access to green space report "less stress [and] lower levels of fear and aggression."[38]

In Japan, they practice *shinrin-yoku*, or forest bathing. This exercise of simply being in nature, engaging the senses, heals, restores, and rejuvenates. Studies done by Dr. Qing Li of Nippon Medical School in Tokyo, and others, add scientific weight to what we've instinctively and anecdotally known for centuries: Being outside in nature simply makes us feel better.[39] Not only does our cardiovascular and metabolic health improve, but our mood lifts as well. The smell of green, growing things and damp earth; the feel of the breeze against our skin, grass under our feet, and leaves brushing our hands; the sound of flowing water, birdsong, and crunching leaves; the blue of the sky, the infinite spectrum of greens, the glimpse of white or yellow of wildflowers; even the taste of fresh air on our tongue—all of these calm our heart rate, ground us in the present moment, and lower our blood pressure. We literally breathe easier in the woods. Our joints thank us for walking on a softer earth. Our brains release calming chemicals. In those moments, we become more receptive to others, more vulnerable in our emotions, and more willing to work in the community. Just as bathing in water cleans and refreshes our bodies, bathing in nature cleans and refreshes our minds and hearts.

Why is that true? Science may not have yielded the answer to that question yet, but perhaps we can theorize that we are intrinsically linked to all the rest of Creation, that being part of the created, natural world, we feel most at home when we spend time in it. Even those urban dwellers who love the rush of city energy and the steel and stone beauty of urban architecture find a different sort of peace when they steal a moment in nature. We might vacation in the city sometimes, but when we are tired or stressed and need a getaway, we seek the woods, the mountains, and the sea. Inspirational posters use nature scenes; sleep or meditation apps use recorded nature sounds. We instinctively turn to nature when we are stressed, just as we turn to the things that comforted us as children. We have comfort foods, favorite smells, and a blanket that reminds us of our grandmother's house. In times of emotional need, we look to those things for comfort. As, too, we seek the natural world.

So, how do we encourage this innate hospitality of wild places? Remember that hospitality can be defined as "offering a pleasant or sustaining environment" and "being friendly and welcoming to guests." While being mindful of the possible dangers in the wilderness, we are indeed welcomed into a sustaining environment when we step outside into the natural world. When life is hectic and emotions are high, sometimes I need to step onto the porch just to take a deep breath. Not nearly often enough, I just sit down on the bottom porch step for a moment and stop thinking. I take off my shoes and feel the stones that have formed a stepping-off place for two hundred years. I listen to the ridiculous chatter of the crows, mindlessly trace the path of wasps in my son's sea of mint. Those little moments are sustaining. We can do the same with others—take a walk, have coffee on the porch, or bring a green plant to the office conference room.

As a mother, I have often found myself shooing battling children out into our yard—in part to run off the energy they've accumulated that is contributing to conflict, but also in part to actually defuse the conflict through time in nature. Sending them outside doesn't solve their problems. It doesn't somehow resolve the issues that caused the fighting in the first place. What it does is hit a reset button of sorts. I can usually tell when one of them isn't ready to let go of some hurt or offense because they stomp back inside and retreat to their room. They seem to realize that they can't stay angry indefinitely outside!

Taking advantage of the reconciliation and healing aspects of the natural world can be done in nearly any context. As more research is conducted into the relationship between conflict, peacebuilding, and natural resources, we are also learning more about how we can go beyond the economic and climate benefits of the natural world to utilizing those resources for the work on conflict resolution itself. One of the many inspiring programs to come out of the work at Glencree Centre for Peace and Reconciliation in Northern Ireland is the experiential Sustainable Peace Network.[40] The network used journeys into nature to promote connection and to build trust and relationships among those seeking recovery and reconciliation from the conflict that shattered Northern Ireland for decades. One participant, in 2006, wrote that "[w]ild is basic—everyone is equal in our natural world. Diversity can be accommodated in nature."[41]

The researchers and leaders of this program found that participants engaged with nature and peacebuilding in four specific areas. First, they reported that nature is calming, allowing for the open space and flexibility to reflect and process. As with the research surrounding Japanese forest bathing, research collected by the University of Minnesota's Center for Spirituality and Healing speaks to the power they term "nature-based therapeutics" in healing trauma. Again, science is catching up to what we instinctively know to be true.

The second area of engagement noted by Glencree participants is the "humbling" aspect of being in the wild. Nature reminds us that we are a part of creation, not the totality. We are faced with the knowledge that though our lives are fleeting, the natural world remains, stretching behind us and before us with little heed to our short time among those trees and rocks and sky. We might be humbled by the realization that we are the part, not the whole, yet in that we also feel a great deal of worth—a comfort in knowing we are a part of something this magnificent and enduring. Madeleine L'Engle wrote of the paradox of this sense of meaning we can find in nature, particularly when we contemplate the night sky, saying, "Rather than feeling lost and unimportant and meaningless, set against galaxies which go beyond the reach of the furthest telescopes, I feel that my life has meaning. Perhaps I should feel insignificant, but instead I feel a soaring in my heart that the God who could create all this—and out of nothing—can still count the hairs of my head."[42]

When a small child is faced with the enormity of the world with all its messiness, noise, and confusion, she seeks comfort in her mother's arms. She finds a sense of belonging and restful comfort, of being known and seen and sheltered. When we as adults feel the same sense of overwhelmedness in the world, we often turn instinctively to the vastness of nature to find that same sense of belonging of being known and sheltered. We creep into the meadows, the parks, the woods to find a place that reminds us of who we are and that we are part of something significant, even in our smallness. Paradoxically, there is an alien sense to the woods and wild places that can cause us to draw near to others in ways we might not in a hotel or conference center. They, like us, are merely a part of this vast natural world, and as fellow human beings, are more like us, despite political beliefs or religion or ethnicity or race, than are the animals that inhabit this place. In contrast to our daily routines, we draw near to them with comfort and trust, so unlike our daily lives. It's the rare hiker that doesn't offer a friendly wave as you pass on a narrow trail, the rare campfire that doesn't draw strangers closer.

But back in our everyday lives, in cities or neighborhoods, in those places we find other people more "like" us for our personal huddles, "the Other" becomes the alien once more, the one who doesn't look like us or think like us. In the stew of humanity, we seek comfort in smaller groups. We look for significance in our jobs, clothes, relationships, and religion, trying to find where we belong amongst the masses. In the wild, we find our significance in our *insignificance*. We are intertwined with the individuals in our vicinity, one tiny subset of life in all the richness and wildness of creation, our human dignity and worth the common ground on which we huddle.

Thirdly, nature is seen as a transitional space. It's neither here nor there. It isn't a battleground or headquarters. Rather, it is an in-between space, suspended from time and specific place. Like a blanket fort, treehouse, or a wardrobe that just might lead to Narnia, nature is a place that allows us a freedom to test ideas, to reset our beliefs. We can be childlike in our wonder out in nature. It is easier to be our authentic selves when we are removed from the spaces in which we act every day. We tend to create roles for ourselves in our everyday worlds. We may be one version of ourselves at work and another with our family of origin, yet another with our spouse or our friends. We often don a costume and play a role when we allow ourselves to engage in debate online. But when we walk out into the woods, we begin to shed those layers of costumes, the masks we wear.

Can we cling to those masks on a three-hour hike? Sure we can. We can begin and end our time in nature just the same if we don't approach our time there willing to allow ourselves to be vulnerable. To allow ourselves to feel our emotions as they bubble to the surface under the influence of birdsong and breeze. In *The Lion, the Witch, and the Wardrobe*, Lucy pushed through the coats in the wardrobe with an air of anticipation and wonder, and she found true magic in friendship and beauty. Edmund, however, entered the winter forest of Narnia harboring resentment and jealousy, refusing to allow himself the freedom to feel the magic. He found a different sort of magic—frosty, hard, and calculating. We need to give ourselves permission to exist in the in-betweenness of nature in order to reap the maximum benefits of our time there, entering with childlike awe and trust in the realness of our emotions and the words and feelings of others.

Lastly, the Glencree peace participants discovered that nature provides the language of peacebuilding. We speak of "journeying" to the mountains or the sea in the same way we journey towards reconciliation. We find new examples of power structures, new themes of vulnerability and freedom. Our language tends to become more descriptive in nature, inspired by the life surrounding us, the colors of leaves and flowers and sky. Relationships are described as "growing" or "thriving." We long to be "rooted" or "grounded" in community. Ideas blossom. Friendships take flight. We compare our communities to a changing landscape of meadow to brush to forest. We talk of weeding out the bad or the strength and resilience found in the flexibility of towering old trees. We see the power in a creek that has carved out a channel through years of steady flow—as well as the destructive nature of erosion that can change its path in one season. We already use these words and images; what is new is the potency they gain when we immerse ourselves in the settings that inspire them.

How does all of this relate to hospitality and the importance of place? Can't we be hospitable in a city apartment? Must we all move to an old farm to properly welcome others into our lives? Of course not! The very question is absurd. Hospitality is about welcome, and the space for that can be created anywhere. I've been welcomed richly in a shanty made of cardboard and tin perched on a smoldering trash mountain with every bit as much warmth as into a gracious manor overlooking the Potomac River. Hospitality never demands a specific setting. Warmth, openness, wonder, and vulnerability can be found anywhere. But there is intentionality to being hospitable, to creating a welcoming space for friend and stranger alike. Gathering in nature—or in a setting that borrows some of the peace and serenity of nature—simply eases the tensions of gathering and helps bring together those who are yet to be friends.

Finding ways to connect with others outside in a natural setting can be powerful in building community, especially a community of people who may be in conflict with one another. A picnic in the park, a hike in the mountains, a stroll along a sidewalk after dinner, a glass of wine on the porch—these are all ways to engage the senses, shake up the routine, and let creation smooth the way. When I was a fresh law school graduate sharing a house in D.C. with four other young women, we instigated Friday Nights on the Porch. Our rowhouse looked across the street into the trees of Rock Creek Park, and we were determined to take advantage of that. We hadn't read a bevy of studies demonstrating that time outside is important to mental health and community building. We hadn't yet reached a cultural moment where songs and stories lamenting the loss of the front porch were common. We simply instinctively sensed that inviting people over for cocktails in our living room was not nearly as welcoming as extending an open invitation to our front porch.

I don't remember a great many Friday evenings with a jam-packed front porch, but I do remember that the nights when friends—and friends of friends—joined us were some of the best evenings of a fun-filled summer. Sitting on our hodge-podge of questionable porch furniture, perched on the old wooden railing, or stacked on the steps, we laughed, told stories, and even (to the dismay of the neighbors, I'm sure) sang. We also sometimes sat in relative silence, listening to the night waking up across the street. Spring peepers, crickets, evening birdsong, and rustling leaves all formed the background chorus to our conversation. We were as hodge-podge as our hand-me-down furniture, but some of our easiest conversations of the time we lived together happened on our urban front porch.

There is something comforting and secure about opening up to others under a night sky. My law school roommate and I had many of our richest, most personal conversations about life, faith, and fears as we walked home to our NYC apartment late at night. It was hardly a pastoral, serene environment, but the city sounds are muted at night, the edges softened, and the air more soothing. Sounds are oddly amplified out of doors at nighttime, and we lower our voices in response. We are hushed, leaning in to hear each other, closing our circle. Outside at night, you tend to draw nearer to other people to feel more security in their presence. In the country, that is likely due to visceral fears of wild animals lurking in the dark. In the city, perhaps, the fear is more attuned to potential bad actors lurking in the alleyways. Wherever we are, we find our security in the presence of others when we are outside in the nighttime darkness. We tend to reveal more of our secrets, more of our worries, or more of our most closely held dreams under a night sky, whether a city street, a suburban deck, or a campfire in the woods.

Even in a home, we tend to draw close to a fireplace. Not always to seek to warm our bodies, but maybe to warm our souls. Stories get told around a fire. Tall tales and ghost stories to make our audience laugh or shudder begin our evenings. But soon, we begin to tell more personal stories—maybe tales about our family or our own personal "once upon a times." We may sit in silent contemplation, staring into the flames, until someone remarks from across the circle that it's good to sit there together like that. Someone else might agree. And the conversation flows into the reasons for gathering, what they are learning, what is good and true and beautiful, and what is still hard or ugly or raw. Even if a fire doesn't lead to the most difficult conversations, it provides a setting in which people can become comfortable with one another, learn more about one another, and begin to build trust. Faces shift in and out of flame and shadow, our expressions muted by the wavering light. It is easier to speak openly when you feel slightly hidden behind a mask made of firelight. This is another way in which nature extends a welcome, provides a pleasant experience, comforts.

Nature is accessible to everyone, everywhere. I am a big fan of a roaring campfire, but not everyone can walk out their back door and have their guests pull up chairs around a fire pit. But even the tiniest of apartments can offer candlelight (even the battery-powered candles can do!) or a tabletop fire pit on a balcony built for four. We can bring nature into our homes and into our lives in all sorts of deliberate and intentional ways. We can meet up with others in a local park and stroll along a walking path to have a difficult conversation. We can engage our broader community and get to know the strangers there by building a community garden at a school or playground. We can simply put a lovely bouquet of grocery store flowers in a jar in the center of the table when we invite someone to dinner. The little touch of fresh flowers can turn a formal table into a welcoming one. Living in the city on a starving student budget, I either bought the wilting flowers from the neighborhood bodega, discounted before being thrown away, or scavenged a few straggly wildflowers here and there along the sidewalk. I could sometimes make my roommate and I meander through the park on our way home from studying in order to clear our minds and calm our hearts. Those precious tokens of the natural world, those little moments of fresh air and sunlight or night breeze, soothed a frazzled, rushed, and harried student. I was more at peace and more open to building relationships when I had those moments than when not. I always tried to find ways to sneak in a little pinch of nature.

There is a stereotype of hermits living alone in the wilderness, men who shun their fellow mankind, seeking to be alone and separated from other humans. I think, however, that many escape to the wilderness to be alone, not to give up their connection to others, but perhaps rather to feel it more keenly and purely than when cluttered with the chaotic interactions of daily life in the outside world. While walking the trails at my farm, I have found myself pulling out my phone to make notes on what I need to get done and realizing I am missing the sights and sounds around me. When I put my phone away, I usually find the clarity and motivation I was looking for in the first place, much more so than when I sat at my desk and tried to make the same list. After allowing my mind to wander, to flit from the cardinal to the greening multiflora rose to the tree that fell since my last walk, I come inside, and my task list writes itself. I file a month's worth of papers, write the email I was dreading, and solve a dialogue problem in a story I was writing. Yet, I thought of none of that consciously as I walked.

When we distance ourselves from the rest of Creation, we find it harder to connect even with other people. The National Mall in D.C. starts with the Capitol and the Smithsonian Museum buildings, but it ends with memorials and monuments. It is busy at the eastern end, with a carousel and food trucks and people flowing in and out of buildings, but as you walk westward, it becomes quieter, greener, slower. The Vietnam Memorial is a dark slash of stone in the green, the Korean War Memorial is startling with its larger-than-life sculptures of soldiers in a rice paddy, appearing suddenly amongst the trees. The trickling water draws you to the World War II memorial to pause and reflect. These places of remembrance and reflection are in the middle of the capital city, but they are purposefully surrounded by nature. We stand in silent contemplation of the Wall while the green grass waves above our heads. We stand there in community with other tourists. Do they search for a family name? Are they Vietnamese or Cambodian? Dutch tourists just taking in the sites? Are they wealthy? White? Black? Do they live in D.C., or are they from out of town? Somehow, it doesn't matter. Traffic sounds are lessened down there along the wall. The grass above helps muffle the city sounds, creating a barrier that provides us space to consider the names, the nature of the war itself—together with all of those "Others" who are doing the same. For a few moments, we are joined in our moment of silence for those young men and women on the Wall. And the space for that is carved out of nature. Walking along the sidewalk on Constitution Avenue just a few steps away, we will hurry past the same people with whom we just joined. We don't look. We don't really see them. Would we take the same time, the same care, if the Wall stretched along that busy strip of concrete? Or does that grass above our heads make a difference?

In Hiroshima, Japan, the site of impact of the atomic bomb is today a vast parkland, Hiroshima Peace Memorial Park. It is an oasis of serenity in the middle of a crowded city. Tucked among the trees and flowers are various monuments and memorials to those who died from the world's first nuclear attack. The atomic dome rises above it, a shattered reminder of the devastation of the bomb and the resilience of the Japanese people. This park is a thriving, green, lush testimony to resilience and survival and the power of green, growing things to heal us and help us flourish. The bomb destroyed buildings and bruised the humanity of the world, but this park, this place of growth, is a reminder that we CAN heal, that lives and relationships can be mended, that life is too precious and too wonderful to be heedlessly destroyed. In the midst of this natural beauty, within the welcome and respite, we are reminded that there are lessons to be learned and work we must do. As you wander the paths between the memorials, you find the stories that need to be told. They are the stories of the lives lost and the life that has risen, literally, from the ashes. There are stories of forgiveness and reconciliation. They are important to hear, and the setting makes it easier. And at the end, if you go to ring the Peace Bell, to call for peace in the world, you will see engraved words from Socrates. The bell, one meant to call us to reconciliation, challenges you to first "Know Yourself." And that is the first and best lesson one finds in the hospitality of natural space—to really and truly, without distraction, see and know oneself.

CHAPTER 3

Community and Space: Place

"...[O]ur full humanity is contingent on our hospitality; we can be complete only when we are giving something away; when we sit at the table and pass the peas to the person next to us we see that person in a whole new way."
—ALICE WATERS, *Forty Years of Chez Paniss*[43]

"In the places where we live and work, equality is better enforced by good manners and common decency than by the courts and the police. But if good manners were to be normally expected and practiced in our neighborhoods, we might more reasonably hope to see them emulated in law enforcement."
—WENDELL BERRY, *The Need to Be Whole*[44]

We are created to belong. Even the most introverted among us tend to have their people—or at least their person, someone to confide in, share a meal with, and do life with. I live in a mixed household of social butterflies and near-hermits. Myself? I fall somewhere in between. As their mother, I need to check up on both the ones who need to go out, absorbing energy from others, and the ones who are more content to check in with a few close friends via text or a game. I want to be sure that they are *connecting* with others, whether many or one, that they are building relationships with other people, sharing their lives somehow. When their friendships seem to falter, I know that something might be wrong. It's a good clue that our children are hurting when they distance themselves from even their closest friends. We need people in our lives—community.

We sometimes romanticize old-fashioned small town living or the joys of large families. Countless Hallmark movies show us the magic of the journey the protagonist takes to shed big-city corporate life to return to her hometown, realizing along the way that though she had felt like an outsider growing up and left to "find herself," her town really loved her all along. The movie ends with her falling in love with her small town, the high school crush she thought didn't understand her, and ultimately, her true self. I'm not sure how accurate that story is, but it's a romance trope we love to watch again and again. Why do we so eagerly follow our heroine or hero, rooting for them to realize how much they love and miss their hometown, how much of a part of them that it is, how loved they are, how well they fit in where they thought they were outsiders? We joke about it. We make Bingo cards during Hallmark's famous Christmas movie season and mock the predictable storylines. I particularly like the online quizzes that have you pick numbers and then read out your own fabricated Hallmark Christmas movie storyline: "Big city lawyer coming home to help save her family Christmas tree farm?" Check. "Rescued by a former high school quarterback when her fancy sports car gets stuck in the snow?" Check. "Learn to accept your roots, make peace with the past, and fall in love?" Check, check, check. We laugh—but then we watch another one.

The allure of community is powerful. We want that deep connection to family and neighbors and even an entire town. Given the popularity of such movies and books, one might suspect that we are, indeed, created for that community. That community can be difficult to find. It is easy to join the increasing chorus of voices decrying the ills of social media and the virtual world we find online. It is easy to blame the virtual for the lack of the real. There is much truth to the accusations, but community has always been elusive to some. Sometimes, that is due to circumstances well beyond our control. A child who moves to a new town following a parent's job change may struggle to find new friends or a place to fit in, no matter how hard he tries. Military families are known for creating community with each move, but some personalities do not adjust well, even in a place where they are supported and their newness understood. Children in the foster care system often face a lifetime of trying to find their place; having lost their early childhood connections in unhappy circumstances, the skills and emotions for creating new communities can be difficult to learn. And unfortunately for lovers of Hallmark, not every small town is warm and welcoming. Nor every big city, for that matter. Wendell Berry writes extensively, movingly, and quite persuasively that we are not only created for that personal community but also that connection to *place*, to the land itself. Considering the number of Hallmark movies that involve farmers and small, rural towns, I think Wendell Berry is right. He asserts that culturally, as we moved away from reliance on and care for the land, we also moved away from reliance on and care for community. As that has become more rare, still we yearn to belong. We crave that cocoon of connection.

Community is a complicated word. Community means where we live, the people geographically close to us. It can mean the other families in our school, our colleagues at work, or the people we choose to spend time with at work, church, or play. Some community is voluntary and some happens to us along the way. In our increasingly geographically rootless society, we are more connected by data bits and bytes over the air than by roads and sidewalks, genes, and the names in a family Bible. We now often choose our primary community, naturally gravitating towards people who are most like us. That's what fits, what is comfortable. But in the end, our choices invariably exclude more than include. It's *this* group, not *that* one. Division instead of connection.

With our link to place severed by jobs and choices in education, our ability to choose a school or a favorite coffee shop, to go to this bar rather than that one, to attend this Presbyterian Church or the one on the other side of the neighborhood, we are not forced to be in the company of those we would rather not be around. My office mates are likely similar to me in education, income, and political affiliation. We likely share the same with our neighbors. We live and work with people like ourselves. Perhaps our choices are unintentional, but the results are the same. And because we choose our neighborhoods, our children are on sports teams with children like them; their schools, youth groups, and friends are all very much the same. In our very transient and mobile world today, it sometimes seems that the most visible difference is the professional sports team sticker on our car. You might live in Northern Virginia, but you grew up in Atlanta or went to school in Chicago. Your neighbor, who drives a similar car, has a comparable income and level of education, votes the same ballot, grew up in Seattle and remains a Seahawks fan. Your biggest disagreement might be over who should win the Super Bowl.

How much of that is true community? How much of that goes deeper than chatting about lawn care, local taxes, and a neighborhood book club? Do you *know* those neighbors, co-workers, and fellow parents? We extend our oft-limited hospitality to these people. We invite them in for drinks or to the backyard to grill. We talk. We enjoy their company. Is that community? It doesn't look a whole lot like those Hallmark movies. Would those neighbors mow your lawn if you broke your leg or rush to care for your children if you had to go to the hospital in the middle of the night? Perhaps a more important set of questions is would we *ask* them to or *want* them to do so? As uncomfortable as that question might be, I think many of us would answer truthfully, *probably not.* As our culture has become more mobile, less rooted, less connected, we've learned to celebrate even more our independence. Despite Hilary Clinton's famous "it takes a village" message, we don't really cultivate the village in the same way that we once did. We curate our villages to meet specific wants or needs, but our current culture discourages the natural development of a village full of different types of people who meet needs and wants we don't even always recognize we have.

Our modern communities are comfortable, familiar, and not too demanding. We ask little of them, and they ask little of us. But what happens to us when our community is so comfortable? Our hospitality so natural? We bemoan our divided culture, yet most of us feel little incentive to change it. Where once Pa Ingalls struck out across the prairie in gloriously celebrated freedom and individuality—yet relied always upon neighbors—now we gather in groups, yet rely little on one another. We celebrate group membership and laud diversity, but only certain kinds of diversity. We may live in a neighborhood that is racially diverse but economically, politically, and educationally homogenous. There is little in such a neighborhood to shake us up or challenge us. Yet the stereotype of close-minded and homogenous small towns has a vise grip on our cultural psyche. Growing up in small towns, I have to argue the opposite. I do not argue that small towns can breed complacency, dislike of "outsiders," a certain arrogance of opinion that refuses to change. Having also lived in large metropolitan areas, I see the same things there. What I also found in my small towns, however, was forced relationship, forced community with people very unlike one another. Wealthy or poor, you shopped at the same grocery store—because there was only one. You attended the same high school, got gas at the same gas station, and hung out after football at the same fast-food restaurant. Farm kid or son of a lawyer, you join the same clubs and eat in the same high school cafeteria. Republican or Democrat, you once went to the same churches, ate at the same pizza place, sat in the same PTA meetings. Not everyone fit in or got along, but everyone was forced to interact in a way that our overall culture discourages today. I wonder if I went "back home," what would be different now that so many can exist in their online silos? Do people still mingle across party lines? Across belief systems, socio-economics, and politics?

So many songs and movies and books have been written about leaving our small towns to go out into the big wide world. When did that start? Why? Some research suggests that dispersion came along with industrialization, as people moved off of farms and into cities for work. The European push to settle the land that is now the USA from the Atlantic to the Pacific was born partly out of the industrial and commercial need for more land and more resources, eagerly carried out by farmers and entrepreneurs who wanted to escape the crowded growth of old Europe and the new East Coast. Women's suffrage and the feminist movement provided the impetus for women to break out of the norms of family life and explore the same independence as men. The exciting world of commerce and industry promoted an ideal of bustling city life, where museums, theaters, and great conversation flourished. There, you could be yourself; there, you could find fulfillment and excitement far beyond the narrow confines of small-town life. One has to wonder if the industry giants building these museums and libraries and bastions of high culture were perhaps trying to entice workers to their cities?

America's Founding Fathers may have been educated, wealthy men, but the farmers and laborers who made up the Revolution were also well-read and well-informed. The *Federalist Papers* were not written for the elite few of the upper class. They were read, analyzed, and discussed at village pubs, town halls, and over fence posts. Tradesmen and laborers alike argued and debated the need for independence from Britain and then, later, the proper form of a new government. Returning to *Little House on the Prairie*, Laura Ingalls Wilder wrote extensively about how important the newspapers were and how the people would gather to discuss the news of the world. They held debates and events where people gave speeches and recited literary works. Frontier towns were not havens for the ignorant and ill-informed. Nor were they built by men and women who believed the same and thought the same and had no room for differences. And always, there were those who wanted to fly and those who were more content to stay. Laura Ingalls, for instance, for all her shared restlessness with her father, settled happily on a farm with her small family and contentedly grew her village. Her daughter, Rose Wilder Lane, was a celebrated journalist who traveled the world, reporting on some of the most harrowing global stories of her day. Yet, in the end, she worked with her mother to bring the stories of her childhood to life. Despite her "worldliness" and her education, her life of adventure and travel (and a reportedly complicated relationship with her mother), Rose seems to have valued the home she had, the rootedness of family, community, and place.

The spirited and independent heroine of *Anne of Green Gables* wanted to remain on Prince Edward Island. It was home. She was content to be there with her community. The *Anne* series by Lucy Maud Montgomery is rich in its descriptions of community. The cast of characters is large and varied, and they disagree on religion, politics, child-rearing, farm practices, modern conveniences, and more. Yet the community is always real and substantial, present. Hospitality is a given—whether to friend, foe, or stranger. Emily Starr, Montgomery's heroine in *Emily of New Moon*, was also content to root at home in her rural village. She found what she needed in her community—even when it didn't understand her, she was part of it.

I read and reread Montgomery's books in high school (and beyond). I wanted to be like Anne and Emily, and I desperately wanted the community and rootedness they had. But I also wanted to flee my small town and stretch my wings. I didn't feel that I belonged in my small town. There was no extended family. No roots. No history. No land. Had my slightly odd self felt belonging in some small way, perhaps I would have stayed—or at least stayed connected. But I didn't feel connected or rooted, and so all of my oddness was a constant friction, a constant rubbing. Instead, I read books about the world, and I wanted to see it. I wanted to be Nellie Bly and travel around the world. I wanted to be a pioneer. I wanted to be Amelia Earhart. By the time I graduated, I wanted to be Sally Ride. I wanted the ultimate escape from a small town—space. But why? What made my experience so different from that of friends who, even after leaving our small town, stayed a part of that community?

When I was an adult, my mother moved back to her hometown, even almost to her land. That's her place of rootedness. Even though I lived there as a small child, I don't have the same connection. That's hard for her to see. I lived there—shouldn't I love it too? But I didn't have the chance to root there in the same way. And my family had moved away. My grandmother lived in Florida. When she visited 'home', she was with us or other family. My great-grandmothers had both passed away. My cousins had moved away long ago and were rooted elsewhere. Once upon a time, we had large, boisterous, contentious, fun family picnics that linked us all for three to four generations. But now, their children's children, scattered across the states, rarely gather. I grew up knowing my cousins, second cousins, third cousins, and cousins once removed. But my children barely know their first cousins. They know the vast extended family only through pictures, social media—and stories. The reason for me to be rooted there is long gone.

I hope that my children can see our farm as a place of root-edness. Our oldest was in high school when we moved here, so for her, it seems like the biggest stretch. Yet, after going overseas to university, she seems likely to come back home. Our boys don't seem likely to take on the role of farmer, but they all assume our home and land will always be here. I've caught them discussing which of them is most likely to move back and why and how they would handle their poor, elderly parents. We still know few people in our new hometown—in part because we are not, in fact, anywhere close to *town* and in part due to the *disease-which-shall-not-be-named* and the isolation of lockdown. But we chose a tiny church full of retirees because it is within walking distance of our land; it was founded by the family that built and lived in our home for over 150 years. We wanted our children to feel connected to a place and have a community. We can walk into the cemetery and see the names of those who lived in our house and of other families that still live in the valley. It's a new sort of homemade rootedness, but it is important nonetheless. And in the six years we have lived in this place, we've been welcomed wholeheartedly into that tiny church home.

Our first fall, we were just trying to sort out baseball for the boys, navigate high school for our daughter, and learn how to live in a 200-year-old house on land that needed our care. We had only attended the church a handful of times, but we saw the announcement for their community spaghetti dinner. And by community, they really meant community. The parish hall overflowed for three hours with people from up and down the valley. The next month, my husband and sons attended the church Christmas potluck and white elephant exchange. They were the only children there and were treated like grandchil-dren all around. The night before Ash Wednesday brought the community pancake supper, and five years later, we ran the pan-cake supper. Those things make a community. They provide the space for relationships to grow. The grace and love extended to my children from the very beginning has given them confidence, made them feel valued, stretched them to serve.

A few years ago, we learned that the annual church picnic used to be held at our farm. We immediately declared we needed that to start again! My boys have learned how to host the fall picnic for our church and our sister parish at our farm. They prepare the house and the yard, help set up chairs and sound equipment, serve as acolytes, and show people where to park and how to find the bathrooms. Our blended church family is a somewhat eclectic crowd, but every year, we are asked again to host, and every year has been a gift. The two congregations mix it up a little and have lunch next to people they do not know—but they expect to enjoy the conversation. The connection to that place has created a beautiful and genuine environment for worship and conversation. We hold the service under walnut trees that have stood for well over 100 years, in the shadow of the house that has seen generations of family come and go. There is something very right and good about that.

Hospitality creates community; community demands hospitality. Imagine a world in which we invite "the Other" in with true welcome? I've sat at the table with Israelis and Palestinians, Serbs and Croats. Hospitality creates community out of division. My family was as dysfunctional as they come. I was never unaware of that, even as a child. But I have wonderfully happy memories of those extended family gatherings. I have had some incredibly weird people in my family, but I love them, tolerate them, and am able to understand a little, sometimes, where their weirder and wilder views come from. I certainly don't agree with all of them. I don't necessarily desire to spend loads of time with all of them, but I love them, and I value them as human beings. What created that? Time, meals, hospitality. Creating community.

Like with our church picnics, opening our doors to the broader church body, we are building a community with people who are otherwise strangers to us. It takes a certain level of vulnerability to do so. The first picnic we hosted, we only knew the regular attendees at our small church. We had never met anyone from our sister parish, and even our priest was new. Were people richer than us? More liberal? More conservative? Were some of them good at landscaping or better hobby farmers? Surely, their houses were in better condition, their kitchens nicer, and their dogs more well-behaved. What would we talk about? What if they were judging us the whole time? And frankly, they probably were. After all, we all observe and make judgments about each other all the time. But we gamely offered up our place and got ourselves ready to host. Our hospitality created a community of the two churches. And that community demands that this hospitality continue for it to thrive. We won't agree on a lot with the other parish. Without having to say much at all, it's clear we sit at different places on the political spectrum than most of them. The hospitality offered by the picnics, however, has created an environment of trust and vulnerability that allows us to have deeper conversations about challenges our culture and our region face—without having the labels of politics and group identities to mask our reason and our hearts.

How can two groups of people, who on paper would appear to agree on very little, communicate productively about poverty, hunger, and stewardship of the land? By building relationships through shared hospitality. There is no other answer. We haven't needed to define our politics because we've become a community of people who share the same concerns. We have come to know we share those concerns because we have talked about them over a meal under our walnut trees. Did we offer to host the picnic for that outcome? Not at all. The purpose of the picnic was to celebrate another year of hope and harvest, to worship together, and to enjoy the company of one another. The purpose was simply hospitality. To welcome everyone, friend and stranger alike, into our home, into a pleasant environment, to share sustaining food and conversation. That welcome is what created the space for a community of folks, very unalike, to form. And that community is what can come together in open discussion of some significant problems facing people in our town and valley.

Without hospitality, we cannot create that space. It isn't found in a sterile boardroom or the private Facebook group. That space for community to form and trust to build is created by hospitality freely offered and freely received. Community isn't just people who like and support one another. Community is made of the hard work of rubbing along together and sharing in one another's lives—even if only for a meal. Community isn't as easy as mere proximity. It involves vulnerability. That vulnerability is nurtured by hospitality.

PART TWO
POWER OF STORY

CHAPTER 1
Shared Foundations and Cultural Rootedness

"Stories are verbal acts of hospitality."
—EUGENE H. PETERSON, *Christ Plays in Ten Thousand Places*[45]

"Stories are the communal currency of humanity."
—TAHIR SHAH, *In Arabian Nights: A Caravan of Moroccan Dreams*[46]

"Reading is the act of listening and speaking at the same time, with someone you've never met, but love. Even if you hate them, it's a loving thing to do. You speak someone else's words to yourself, and hear them for the first time."
—DANIEL NAYERI, *Everything Sad is Untrue*[47]

Stories root us. They create a web of interconnectedness that helps shape both our group and our individual identity. What happens at a wedding rehearsal dinner? Story after story of the bride and groom are told. Those stories may be funny or sad or embarrassing or tender—but they all serve to more deeply entwine the new couple in the bonds of both families, joining them well beyond the legal creation of a marriage. Their new life together is being built on this shared foundation of stories, reflecting the values and beliefs they bring to their relationship. When an only child marries one of ten siblings, the stories their spouse and new family share help the only child to understand better who her new husband is and how he came to be that way. A woman who grew up on a farm tells stories as a way to clue her suburban husband in on a part of her identity he might not otherwise realize is there. Those family stories shared in celebration add to the foundation. Grandma, sharing the story of how the bride once spent the night in her horse's stall watching a difficult birth, tells the groom his new wife is compassionate, loyal, brave, and unflinching. And he learns that her grandmother is proud of her for those things, her family values those traits. And so another set of stones are added to the foundation.

The young narrator of *The Many Assassinations of Samir* by Daniel Nayeri spins tales within a tale in the tradition of Arabian Nights, buying his freedom like Scheherazade with his stories. If stories are the "communal currency of humanity," why? And what does that mean? Stories hold value as social currency, a way to exchange ideas within and across cultures. This currency identifies us and gives us something to exchange in order to forge a connection with others. Who I am and what I know and believe are shaped and matured through the stories I have heard or lived. Who I am and what I know and believe also can be understood through the stories I choose to share.

My family told stories at every holiday gathering or reunion. I used to ask them to be repeated year after year. These stories created a family anthology that told me our identity and origin. Whether the stories were true or not mattered little to my younger self—or, to be fair, my older self. The stories themselves were what mattered. The telling and the sharing of them. In *One Writer's Beginnings*, southern storyteller Eudora Welty wrote, "Long before I wrote stories, I listened for stories. Listening for them is something more acute than listening to them. I suppose it's an early form of participation in what goes on. Listening children know stories are there. When their elders sit and begin, children are just waiting and hoping for one to come out, like a mouse from its hole."[48] The child listening for stories was me. I did run and play and steal cookies and chips from the picnic tables with my cousins, but just as often, I found myself creeping back towards the adults, finding my quiet corner with a book to mask my interest, and listening, just listening, for the stories to start.

To Kill a Mockingbird hauntingly captures the small town life of its author. Harper Lee's protagonist, six-year-old Scout, spends much of her time with the adults around her, asking questions, listening to gossip, and hearing stories about her town and its people that sometimes shocked and sometimes encouraged. Like Scout, I heard stories that were funny, tragic, and scandalous. And like Scout, with her gossiping neighbor Miss Stephanie, I had to learn to distinguish between the good and the pure gossip, whether well-intentioned or malicious. The more I listened, the more I learned to discern which family storytellers had integrity and empathy, who understood the value of passing along the stories of our family, and which were purely engaged for the purposes of passing on gossip for entertainment or attention. Listening for stories is active. It's more than a passive intake of information. I was waiting, bated breath, hoping to hear a *good one*. The storyteller would start, and I'd listen closer. *Had I heard that one before? Is it about my mom's cousin Bill or a Bill from another generation? Then, wait? The story is different this time. How? What is different?* Which storyteller, which time, was true? What were the motives in telling the story that way? The family web would grow more elaborate, larger, the pattern more defined. Every story told me a little more about this group of people into which I had been born, which told me a little bit more about who I myself could be. Madeleine L'Engle wrote, "We turn to stories… because they show us who and what and why we are…"[49] They help us "to become more whole, to become Named."[50] Not every family story was true or consistent or "good," but all of them together formed a foundation for my identity. They placed me within a family, a community, a timeline of history.

This placing gives us a sense of how we fit into the world at large. Listening to these family tales teaches us that while each of us is an individual, we are also part of something else. Our first "group" identity is usually within a family. That family is within a community—geographic, ethnic, religious. Perhaps it is in multiple communities. We learn how to navigate those different communities, different group identities, in part through the stories we've heard. As we move out into the world beyond our family, that story foundation is built upon through the people we meet, the places we go, adding more stories of our own lives and the lives of those we get to know. With the stories of our childhood remembered, we forge connections with others as we relate our experiences and histories to theirs. Did their great-grandmother also have distant cousins in another country with whom she corresponded her whole life? Did their grandfather have a moonshine still in West Virginia? Did they have a change to the family surname as their relatives came through Ellis Island? Or an uncle owns a restaurant, another was drafted in the Vietnam War, and an aunt was loud and flamboyant. Maybe they grew up on a farm or were teased by their family for reading too much. Maybe they got kicked out of preschool or had an uncle who was a first-grade dropout. Each story brick in our foundation is a possible link to someone else and a way to build our lives together.

We relate best to other people when we dig into the stories that make us who we are. No matter how many things we do or do not have in common on a surface level, it is at the foundational level of stories that we truly connect. Conference hosts often make the participants do an ice-breaker activity or to introduce themselves with "an interesting fact," such as their favorite ice cream or where they grew up. Sometimes, these icebreakers might do their job of cracking the surface formality and tension, getting attendees to relax a little, but often, they fall short of their deeper purpose of inviting vulnerability and openness. Conferences that take the time, however, to have people actively share within a smaller group tend to build deeper connections among participants. Guided conversation starters at a table, for instance, can prompt the kind of storytelling that begins to forge bonds that knit an otherwise unfamiliar group of strangers into allies and potential friends. The same human nature that uses dinner table storytelling to develop strong family bonds and shared identity works to create strong community bonds and identity as well.

Peacebuilding work at a high level is done at conference tables with formal documents, lists of requests, concessions, needed outcomes, etc. The participants are necessarily more concerned with the formalities of the peace agreement than with reconciliation and relationship. But as you get further down the hierarchy of organizations and people doing the actual work of peacebuilding, you find more stories than spreadsheets. The Dayton Peace Accords of November 1995 formalized the end of the Bosnian War, part of the larger wars among the former Yugoslav Republics. After years of negotiation between various world leaders, the final peace agreements were signed at Wright-Patterson Air Force Base near Dayton, Ohio. These accords established a new Bosnian national government and settled territorial questions. The systems put into place by the Accords were unwieldy, poorly designed, and even more poorly instigated. They were the result of years of increasingly frustrated international leaders attempting to put a halt to the ongoing fighting. But these agreements did little to solve the problems facing the people of Bosnia-Herzegovina. At the heart of rebuilding a shattered nation are the people who must move forward with former brutal enemies now their co-citizens, sometimes even still neighbors. Today, thirty years since the Dayton Accords were signed, tensions still flare, and the fear of open and violent conflict remains.

How do they actually *make* peace once the papers are signed? In the years following the various Balkan conflicts, I got to know personally and professionally many of the ordinary people trying to reconcile and to make peace—to rebuild community—by creating that critical space to hear and be heard. One such group of people founded an organization called ROM: Renewing Our Minds. With their name taken from Romans 12:2 ("...do not be conformed to this world, but be transformed by the renewing of your mind"), their mission was to bring together young people from around the former Yugoslavia and create an opportunity for them to hear one another's stories and build relationships with "the Other." For three weeks each summer, a couple dozen young people would gather in the small mountain town of Fuzine, Croatia, and work out the relational aspect of reconciliation. They talked about identity—their own and that of the other participants. They wrestled with how much of their own identity was informed by how they were seen by others or by, as written about so eloquently by Amin Malouf, the part of themselves feeling the most defensive.[51] They told the stories of their own experiences in the wars that devastated the Balkans and learned to listen to the stories of their roommates and tablemates. More than that, they shared favorite books and movies, favorite foods, and their love for family back home. Though ROM packed countless speakers, team-building exercises, and workshops into those three weeks, much of the real work of reconciliation happened in the everyday peace of storytelling around the communal tables. Participants were not only encouraged to spend time with young people from the other ethnic groups represented but were sometimes given little choice in the matter.

Faced with the challenge of sharing meals and games with other young people they had been given reason (some all too real and some not) to hate, they did what we humans do in such situations: They told each other stories. Some of those stories were hard to share and harder to hear. These young adults had lived through the absolute terror of bombings, militia groups retaliating on the women, children, and elderly left unprotected in small towns and rural villages, and the loss of fathers, mothers, siblings, grandparents, and friends at the hands of soldiers and terrorists that spoke with the accents of the people looking at them across the table. They didn't usually start with those stories. Instead, they talked of commonalities of school, sports, and pets. They formed bonds of laughter, poking fun at the older adults shepherding them. And as they broke through the distrust, the fear, and the animosity, they began more guided conversations into their shared history of conflict. They acted out one another's stories, leading to more sharing. The young people of the first few ROM gatherings are now parents, teachers, and community leaders. They have taken those stories from those three impactful weeks and used them to build communities of peacebuilders and reconcilers across the Balkans nearly three decades later.

One of the most inspiring groups I encountered during my work in the former Yugoslavia were the teenagers of Kids for Peace in Mitrovica, Kosovo. Mitrovica is a border city divided into the Kosovo-Serb community north of the Ibar River and the Kosovo-Albanian community to the south. The bridges connecting the two halves have long been flashpoints of violence, tangible symbols of the division and conflict. As the international community debates the future of Kosovo—and particularly the future of Mitrovica relative to Kosovan and Serbian claims to the region and the people living there—the people themselves go about the ordinary, everyday tasks of peacebuilding.

Today, those communities, still living in tension, still wary of the occasional violence, distrustful of political leaders from both sides, are filled with people who live and work side by side, sometimes as community acquaintances and sometimes even as friends. In 2004, these communities were struggling even more to find a sense of normalcy, while rebuilding from the violence of the preceding years. Three Kosovo-Albanian children drowned in the Ibar when they were reportedly chased by Kosovo-Serbian youth. Violence erupted across the city. But one group of young people refused the narrative of violence. Led by Fatmire Feka, an ethnic Albanian teenager who had lost family to the violence of the war in 1998-99, Kids for Peace raised their voices in protest. Begun by Fatmire with the support of World Vision in 2002, Kids for Peace organized clubs for ethnic Serbian and ethnic Albanian youth to come together to get to know one another. They told stories, wrote poems, and built a community of shared understanding. In 2004, when the world feared Kosovo would descend into sectarian violence again, Kids for Peace began publishing a newsletter of these stories and poems. Instead of violence, they chose stories. Instead of sharing hatred, they shared poetry. Their example spread to their parents, teachers, and community leaders. The tension in Mitrovica, as in most of this region, remains unresolved, but these young leaders are doing everything in their power to build community by communicating through stories, developing trusting relationships that may someday be the means by which the conflict is permanently dissolved.

Most of my engagement in the former Yugoslavia took place as I worked with World Vision in Washington, D.C. From there, I attempted to translate those faraway stories into words that political leaders in the United States could hear and understand—words that would move them to continue engaging in the critical work of peacebuilding and development there. I got to know my Balkan colleagues and the communities in which they lived and worked through their stories. And when I traveled there to meet with them in person, we connected through even more stories. I traveled with my daughter, then one, which made for a natural point of connection. We shared stories of our children, challenges faced by working and finding childcare, rolled our eyes at the things the grandparents expected or the gifts they would bring. My mother is far from a typical Bosnian grandmother, yet somehow, it turns out that grandmothers are recognizable the world over.

Though in some sense this is as easy as it sounds, we must take the time and the care to understand the culture in which stories, personal or otherwise, are shared. We need to find the cultural keys to unlocking the meaning of these stories. We may not grasp every nuance or understand every metaphor, but we can listen and observe and ask the questions that lead to understanding. Yes, I could have a good conversation with my Bosnian colleague about how ridiculous loving grandmothers can be, but that does not erase cultural differences, and I do not mean to imply that it does. Our mothers do not act the same, do not treat their grandchildren the same, and do not share the same definition of spoiling when it comes to those grandchildren. There are distinct differences in the familial relationships in western Pennsylvania and southeastern Europe and differences in how love is expressed, how children are treated, and how the generations interact. Those differences are not insignificant if one is not mindful of them. Still, sharing those stories did create common ground. They did allow us glimpses into each other's lives and hearts. They gave us a way in, a doorway to get to know one another better and build trust.

More than our shared personal stories, we could relate to the stories we all loved from our own childhoods. How many cultures have a story about a beautiful youngest daughter who must marry a beast or a bridegroom disguised as an animal? In each, the daughter's beauty, love, and kindness are a blessing to her family, yet her beauty causes her the distress of what seems an unhappy marriage. Always, the beauty of the bride is revealed to be as much of her heart as of her face, and through her love, she transforms her beastly husband into a prince. The modern European fairy tale *Beauty and the Beast* has a direct lineage to a French tale from the 1700s, but that was likely derived from other tales common throughout Europe—Russia, Norway, Romania, Italy, Spain, Portugal, England, Scotland, and others have their own versions of beautiful, virtuous maidens marrying beasts. Perhaps one might trace these back to a common ancestor in the Greek tale of *Cupid and Psyche*, but that cannot explain an Israeli tale, one from India, and others throughout Asia. Just like with Cinderella tales, I can reference "beauty marrying the beast," and friends and colleagues from around the world will have a similar tale brought to mind. We can use that story to remark that true beauty comes from within and makes everything around it beautiful. Or we can say that even a beast can be won over and changed by the inner beauty of someone generously loving and kind. The details may be different—a beast, a white bear, a snake—but the heart of the story remains and is a point of shared understanding.

Children's stories—fairytales—are not merely a form of entertainment. In the pages of any traditional collection of fairytales (most particularly older versions), you can find tales of courage, faithfulness, sacrifice, and great love. Following the twelve king's daughters down a hidden staircase to a magical land where they dance until their slippers are worn out inspires children to be brave, resourceful, and loyal. Lying in bed with an ailing emperor and listening to a nightingale sing inspires a search for true beauty and friendship. Welcoming Edmund back as a knight and hero inspires forgiveness, compassion, and love. These aren't lessons to be learned through watching a slide deck or reading an essay. They are taught through stories that allow children to become the characters they wish to emulate. I read voraciously as a child—classics, great literature, frivolously fun books, and stories that perhaps should never have made it onto the shelves. As I read, I imagined myself in the world of the stories. I wasn't just reading about Anne Shirley and her search for a bosom friend: I *was* that abused and neglected yet ever-hopeful redhead desperate for a chance. I was Edmund—and Lucy and Peter, too.

We communicate better when we find ways to relate to one another. In high school, we may learn to identify in a formal manner such figurative literary devices as metaphor, symbolism, allegory, and simile. Without thinking of them by name, we use them in everyday language to communicate ideas. Our descriptions are richer, and our understanding is deeper when both parties to a dialogue are able to decipher that figurative language. That comes most naturally in a shared cultural setting. When we grow up alongside one another, sharing the same television shows, the same fairytales, the same sporting events, the same religion, and even the same dialect and slang, we can communicate in a sort of cultural shorthand that allows us to bypass some of the small talk of getting to know one another. In a sense, we feel like we *already* know one another thanks to the shared cultural foundation. I was a slightly older mom by the time my youngest child was born, but I can ferret out my same-generation fellow mothers by such things as shared laughter over our horror at our middle school obsession with *Flowers in the Attic* or our high school celebrity crushes. Gen-X is fiercely protective of their childhood movies, and I know my people as soon as I say, "You keep using that word. I do not think it means what you think it means."[52]

We instinctively seek that common ground. One of the best friends I've had was my law school roommate. Having grown up on Long Island with, as she put it, a caricature of a Long Island Jewish mom, she easily found ways to relate to anyone with a similar experience. But more than that, she used that phrasing to give people insight into who she was, using the familiar cultural trope to help people understand her background and identity. She gave people a way to connect with her through their own experiences, whether that was the significance of food in family gatherings, the role of religious holidays, the drive for success, the assumption of a certain kind of spouse, or a sense, at times, of otherness. She could use that description of her mother as an opening, a doorway through which others could enter into a relationship with her. Over and over again, I witnessed the effect of her breezy and exaggerated stories of her mother and her family life on new acquaintances who often turned into friends. She shared little in common on the surface with some of them, but she used her humorous stories to find ways to connect.

Far more outgoing and social than me, she once dragged me to an evening coffeehouse of Christian music because she knew I wanted to meet people outside of the law school but didn't want to go alone. I met the lead singer-songwriter of the band performing that night, and it was largely through the efforts of my roommate that we were able to get to know one another. At first glance, Karen and this musician had very little in common. She was from a comfortably upper middle-class secular Jewish family from Long Island. She had an undergraduate degree in engineering and was attending Columbia Law School with me. She had no interest in evangelical Christianity and was a bit baffled at times by my lifestyle choices. He was from an Italian-American family from New York City and was working an office job while trying his hand at getting a Christian band off the ground. Yet she bonded with him easily, paving the way for me to overcome my reserve more slowly. She was able to find and use the social currency of their shared cultural foundation, however different they seemed to be.

We can't build without a foundation in place, whether that's a house erected on a foundation of cinder block and cement, a career in engineering forged on a solid foundation of mathematics, or a community painstakingly constructed on shared experiences and values. We identify those building blocks through the stories we tell or the stories we reference. Sometimes, they are the stories of our lives, crafted from the memories and experiences of ourselves and our parents, grandparents, and great-great-great-grandparents, the stories that created us. Sometimes, they are the stories of cultures—fairytales, folklore, myths or movies, books, and television. Without stories we can tell, tales we share, we are fabricating a community on air. Like a house without a foundation, the community is temporary, doomed to fail at the first storm of conflict.

One of our first acts upon meeting someone new, whether for work or for play, is to exchange stories. We might look for a point of connection—discovering a shared love of fishing or rom-coms. Or we might try to relate to one another by career path or education, by place of origin, current neighborhood, or favorite sports team. We leave the trickier topics of religion and politics for later. I have often struggled in these first social meetings to find that point of connection, particularly within that absolute labyrinth of parental relationships associated with kid sports and other school activities. I do always manage to find an entry point, a shared story that gains me admittance to the team parent circle, but I am challenged to move past that. My foundation often remains rather shaky. If we want to forge the sort of community that weathers storms, we must build the sort of foundation that can handle them. The first step is simply swapping easy stories of introduction. We follow those with deeper, richer stories that reveal more about us or our backgrounds, finding common points of reference, familiar waypoints.

What are the signposts that link you to your fellow travelers within your community? I don't often encounter fellow college alumni in my field, but I do find others who attended college in the Boston-Cambridge area. Going deeper, I make a path to peers or colleagues by relating my experience intending to pursue a major in engineering but ending up with a degree in cognitive science. Deeper still, I may tell the stories that led to that change and to a concentration in political science, a faith awakening, and a career in human rights advocacy. Which part of that story I tell reflects my level of comfort and my desire to take a relationship further and build a strong foundation of community with someone.

What stories do you tell that set the foundation? How do you build on that? The details we include are important, but the nature of the stories matters just as much. Yes, I want to tell people my own personal story, adding more detail, more color, as the relationships deepen, but what about the cultural stories, the references to the stories of others? How much do they reveal about me, and how do they strengthen the foundation? Think about what stories you might reference talking to fellow parents at a Little League practice. You might use pop culture, children's stories, and movies. You reveal a lot about yourself when you reference pop culture from your own childhood. With my youngest, I often find myself relating more to the grandparents than the parents when I bring up my childhood favorites. There is a subtle risk I take when I do: Will those "young" parents accept me and invite me into their circle? Or will I be an outsider, orbiting at a slight distance all season? What about a new church group? Do you find that sometimes you choose your stories as a bit of a litmus test, even if subconsciously? Perhaps you reference a book or a game that is just a tiny bit controversial to see how compatible the group might be. Or perhaps you deliberately refrain from certain stories, aware the contents could cause offense or alienation. The most naturally socially adept among us make these calculated decisions subconsciously, instinctively pairing their stories and their audience in ways to best build connection. For the rest of us, we must sometimes take an extra moment to listen to those around us and choose the best way to create that foundation of relationship and community, whether that be personal stories, books, fairytales, or shared history.

Use that social currency of stories to lay solid foundations of community. Actively seek stories that connect and ultimately bind you to one another. Move beyond the bricks and stones of your own basic story to the mortar formed of shared stories and deeper personal stories that create vulnerability—and trust. The reward for taking that step is the beginning of a community that has the strength and resilience to utilize conflict for growth rather than be destroyed by it.

CHAPTER 2
Imagination and Art, Creativity, and Wonder

"As the sensible mind needs eyes to see, so reason needs the imagination in order to behold mystery and to perceive the true quality of things."
—VIGEN GUROIAN *Tending the Heart of Virtue*[53]

"Because when we read together, we open our hearts to a story, open our hearts to each other.
We connect.
And that's miraculous."
—KATE DICAMILLO[54]

"[W]onder (which is the seed of knowledge)..."
—FRANCIS BACON[55]

We human beings instinctively seek the beautiful. As children, we are drawn to the happy brightness of a dandelion and the rich varieties of brown found in an everyday rock, the evening symphony of spring peepers, and the fuzz of an elm leaf. If we are encouraged to look with eyes of wonder, our appreciation for beauty grows and matures. From the easy appreciation of a child, we mature to admire a Monet, we rejoice with Handel's "Messiah," and we marvel at the velvet of a baby's cheek. We grow into people who are touched when a room, a garden, or a meal delights our senses.

As created beings, we also are born to create. But imagination that drives us to create won't survive childhood unless it is nurtured and encouraged. Stories are one of the foods necessary to grow healthy imaginations. Stories that challenge the curiosity and creativity of a child—or an adult—stretch and nourish them. When a child confronts a dragon in a story, she becomes a dragon slayer—or a dragon friend—in her deepest self. When a child pulls a sword from a stone, he is filled with the wonder—and responsibility—of becoming a boy king. Imagination, creativity, curiosity, and wonder—those are the things needed in a troubled world where problem solvers are few and divisions are growing. Children who see themselves as both the Beauty *and* the Beast—the pure, goodhearted heroine *and* the cursed monster who grows and changes—mature into adults who can see themselves in the political, religious, or ethnic "Other." Children who try to find a way into Mordor to destroy an evil ring grow into adults who seek to build partnerships to build a better world.

As G.K. Chesterton so eloquently wrote, "Fairy tales do not give the child his first idea of bogey. What fairy tales give the child is his first clear idea of the possible defeat of bogey."[56] Just as we are drawn to beauty, we are born with the knowledge that evil lurks in the world. We may not be able to name it, but the smallest children can identify it. No matter how carefully we screen their world, children still know there are monsters. They hide under the bed, in the closet, in the shadows. Who teaches a toddler to be afraid of the dark? Who paints the word pictures that become the nightmares they cannot articulate in their waking? Children know there are evil things; they just don't know what they are. Nor do they know *how* to defeat them without becoming the thing they fear.

Our children look to the adults in their lives to give context and meaning to the shadows that slink around at the edge of their vision. What are those shadows? Do they need to be afraid? Can they be overcome? Sometimes, in our rush to soothe and protect, in our desire to let our children be carefree and happy as long as possible, we try to brush away the shadows or pretend they aren't there. We tell them monsters don't exist, and we push the idea of evil back into the closet. We tell ourselves that they don't need to know that there are bad people in the world or that bad things happen. We can keep them safe until they are "old enough to understand." Unfortunately, we can't always protect our children from evil, and we can't always keep them safe. And in smoothing away their fears, we add a lie to them instead.

I have a child who has always been curious, who always wanted to know the "why." But she didn't stop after the first question and answer. She wasn't satisfied with hearing everything was okay. She learned a few basic facts about World War II in first grade, and we read the book *Twenty and Ten* about twenty French children in a boarding school who hid ten Jewish French children from Nazi soldiers. She asked, of course, why the children had to hide the other children and why the Nazi soldiers were looking for them? Children only ask as much as they want to know (or so parents are told), so I gave her a simple, age-appropriate answer in line with the story in the book. She was six. We had the luxury of being able to refrain from giving a six-year-old too many details about the horrors of war and the Holocaust. My daughter wasn't satisfied. *Why?* she asked again. *Why?* What answer can you give to explain the evil that took millions of lives, destroyed countries, caused terror that lingers in hearts and minds eight decades later? My daughter knew that evil existed. She knew monsters were real. She didn't want me to tell her it was over. She didn't want me to tell her it would never happen again or that it was just one bad man. She needed me to tell her what happened and that, yes, evil can grow and thrive in the dark places of the world—but yes, good people can fight it and *win*. That heroes surround us every day. That *she* could be a hero like the schoolchildren in that story. She could be strong and brave and loyal and loving. She could fight back and she could defeat that evil if it ever poked its head out of the shadows again.

Not every child wants the most horrific of details about Nazi evil before they even turn seven. Details trickled down more slowly to my second child. Most of his metaphorical dragons were the "bad guys" in the original *Thomas the Tank Engine* tales or the mishaps encountered by mischievous little brother Sam in the *Poppy and Sam* stories. He waded into the world of monsters slowly and carefully, testing the waters at every step. We read stories about evil dragons and good dragons, brave knights and not-so-brave knights. He wanted to know who the good guys *really* were and who their helpers were before he was ready to slay dragons. Yet even here is a bit of a paradox: My son, who preferred the gentlest of children's stories, was enthralled with the Margaret Hodges' version of *Saint George and the Dragon* from the epic *The Faerie Queene*. The story is beautifully illustrated and softly told, but Hodges does not downplay the dragon's evil or its strength and fury. The brave knight, St. George, doesn't easily slay the dragon in their first encounter. He lies bloodied and spent through the cold night. My tiny, cautious son admired the knight for his determination to do right and his courage, even in the face of sure defeat. He wanted the princess's family and village rescued from the dragon's clutches, and he respected Princess Una, who rode away alone to find help and then braved the dragon to care for the wounded knight that long night. If Una and George could defeat that dragon, then maybe he could too.

Our children want heroes. They want to see people who feel afraid but act with courage. They want the good guys to win. They want to cheer when Hansel and Gretel defeat the witch and make their way home. They laugh at the Emperor who struts naked down the city streets while they internalize the message that hubris and arrogance are wrong and that one person standing up for the truth can make all the difference. Who is the hero in *The Emperor's New Clothes*? The false tailors who trick the king are brave and cunning, but what of the little boy who says the fatal words out loud, "The Emperor isn't wearing any clothes!"? As an adult, I simply see a child who doesn't realize what is happening and speaks without thinking. That's all too familiar to most parents! But to the child listening to the story, the little boy who cries out is the one brave enough to speak.

Most of my personal references are from Western European collections, such as Hans Christian Andersen's 1837 fairytales. However, he adapted many of his tales from a much older collection that included stories from the Middle East and around the Mediterranean. You can find similar tales from around the globe. Indian folklore, for instance, tells a story similar to the *Emperor's New Clothes*. It's a literary reference that resonates across different cultures, highlighting the universal lessons about willful ignorance and false logic. Fairytales and folktales around the world share themes and even plots. Pick up a collection from China, India, or Peru and you will find familiar friends and foes inside. We can learn much about our own shared humanity in the words of these simple children's stories.

In children's stories and fairytales, the bad guys aren't always dragons or dark wizards or evil masterminds. Sometimes, the bad guy is an old man named Sneep with a grudge against an old schoolmate and who sucks a lemon to ruin his homecoming celebration. And the good guy with courage is a young boy who knows how to play the harmonica to lead the celebratory song. The story *Lentil* by Robert McCloskey also teaches something of freely given forgiveness when the sour old man gets to enjoy an ice cream cone along with the rest of the town. One short book about a boy without many talents who learned to play the harmonica. One small boy who had the courage and presence of mind to stand up and take the lead so a celebration could happen—and an ego stroked so the town could get the money it needed—and a town that didn't hold a grudge. It's not a long book or a deeply profound book or a book with much action. It's simply a good story with an unlikely hero and a satisfying resolution. My son and I used his wooden blocks to build Lentil's little town, complete with the statue in the town park with a pencil sharpener cannon on top, and we acted out the story with harmonica and much pretend lemon slurping. My five-year-old didn't really like the object of the celebration and thought the old man probably had good reason for his grudge, but he knew the celebration was important to the town. He thought, even at five, that Ol' Sneep's bitter plan to ruin the day was silly and petty. How much more did he learn from that sweet little story than from any lecture I could give about standing up to bullies, courage, and forgiveness?

Children's stories do not just teach good and evil, but they also encourage the development of wonder and the appreciation for the beautiful. One of our family's favorite picture book authors and illustrators is Barbara Cooney. From her Maine stories like *Miss Rumphius* and *Island Boy* to the incredible illustrations in *Ox-Cart Man* and *Roxaboxen*, Cooney captured the wonder, joy, and beauty of childhood. Is there any other story that, more explicitly yet gently, tells us all the importance of bringing beauty to the world than *Miss Rumphius?* Miss Rumphius didn't add beauty by painting, sculpting, or doing something grand. She scattered seeds—seeds that became flowers that covered her town. Cooney planted seeds of beauty and wonder in children around the world for generations.

Like his fellow Maine author, Robert McCloskey gave us stories of wonder. The illustrations in *One Morning in Maine*, *Blueberries for Sal*, *Make Way for Ducklings*, and *Time of Wonder* are exquisite. The first three are largely monochrome, which makes the lavish color of *Time of Wonder* so astonishing. All of these books are ones that can be poured over again and again without words, but then you come to the words, and you want to read them slowly, reveling in the world they create for you. There is the beauty of familial love and protection, the beauty of community, the thrill of independence. When Sal loses her tooth, her father is sympathetic but not maudlin. "It's okay," is the message imparted. "Disappointing things happen, but you will be okay." And Sal *is* okay. She proudly shows off her gap and is thrilled to find that her wish for an ice cream cone is fulfilled. She accepts her new role as being "almost grown-up" and helps her little sister and her father. My kids all wanted that freedom—and responsibility, too. Imagine riding a boat across the bay to get groceries! Imagine running along the island shore alone, talking to seals, and laughing with loons? Robert McCloskey's books are good at reminding children—and their parents—that bad things happen, but good things do, too. His stories remind us that helpers exist: That sometimes policemen will stop traffic to allow a family of ducks to cross a busy intersection; that teeth may fall out and we may grow up, but growing up can be fun; that sometimes small children get separated from their parents, but they can be found; and that even when storms hit, the sun comes out the following day.

The lessons from children's stories do endure. It is through their example that we learn patience, wonder, resilience, creativity, forgiveness, and the power of beauty. I will never be an artist or an interior decorator or a landscape architect. I will not suddenly discover a talent for dance or acting or sculpting. Yet paradoxically, I write that we are created to seek beauty. I can unequivocally say that I will never win awards for creating a beautifully and artistically decorated birthday cake. My children, however, assume I will decorate their birthday cakes to their specifications. I suspect my youngest may be secretly taunting me by asking for such things as a griffin or a "red dragon in a green field with a blue sky and a red knight." He asks for the seemingly impossible every year, and every year, I gamely do my best. Are they Pinterest worthy cakes? Most assuredly, they are not. They are, however, beautiful in the eyes of my son. I do not claim they are particularly well done or artistic. My son, truly an artist, has no problem critiquing my design and execution. Still, he loves my cakes and asks for them again the following year. Why? I don't pretend to fully understand the workings of his clever mind, but I offer that perhaps he appreciates the creative effort. Yes, we want to rest our eyes on beautiful things, but we also want to experience the joy of creativity. He wanted that red dragon because we were reading stories about knights and dragons. In that elaborately drawn, somewhat messy cake top, he saw the stories come to life. And I get to live out with him the idea that imagination doesn't have to be shunted away down a side track, hauled back for special occasions and true artistic endeavors: Imagination is for the everyday. Imagination is for messy birthday cakes, sun prints made with bent paperclips and dandelions, funny voices when reading aloud, or made-up stories about the lives of the squirrels in the tree across the way. Imagination, nourished and cultivated and celebrated, becomes the key to building bridges, both literal and figurative, in the complex world of adulthood. Imagination allows us to envision solutions and relationships beyond what already are to the beautiful things they might become.

The book *Harold and the Purple Crayon* is now a movie. Does it capture the wonder of and imagination contained in a simple crayon? It is able to convey the silliness of the clever wordplay in the book? We always got a particularly good giggle out of the line, "Then he drew up the covers..." The imagination of Harold didn't need special effects and flashy colors. With one simple crayon, he could go on a walk, meet a dragon, sail the ocean, enjoy a picnic, feed some animals, climb a mountain, ride in a hot air balloon, and eventually find his house, his window, and his bed. There is beauty in the simplicity of that story. There are also great lessons to be quietly absorbed. Harold is bored, so he goes for a walk with his crayon. He makes a moon when he needs moonlight, an apple tree for a walk in nature, and a dragon to guard the apples. He thinks quickly and makes himself a boat when he falls in the water. He is kind, drawing a hungry moose and a deserving porcupine to finish his leftover pie (does everyone try to name their nine favorite pies when reading this part?). He knows to ask for help when he needs it, but when the policeman is unable to help, he doesn't give up. He solves many problems along his journey with creativity and resourcefulness. Those skills aren't innate; they must be learned. And how better to learn them than through the subtlety of a clever story? How better to demonstrate the power of imagination?

Keep wonder alive. In our homeschool community, my younger children would celebrate with costumes around Halloween, but they had to be costumes of a book character. My youngest two boys would throw themselves into creating elaborate costumes: Elrond, Faramir, the Nazgul King, Gandalf, and even Sauron (yes, there was a several-years-long theme). One year, I spent the day as Mrs. Whatsit from *A Wrinkle in Time*, draped in scarves, complete with rubber boots and an old hat. The following year, my older son, who was beginning high school, had no intention of dressing up. He wasn't going to be one of the few high school kids in costume. I decided that was nonsense. I love a good costume. We happened to be reading aloud the *Fablehaven* series by Brandon Mull. One of the characters is Bracken, the son of the Fairy Queen. In human form, he is described as an impossibly handsome teenage boy. He also appears as a unicorn. So, of course, I went to school that day in my daughter's pink unicorn onesie, plastic sword in hand. I popped into my oldest son's class and asked if his classmates liked his costume—Bracken, the fairy prince disguised as an impossibly handsome teenage boy. While I enjoyed teasing him, I also enjoyed reminding a class of teenagers that imagination isn't something you leave behind after middle school.

Creativity isn't limited to childhood, only to be indulged in by adults working in the arts. A parent can dress in costume or decorate a funny cake. Or even write songs, as my husband does, for every child. A handyman repairing a hole in your porch floor may scavenge for scrap wood he can puzzle together to create the perfect patch, or a plumber turn a pipe fitting 90 degrees to create space for insulation. Simple problem solving, right? But done with creativity by someone who had the imagination to look beyond what they could see to find a better solution! Engineers can be focused on their numbers and their computer code and their logic-based analysis of a problem, but the very best engineers are also the ones who add creativity (and beauty) to their skill set.

When I entered college, MIT was ranked the number one college in the United States and, for some areas of study, the world. It was the pinnacle of STEM higher education. I was drawn to that, of course, but more than that, I was intrigued by its reputation for play. As much as MIT is known for turning out engineers and Nobel-prize-winning scientists, MIT is also known for its culture of hacking. Not computer hacking—though I'm sure there is just a little of that, as well. What fascinated me was the apparent celebration of humorous, large scale pranking that was also referred to as hacking. Known almost as much for putting a police car on the Great Dome or the bridge measured in Smoots as for Nobel prize winning professors, MIT has a history of encouraging creativity. Long hours of work on problem sets meant long hours of conversation and, inevitably, storytelling. We marinated in an atmosphere of wonder, fueled by stories of professors who let students tool around in their labs (how many of my class were sad to learn we just missed the opportunity to play with Doc Edgerton in his stop motion photography lab!), stories of hacking from decades past, and stories of inventions or discoveries about which we had read or dreamed. There was a thriving arts community at MIT, as well. Theater, music, photography, and sculpture abounded. I took a creative writing class, had classmates who went on to Hollywood or played instruments in community orchestras. If you are used to creative thinking in one area of your life, it spreads outward to touch every aspect, as long as you don't try to contain it.

When I talk with my children about my time at MIT, I nearly always end up telling some stories of how we would just talk. I tell them about my professors and about my classes. I tell them about freshman year physics problem sets that took all night. I tell them the work was hard. But mostly, I talk about the way my classmates emanated wonder. There was a curiosity to learn and a sense of wonder retained from childhood, refined by knowledge and maturity.

It is not surprising to me at all that I found God at MIT. What better place for Him to be found than where people devote themselves to studying His great world with such a sense of wonder and awe? Creativity of thought, imagination at work. These open the mind to the possibilities beyond our immediate sight. That openness might lead to grand discoveries in microbiology—or it might lead a young student to the greatest Creator of all. I do appreciate the shock value of declaring I found God at MIT, but to me, it isn't shocking in the slightest. The imagination that was fed and grown through a love of stories that no one ever convinced me that I needed to outgrow, the imagination that found a ready home at a university that understood that science is intimately, deeply, intrinsically connected to imagination and wonder, the imagination that reveled in the stories of my peers—that imagination also left open the door to faith. Is not the Bible a storyteller's dream? Rich with details of people and places, big emotions, drama, and pathos, the Bible is the ultimate story of humanity. *Yes!* My soul cried when I read the words of John 1: "In the beginning was the Word, and the Word was with God, and the Word was God. All things were made through Him, and without Him, nothing was made that was made." (John 1:1) God was a WORD. He spoke the Story into existence. And wasn't it marvelous, I thought, how that story unfolded in all the glorious cellular biology and chemistry and astrophysics? Faith and science are forever intertwined in the grand story of Creation itself.

CHAPTER 3

Morals, Empathy, Vulnerability, and Virtue

"It has lessons that don't feel like lessons."
—CHAUTONA HAVIG, *Clock Tower Bound*[57]

"Little by little, he began to feel the joy and sadness of others.
He became less immune, less numb, because of the stories."
—DANIEL NAYERI, *Everything Sad Is Untrue*[58]

"We rely upon the poets, the philosophers, and the playwrights
to articulate what most of us can only feel, in joy or sorrow.
They illuminate the thoughts for which we only grope; they give
us the strength and balm we cannot find in ourselves. Whenever
I feel my courage wavering, I rush to them. They give me the
wisdom of acceptance, the will and resilience to push on."
—HELEN HAYES, *A Gift of Joy*[59]

People in conflict struggle with being vulnerable. If the conflict is already hurtful, no one wants to risk more pain. Whether the ones at odds are twelve-year-olds trading barbs or neighbors arguing over placement of a fence or family members on opposite sides of the political aisle, we carefully manage our emotions to minimize our vulnerability. Empathy sounds lovely in theory, but when you empathize with your opponent, you risk losing your edge. What if they don't reciprocate? What if they take advantage of your empathy? Not to mention how difficult it can be to even muster empathy in the first place.

Seeing that play out powerfully in the person of a teenage girl in Mitrovica, Kosovo, challenged me to reexamine the power of empathy. Fatmire Feka and the other young people in the Kids Clubs for Peace in Kosovo showed incredible empathy to their enemies and allowed themselves to be vulnerable enough to step up and firmly, unequivocally declare that they wanted peace. Led by the youth, the leadership in Mitrovica followed their example in both empathy and vulnerability. Teachers impacted by the peace clubs in their schools reached out to teachers on the other side; parents were encouraged by their children to choose peace over hate; and community leaders redoubled their efforts to restrain violence, joining together in the Council for Peace and Tolerance, of which teenaged Fatmire was a member. Over and over again in conflict areas, we see this same dynamic at work: The young people reach out to one another, and the adults follow.

And I think we can understand why. Besides all of the practical and political reasons for adult hesitance, I suspect that children remain closer to their imaginations, closer to wonder, closer to their emotions. If you can be Peter Pevensie forgiving his brother for betraying his siblings to the White Witch in Narnia, if you can be Beauty seeing the good and the true in the Beast, or even Ol' Sneep humbly and happily enjoying an ice cream cone and the town's forgiveness, you can see yourself reaching out to those who stand on the other side of a chasm of painful conflict. It's not mere naivety that fuels such outreach. Rather, it is the willingness and ability to be "the Other," to use our moral imagination, to get our purple crayon, and to be open to reconciliation.

Our culture today is in a near-constant state of conflict, even self-feeding high conflict. With emotions high, we don't want to risk appearing weak or stupid. We often learn to protect ourselves and to guard our emotions. Even the most emotionally healthy of us are adept at concealment. Not everyone should be privy to our innermost thoughts or every feeling. Keeping some things close is not a fault. Yet, we must learn how to be vulnerable and open when warranted in order to build trust in challenging situations. We can never truly engage in reconciliation if we do not know how to be appropriately vulnerable. As well, we need to learn how to understand, interpret, and empathize with the emotions of others. We can learn those lessons, in part, through our relationships with the characters in stories, relationships that we have nurtured and developed as children.

Stories that bring us to laughter or tears, to anger, sorrow, compassion, or pity help us learn those emotions. Children who identify with Lucy's anger and sense of betrayal when Edmund lied about Narnia learn that it is okay to be angry sometimes. And when Edmund leaves to go to the White Queen, his defensive anger to justify his betrayal of his siblings is understood to be different from Lucy's justified anger. They can wrestle with Peter's anger at Edmund and with Lucy's forgiveness. It is easier to understand their own emotions when they are mirrored in a story they love. It is easier to see the humanity in an enemy in a story than the one sitting across the classroom, the boardroom, or the social media page.

Much of the focus today is on teaching "values," but values is such a vague and imprecise term. Whose values? How are they labeled and defined? I value free time to read; reading books for hours is a personal value of mine. Is that a virtue? Does that make me moral? I don't particularly value exercise. I do value my health and take measures to stay reasonably fit and healthy—but those measures will never involve long hours in the gym or miles of running. What about valuing financial stability? Being close to extended family? Owning pets? All of these can be considered values, but they are hardly universal—even within one family.

Morals and virtues, on the other hand, translate across time and place. Honesty, loyalty, prudence, compassion, justice, and courage are admired nearly everywhere in every time. Not that their relative weight or exact nature are the same—some cultures value loyalty above compassion or see more justice in mercy than in retribution. If we recognize the virtue of honor, we can learn the importance of it in cultures other than our own. If we recognize the virtue of mercy, we can appeal to that no matter the circumstance.

The Declaration of Independence and the Preamble to the Constitution of the United States are based on a set of virtues and the premise that our rights as human beings come not from a determined set of values, vulnerable to the whims of time and place, but from our very beings as created by God. If we do not understand that, we risk losing everything that our Founders fought to preserve. Life, liberty, and the pursuit of happiness are considered innate possessions of the human race—not gifts bestowed by a government because, in that time and place, they are valued. We, as mercurial humans, sometimes value things temporally that would bring harm in the long term. Coming out of conflict or trauma, we might value personal safety and security over liberty. Of course! But as our safety and security grow and our memories of trauma fade, do we not long again for freedom and chafe against restraints to our pursuit of happiness? One is a value, something we place importance upon at the moment, but the other is akin to virtue, something more deeply ingrained in our humanity. The pursuit of happiness itself is a virtue; Jefferson enshrined the right to live a life of worth in the Declaration of Independence. How we live that out is a mix of virtues and values. I may live with the virtues of integrity, compassion, loyalty, and thoughtfulness and do so by engaging in things I value, such as work I find meaningful, building a home filled with things I find pleasant, and relationships that bring joy. All of those are specific to me, things I value, but the virtue of pursuing that life of worth is universal.

Our values change as we move through different stages in our lives. As a twelve-year-old, one might value making every play in baseball and being on an All-Star team. At twenty-seven, that is most likely no longer seen as important unless you happen to play for a Major League team. But the virtues of determination and perseverance that led to the twelve-year-old practicing for hours every day help the twenty-seven-year old doggedly pursue victory in a legal case or solve the problem of a weird plumbing angle.

Someone growing up in a large Italian-American family in New York may have a set of values that includes marrying young, being a faithful Catholic, having children, making time for family dinners, and working hard. Growing up African-American in a conservative Baptist family in South Carolina, one might have a similar set of values. But the values might diverge. The second family might find another set of values in common with other African-Americans growing up in New York City, and the Italian-American family might share some of these values with descendants of Polish mill workers in the Rust Belt. A farm kid might share some values with a kid growing up in Baltimore, and a teen in the suburbs of Washington, D.C., might share some with a Cuban immigrant in South Florida. Which values define you?

Political rhetoric depends on value statements. The value of education, the value of health care, etc. Politicians appeal to the things we hold important. Value, though, is an economic term. It defines what we consider important, that on which we place a price and something on which we can trade. And isn't that what our political world is today? It is a constant trade of things of value. Aid to a foreign country? What will you give me? If you vote for me, I'll make sure you get more money for infrastructure and less for foreign aid. What do you value?

That emphasis on values has a significant and not always helpful impact on our attempts at reconciliation and living with healthy conflict. My values may be in conflict with yours, so our discussions become one of trade-offs. The economist Thomas Sowell wisely said there are no true "solutions" in politics and policy, only trade-offs. We fight about an economic exchange to see how to maximize the benefits to each party. But when we live in a state of high conflict, we place an outsized value on our position, making it nearly impossible to come to a compromise. We find that we *must* stand our ground to protect and defend something of such worth. Unfortunately, when both sides are encamped on the hilltops, firmly convinced that they hold the position of highest value, neither side will back down—but neither side can win.

Some conflict resolution tools teach a values-based process, wherein parties to the conflict assess their relative positions and negotiate an outcome. There is nothing wrong with approaching some conflicts with this mindset. Sometimes, conflict must be mediated in this way to achieve a working solution. However, this type of resolution process should be reserved for specific conflicts that can be managed by a series of trade-offs and bargains. This approach is not appropriate for broader cultural conflicts, familial conflicts, or anything rooted in identity. Our identities are not values to be traded on the market. Our relationships should not come with a price tag. The tools and processes we learn for conflict resolution are meant to assist in situational conflict, not to address a state of conflict or a culture of conflict. They are tools only—not an end themselves.

To reset our approach to conflict and reconciliation, we should look to the virtues rather than our values. In my own life, I place a high value on family game nights. Those aren't always shared values with a husband and four ever-older children. When I propose one, what virtues underlie my suggestion? Perhaps love, cooperation, and unity are driving my desire. I want to bring my family together to strengthen our family by spending time together in fun. If I cling to what I value, I may miss the opportunity to strengthen our family virtues through the counter suggestion of a movie night. As my children have grown older and more empathetic, they will sometimes protest, "But Mom, if you really want a game, then you can *make* everyone play." I appreciate their concern, but I am trying to teach them that deferring to preference is often putting the family virtues I wish to strengthen over the things I personally value. Since I also want to strengthen virtues such as respect, sacrifice, and kindness, sometimes I insist on game night. Regardless of our activity, resolving the conflict means addressing the virtues we wish to see rather than the surface-level values onto which we are holding.

A statement of values does not infer the truth of the statement. What are "family values," for instance? Do those words have the same meaning across cultures and subcultures? I value family. I value certain characteristics implied by the term "family," but are those characteristics the same as yours? What I might say instead is that I value love, compassion, charity, kindness, patience, hospitality, persistence, faithfulness, and hope. Those virtues are part of the package I see as "family values." They define that which I hold important, how I approach others, and how I want to live. In other words, virtues define our character; they define who we are. That character then chooses what we value.

Storytelling is perhaps the best medium to teach the virtues. As any teacher or lecturer—or boardroom presenter—knows, our audience remembers best what they've absorbed through a story. No lecture on the numbers needed to reach a sales goal will stick as well as a story told about the year a lowly salesman broke the record and put the company on the track to success. We learn through stories—history, science, even math (remember word problems?), and most especially virtue. Our moral imagination is awakened and strengthened through stories.

A quick internet search for children's books on kindness brings up a seemingly endless supply of picture books with the words "kind" or "kindness" in the title. Do they all truly teach the virtue of kindness?

Picture books that provide a step-by-step lesson on how to be kind are more likely to put you to sleep than inspire you, much like a management meeting that emphasizes lists of tactics and wields the word "sales" like a hammer. Children absorb the message of "be kind" or, in other words, practice the virtue of kindness better through books like Marjory Flack's *Angus and the Cat* than any how-to book on kindness. They can learn about friendship and kindness in *The Reluctant Dragon* by Kenneth Grahame or William Steig's beautiful *Amos & Boris*. They learn about the importance of being true to oneself in *The Story of Ferdinand* by Munro Leaf. My boys howled with delight at the fierceness and wits of the *Paper Bag Princess* and cheered when she told off her wimpy, stuck-up prince. They didn't need a lesson on how girls can be strong and independent. They needed a story.

Recently, I was reminded of the old *Sesame Street* cartoon short called *I Remember*, which is about a little girl going to the store for her mother. My kids all had a good laugh when I told them I still chant along with the little girl in the cartoon, "a loaf of bread, a container of milk, and a stick of butter," when I am running through a shopping list in my head. We talked about how the technique of repetition helps us remember, but then we also talked about how the mother offered her little girl a different tool to help her with the shopping: Her mother offered to write it down. The little girl refused and skipped off, chanting her list to remember. Once at the store, however, the little girl forgot the final item. Rather than run home without it, she thought hard and repeated the list to herself until the final item—a stick of butter—was recalled. Then she happily ran home with the shopping completed. I readily learned the lessons of that little short: I could be responsible, and I could help mommy. I learned that I could be independent and I could do hard things. I learned a trick to help me remember. And I learned what to do if I forgot—and what to do if I couldn't do something entirely right on the first try. Responsibility and persistence, independence, resilience, and remembering. I learned those things by skipping along with a tiny girl in a yellow dress, repeating with her, "A loaf of bread, a container of milk, and a stick of butter." Decades later, I recall both her little chant and the lessons it imparted. Would I remember as well if *Sesame Street* had taught me "three tricks to a better memory" or if the little girl had gone home crying and her mother went back to the store for her? I didn't learn the lessons because they were explicitly spoken. Rather, I learned them because I was drawn into that little story with that little girl running an errand for her mother.

It is through stories that we can experience challenges and relationships that we cannot in our real lives. I didn't grow up in an urban neighborhood where I could run down the block to the store to pick up a few groceries for my mother. I didn't need to for me to be able to relate to the little girl in the cartoon. More than the experience of skipping down a city street, however, I could live through war on the home front in books like *Rilla of Ingleside* by L.M.Montgomery, the death of a family member in Madeleine L'Engle's *Ring of Endless Light*, the death of a friend and questions of faith and doubt in *Terabithia* by Katherine Paterson, and the horrific lives of mill workers in the early part of the Industrial Revolution in her *Lyddie*. I was able to see that being shy and out of step with my high school peers wouldn't last forever as I walked alongside Meg in L'Engle's *Wrinkle in Time* series. That's a perspective you can't find on your own at fifteen, but it is one that is sorely needed as you navigate that challenging period in your life. Stories gave me access to the reality of "the Other."

Of all the protagonists I adventured with, I resonated most with Meg in *A Wrinkle in Time*. She was unpopular, didn't feel like she fit in, and was angry and frustrated with school and the not-always-so-subtle push to conform. She was the object of the bullies. But I know others who read *Wrinkle in Time* were not Megs. Maybe they identified more with Calvin, who, though also a bit unlike his peers, managed to camouflage his differences and attained popularity by being a basketball star. Or perhaps they identified with Meg's twin brothers, who were happily "normal" and didn't understand why their sister didn't just try harder. As they read the story, did they learn empathy for Meg—and, by extension, the Megs in their lives—as they followed her journey?

When children read books about characters very unlike themselves, they learn to look through their eyes, however briefly. My daughter was born in Washington, D.C., and we were an average. well-educated, middle-class family. She had never known poverty, war, hunger, or the real terror of military occupation. But through my stories from my colleagues in the Middle East and reading books with her such as *Sitti's Secrets*, she learned a little bit about what it might be like to be a child in Israel-Palestine. When a colleague with a daughter close to her age visited, my then-six-year-old sent him home with a booklet of pictures and words of hope for his little girl. She could see through the eyes of a conflict-traumatized child and wanted to offer what comfort she could. In another story lesson, as the only white child in an all-Black school, she faced some hostility. She could see herself in the story of Ruby Bridges, but she could also see the history her bullies were fighting against. Rather than anger or prejudice taking root, empathy and grace prevailed.

Racism isn't resolved with a picture book, but children who are immersed in a world of stories with diverse main characters learn to look at the whole person and not just race or ethnicity. Children don't have to read a biography of Ruby Bridges (though her autobiography for children, *Through My Eyes*, is fantastic) to identify with a child of color. *Corduroy* and *Snowy Day* were classic favorites of mine, and my children in turn, that allow any child of any race to enter into the experience of the African-American protagonists. Will that solve racism in the United States? Of course not. But white children who love Don Freedman's Lisa and her care for her bear Corduroy are learning to find a friend in someone the world can deem "other." They don't need ham-fisted lessons on anti-racism in elementary school if they have been making story friends of all races and ethnicities their whole lives. Those story friends—and their real-life friends—help prepare them for more challenging books that deal more openly with issues such as racism. From picture books to novels like *The Watsons Go to Birmingham* by Christopher Paul Curtis to Harper Lee's *To Kill A Mockingbird* to Ralph Ellison's *Invisible Man*, children who have not experienced racism themselves develop empathy and understanding for those who have, and they have learned to hear the stories of real life friends with those experiences. I was a poor white kid growing up in a very white rural world. But when I entered the world of MIT as a young adult, I was better prepared to enter into the space where difficult conversations on race can occur. Not because someone described racism to me in a classroom lesson in second grade or because I saw a bullet-pointed slide show, but because I had walked alongside characters I loved who were living those experiences. Empathy doesn't develop from a lecture. It grows naturally from stories.

I have what my daughter sometimes believes is too much patience for belligerent, cranky, and misogynist old men. Sometimes, she has a point. But sometimes, even the most cantankerous and mean old man has a story that helps you understand, and that empathy grants you that extra measure of patience. I have learned to listen for those stories, in part due to the dozens of stories I've read over the years with a character whose nasty exterior masks a hurt or misunderstood heart. In *Heidi*, no one liked Alm-Uncle for his meanness, his hatred for women, and his desire to be left alone. That is, until his granddaughter came along and gradually uncovered his past, and the reader came to understand him. No, not every old man spewing racist vitriol at the world is covering past hurts with a hard shell. Some people really are just mean. And sometimes, our first priority must be to protect someone else from their hate, regardless of what lies behind it. Still, when I can, I am willing to entertain grace for even the most venomous jerk because I know everything is not always as it seems. Sometimes, that jerk is really an Alm-Uncle who hasn't come to terms with his past.

A parent might read *The Story About Ping* to their five-year-old, who, many years later, recalls his fascination with the boat boys on the Yangtze River. Though *Ping* is simply a picture book written by an American woman in 1933, the story is a little window into pre-Mao life on the Yangtze River. Pre-WWII China may be taught in a history class one day, and that young boy remembers the sweetness of that story. Because of his curiosity and empathy, he might pay a little closer attention in that high school class. He might learn more deeply the lessons regarding the Second Sino-Japanese War and the impact of WWII on China. That little picture book by Marjorie Flack created the space for an older student to learn.

Story characters don't have to be paragons of virtue to teach the virtues. Flawed characters who change and grow teach best.

The little trains in Rev. W. Awdry's original *Thomas the Tank Engine* didn't always do the right thing on the first try. But they demonstrated perseverance, kindness, generosity, thoughtfulness, humility, and patience with each other and learned their lessons along the way. My children all preferred the old stories to new ones, saying the new ones were "too lecture-y or too silly," to quote one irritated young son. He preferred the stories where the trains went on adventures doing their jobs and learned their own lessons. Alongside Thomas, he learned the lessons, too. As with *The Wizard of Oz*, stories that define the characteristics that make up a virtue teach more than a series of acts. The lion wanted courage, but he didn't know how to define it until the Wizard showed him how brave he had been all along. He demonstrated courage because he did brave acts while afraid. The Scarecrow wanted brains, but the Wizard helped him see how he had been thoughtful and wise all along as he helped Dorothy make decisions about how to proceed on their journey. The lesson learned wasn't that one must do a certain thing to have courage or think a certain way to have brains. The lesson was to cultivate the habit of bravery or critical thinking. Older children rereading *The Wizard of Oz* may also pick up on subtle barbs aimed at a society that equates a medal with bravery and a diploma with wits.

Stories in which the characters grow to embody the characteristics we wish to emulate or who act in ways we wish to act help us envision what could be. I'll never be a young girl growing up on a farm in upstate New York, riding horses and solving mysteries with my best friend, my brothers, and our gang of friends, but I learned more than a few life lessons from Trixie Belden and the Bobwhites. Reading through that old series, I could see how friends stick by one another, forgiveness makes it possible to reconcile, being bold needs to be tempered with wisdom and patience, and hesitance can be caused by fear or lack of understanding and doesn't always equal wisdom. Who wouldn't want friends like the Bobwhite gang? Trixie's idyllic life may not be realistic for anyone—if it ever was—but we don't have to live that life or even to want her exact life to step into her world and absorb its lessons of loyalty, service, and generous love. I didn't love Trixie because she was a heedless tomboy who wanted to be a detective. I loved Trixie because she was a good friend and had good friends. Just as I was unfamiliar with Trixie's farm life, I didn't have any experience with the city life in *A Tree Grows in Brooklyn* or frontier prairie life in *Little House on the Prairie*. Yet each of those books taught me valuable lessons, as well.

It isn't only picture books and novels that teach us. We learn to empathize, and we learn the virtues that form our character through the stories we hear from others. Another story from our family tradition is that my mom's family, like so many others assert, has a great-great-grandmother of Native American ancestry. We can find no documented evidence of that. On the other hand, we can't find any conclusively documented evidence that story is not true. That ambiguity is a lesson in itself. While it seems increasingly unlikely that my great-great-grandmother was, in fact, Native American, the search for her records was illuminating. For many people with Indigenous ancestry, the family tree has entire branches that will remain blank because their stories were erased, their ancestors either forced to assimilate and pass as white or remaining undocumented, nothing more than a name on a census record or a child's draft card.

Growing up hearing the story of my great-grandfather's reasons for leaving his family while a teenager and working his way hundreds of miles west alongside his younger brother, I wanted to learn more. Was I really descended from a Native American woman? Who was she? What was her tribe? Was she mixed? How did she meet and marry a German immigrant? Did his second wife really dislike my great-grandfather because his mother was an "Indian?" That short tale has so many elements that are familiar to many different American families. Part of it is a desire to be a part of something, to be rooted in our nation's past and place. We want to belong to this place and we know that while the European settlers were brave, adventurous, and committed to liberty, we know, too, they were sometimes cruel, arrogant, and greedy. Yes, we think we are the intrepid settlers who built a great country founded on ideals it still struggles to achieve, but also, we are the people who were displaced, lived here first, loved the land, and honored it.

It is a sad reality that many families were torn apart by racism, fear, and pride. I don't expect to ever have a clear answer about my great-great-grandmother, but I do know that hearing that story throughout my childhood, I developed a fierce desire for justice for those who lost their identities, who were forced to hide their heritage and lived invisibly with the hate around them. That little snippet of likely false family history gave me the impetus to learn more. It provoked empathy for those who really lived through that erasure. I don't have the firsthand family knowledge of assimilation schools that others do, but my growing up with those stories created the space to learn and empathize.

Not everyone absorbs their family stories in the same way. For those stories to create space for hearing others, I have to step into them with vulnerability of my own. I can't share the family lore without also being open to saying, "But we don't know if that was true and we didn't live that experience as if it was." My great-grandfather passed away young, long before my generation or the previous one could ask him the questions that would give us the answers and help us understand him. If he was, indeed, the son of a Native American woman who passed as white, the impact of that will remain unknown. I can't pretend to join the experiences of those whose family members have recounted the trauma they endured and the stigma they felt. It is important that I approach those conversations with humility and vulnerability rather than focusing on my story and my identity and my pride. And hopefully, those with whom I am speaking are able to hear my story, as well. I hope they could hear that I wanted to learn—more of him, of course, but more of them and more of their stories and their impact. I hope that in my story, they could hear that I understood even a small part of their story, and I hope we can find common ground in our care for those stories and for the dignity and humanity of the people who lived them.

Too often, we isolate ourselves in our silos of identity. Our family stories become our armor, our community stories our weapons. Amin Maalouf, a Lebanese-born French author and scholar, writes in *In the Name of Identity* of how we tend to hold most dearly that aspect of our identity most under attack, and the wounds we suffer due to various allegiances ultimately set up our hierarchy of identity within ourselves. Am I a woman? Italian-American (thanks only to my last name)? Rural? Appalachian? Poor? Middle-class? White? Smart? Short?

Christian—evangelical, Presbyterian, Anglican, Episcopalian? Which identity dominates? My father, adopted as an infant by his Italian-American stepfather, has never identified as Italian-American. So, what identity does matter most? What stories did he hear as he grew up? Today, he is a kilt-wearing bagpiper who is creating his Thoreau-inspired wilderness buffer around his house. As writers like Mitali Perkins and Daniel Nayeri express so beautifully, growing up in an in-between space can gift us with the kinds of stories that cultivate empathy and understanding.

Stories ground us. They root us in our past, our families, communities, and places. They help us retain wonder, deepening our imaginations while we learn how to hang on to the creativity of childhood. They help us develop our character by demonstrating the virtues we learn to emulate, forming those habits alongside the story characters we love. And stories let us step inside and walk in the shoes of others, exploring their emotions and experiences, expanding our capacity for empathy. Whether a child is listening to bedtime stories and turning the pages of a favorite picture book, crouched on the stairs listening to family stories make the rounds at the end of the holiday meal, getting lost in a novel that transports them to a different place or time, or swapping personal stories with a new friend, those stories make us people who can walk fearlessly into conflict.

PART THREE

POWER OF CRITICAL THINKING

CHAPTER 1

Critical Thinking and Socratic Questioning

> "The worst of all deceptions is self-deception...when the deceiver is always present..."
> —SOCRATES, PLATO, *Cratylus, 428D*[60]

> "...[T]he unexamined life is not worth living."
> —SOCRATES, PLATO, *Apology 38a*[61]

> "Behind the logical form...often an inarticulate and unconscious judgment...the very root and nerve of the whole proceeding."
> —OLIVER WENDELL HOLMES, JR., *Path of the Law*[62]

I have a confession to make: Though I've spent most of my adult life orbiting the political sphere in Washington, D.C., married to a man deeply engaged in politics, I cannot watch televised political debates. Perhaps I should say that my family prefers that I do not watch them. I do appreciate a good debate. I even teach a class on Logic in Mock Trial. I do not, however, find much "good debate" or logic in our modern political debates. Nor do I find much of it online. I have tried sporadically, and optimistically, to engage in thoughtful discussions on social media. Cue the laughter. Even in person, I often find that discussions of potentially contentious subjects are minefields of judgment, self-defense, and misunderstandings. I, like many others, am uneasy at the thought of bringing up health care, social security, education, religion, foreign policy, immigration, gun control, abortion, sex/gender/sexuality, or, tragically, the presidential election process. The list could go on indefinitely, a damning inventory of our inability to metabolize, to digest, conflict.

I once asked one of the high school classes I taught if conflict was good or bad. Every single student announced with certainty that conflict is indubitably bad. "Really?" I asked. "Are you certain?" Yes, they were. Every head nodded. I pressed on. "So, if you—"pointing to one particularly vocal student—"think homeschooling is wrong and should be illegal and she—"pointing to a quiet girl across the room—"thinks homeschooling is wonderful and must be protected, are the two of you in conflict?" Without hesitation, the first student declared an emphatic no. "Of course, we're not in conflict if we just don't say anything. I just wouldn't talk about it with her." Again, affirmative nods from every head.

I pushed on. "So, what happens if you are now legislators considering a new bill that would make homeschooling illegal? Are you now in conflict?" This time, I got a few reluctant yeses from unhappy students.

My vocal student tried to find a way out of it. "Well, technically, we would be in conflict, but we could probably just figure out a way to work around it." Murmurs of agreement followed her around the room. I waited, letting the idea simmer for a minute, looking for more answers. I got a few hesitant suggestions about how to hold opposing views yet not be in conflict. My tenth graders looked increasingly uncomfortable, but I didn't have a rescue. I had another question. "So, you are holding a debate on the House floor. One of you introduced the bill, and the other one has introduced a second bill criminalizing any curtailment of homeschooling by the State. You each need to state your position and offer supporting arguments. Are you now in conflict?"

I drew reluctant nods from everyone. Another outspoken student wondered if perhaps they are not in actual conflict unless they are being rude or argumentative or if they are getting violent. Her classmates seem to like that suggestion, a way of once again pushing conflict back to something *more*. This high school class has studied history and Great Books, taken formal logic, and been exposed to ideas from across the world, yet they refuse to entertain the thought that conflict is anything but bad. After all, they don't want to *fight* with anyone. They want to be *nice*.

I let them talk for a minute, and then I announced that they were all completely wrong. "You and you," I said, pointing back to the original two, "have been in conflict the very moment you had opposing thoughts about homeschooling. You do not have to be having a fistfight on the Capitol steps to be in conflict. You do not have to be standing up in opposition to one another in a formal debate. You are in conflict when you hold opposing viewpoints. Now, is conflict good or bad?"

Is conflict good or bad? Neither, depending on the circumstances. Conflict is simply a state of opposition, disagreement. The second entry on Dictionary.com is "be incompatible or at variance; clash." In that case, we are all in conflict with nearly everyone, nearly all the time, in some form or another. And that's not a terrible state in which to be. Arguments, debates, discussion, conflict—none of those are dangerous or wrong. In fact, those are necessary for a healthy community. Conflict pushes us to solve problems, produce new ideas, and build new strengths as individuals and communities.

I value Benjamin Franklin's truism, "Early to bed, early to rise, makes a man healthy, wealthy, and wise." I married a night owl who takes issue with the very idea that anyone can enjoy living that way. That is simply a point of conflict for us. It is sometimes a joke between us, sometimes a source of amusing stories for friends. Sometimes, true, it bubbles up into the sort of serious disagreement of the kind my students seemed to suggest is bad.

Even then, the conflict itself isn't bad or wrong but depends on how we handle the disagreement.

How we handle conflict, opposition, disagreement—all require critical thinking in order to discuss reasonably. Sometimes, we don't manage that. We wield our different internal clocks like weapons until we find ourselves in a state of high conflict, where every negative thing that happens must relate back to the source of disagreement, whether that be what to have for dinner or who is taking our son to a practice. I am sure most couples have those moments where a simple disagreement is suddenly so much more, and our feelings begin to fuel the conflict until the conflict itself is in control. Usually, however, no matter how much our different approaches to sleep and wake cycles conflict, we are able to approach the conversation thoughtfully. Over the years, our more or less thoughtful approach to the conversation has led to some creative problem solving, a bit of compromise, and even some personal growth in both sleep desires and flexible thinking.

The first step is always to check myself. Is my faith in Ben Franklin based on the absolute truth of his statement? Or is there perhaps room for other views? In *The Socratic Method: A Practitioner's Handbook*, Ward Farnsworth lists the "Rules of Engagement" for Socratic dialogue.[63] He starts with "the open table," in which no view is immune from questioning. *No view.* Not my clear preference for waking by dawn nor my husband's fondness for a productive writing session at 2 am are exempt from examination. No matter how strongly I feel about the value of an early bedtime or how productive it makes me the following day, my *belief* in the truthfulness of that statement attributed to Franklin should be on the table for discussion and testing.

Farnsworth follows with eleven more "rules of engagement." They are but one interpretation of the practical application of Socrates' dialogues, but they create a valuable resource for anyone wanting to dive more deeply into the how-tos of such dialogue. An important second rule is that the purpose of dialogue is always to seek the truth. Despite taking multiple classes in formal logic, when my son studied debate, the goal was always to "win." Each side, whether partner debates or solo, presented their position as "truth" and sought to discredit and disprove the arguments of the other. My mock trial students automatically approach each case as adversarial—which, indeed, they are—without considering the purpose of seeking the truth of the matter. My students often question how someone can be a defense attorney knowing many of the clients will be guilty. As a prosecutor, I tell them I wanted my opposing counsel to force me to do my job well, to present a case that sought the truth of the matter and proved guilt beyond a reasonable doubt. I didn't want to win for the sake of winning; I wanted to win because the defendant was truly guilty. And if they were not guilty, I wanted a defense attorney who could show the jury the inconsistencies in my case.

Does that seem to be the purpose of most debate today? One can pick nearly any topic of national interest, from race to gender to education to gun control to simply political party affiliation, and find posturing, grandstanding, and vitriol but very little true and earnest debate. For instance, the health care debate in the United States has been of varying degrees of contentiousness for the past twenty years with increasing polarization of opinions. When we step back, it's safe to assume everyone wants good health care for themselves and their family members. No one is cheering for bad health care. All decent people feel some measure of empathy and concern when they learn of a tragic diagnosis from a mere acquaintance. Yet, it's very difficult to see this good faith desire for good health in "the Other" when it comes to health care policy. Instead, we see a debate dominated by demagoguery and demonization.

During one flare-up in the healthcare debate over the Affordable Care Act, I waded into the Facebook discussion with a few questions: If you are pro-ACA, do you believe it adequately addresses the healthcare needs of Americans and can withstand rigorous scrutiny and debate? Do you believe it was passed in full transparency and good faith? If you are against the ACA, can you explain the points with which you disagree and how to address them? Are you willing to acknowledge ways in which the ACA has improved health care access for some? If you don't have answers for these questions, then perhaps you should not be attacking someone else or posting nasty memes. My post garnered little attention in the rip current of irrationality that passes for discussion on social media. Many people say they want to have good debates, yet the blame always lies with others. I have yet to see good faith debate on the topic of health care access in the United States. Instead, I see finger-pointing. I see suggestions on how the other side should be thinking about or speaking on the topic. I see anger, frustration, self-righteousness, and demonization. I also see sadness. People see a broken system of health care access, and they want to see it fixed, yet it is rare for people to ask hard questions about their own positions.

If "both sides" truly desire affordable healthcare access for everyone and see it as a social good, then should not *all* positions and options be on the table for scrutiny, and should not the object of the discussion be finding the best solution for the most people with the least harm done? I have yet to see that be the dominant approach in government, media, think tanks, or education. I see fortified defensive positions and offensive attacks aimed at winning the argument, not seeking the truth and solving the problem.

Too often, I hear people backing away from open conflict because they refuse to "dignify [the other] with a response."

That sounds so rational, so thoughtful. No point in arguing with someone so clearly wrong or so clearly offensive. Like many parents, I used this approach with my young children. I am not going to argue with a four-year-old about bedtime. To do so would lessen my sense of authority and remove me from a position of leadership. The four-year-old is not my equal in the decision about bedtime. The seventeen-year-old, however, is given the opportunity to make a case for staying out later than curfew. No, he isn't quite sharing my place of authority, but he is closer and is ready to make more decisions for himself. Allowing the debate gives him a chance to test his reasoning. I grant him the dignity of engaging with me as a fellow adult human being with ideas and opinions of his own.

When it comes to a question of politics or religion or economics—is my neighbor more like that four-year-old or the seventeen-year-old? Or, dare I suggest, myself? If I refuse to discuss an issue with someone because I find their position reprehensible, I am essentially declaring them less than. I am denying their inherent worth and dignity as a human being. We do affirm their dignity when we engage or respond. And yes, sometimes, that feels difficult. Or perhaps even wrong. But it is not my place to declare someone unworthy of human dignity. Arguments must be decided on their merits—not on the assumed worth of the ones making them. The only way to approach a conflict is to engage, to be willing to hear the other side and answer with your own argument in return. Anything else risks my own dignity as I become more insulated from disagreement, and my heart becomes more hardened to dissent. Admittedly, sometimes this doesn't work. Some people are so enmeshed within their conflict that they are unable to discuss the subject in good faith. It's okay to bow out gracefully when an argument becomes circular and your opponent illogical and aggressive.

One of the most important things I can do for myself in conflict is to engage in self-critique. I cannot go into an argument (and here I am viewing this from the perspective of logic, with an argument being the set of reasons given in support of a belief) believing that I am, without a doubt, correct in my views. To return to the early to bed, early to rise debate: If I approach my husband absolutely certain that my position is the best one, the right one, the true one, and I must convince him of that, how will I be received? No doubt, my husband believes quite firmly that he feels better, is more productive, and enjoys his time more when he is able to stay up late and get a little more sleep after the sun is up. He may be willing to concede that my view has some merit, but that's less likely if I hold my ground and start off by telling him he's an imbecile for thinking as he does. Is it possible that my view is wrong? Or is it possible that there are other factors I must consider in making a determination? Of course!

Why do I believe what I do? Well, when I reflect on my position, the obvious point is that I personally turn into a pumpkin by midnight. I valiantly attempted to live up to my alma mater's mascot during my first few years at MIT. A beaver is nature's engineer—and is nocturnal, doing its best work at night. Not atypical of most colleges, MIT came alive after dark. At some point, I had to concede that starting a problem set at midnight was not going to work for me. Some of my favorite college memories are squabbling with my floormates in the floor lounge at 11:00 pm over whether to watch the sitcom *Wings* or *Star Trek: The Next Generation*. We would eventually settle on one or the other (usually determined by who managed to snag the TV remote first and withstood the inevitable attempts to wrest it back) and happily watch for an hour, trading banter, venting about work, teasing, snacking, and generally relaxing. At midnight, the show would end, and my friends would peel off to join various study groups, prepping for a night of math or research.

I, however, would take myself off to bed, happy to get my eight hours of sleep to prepare for the following day. That hard-earned knowledge of what works best for me provides evidence that my position is correct. If I dig a little deeper, I recall that my father is a morning person, believing heartily in rising early and tackling his work for the day. I did not have a set curfew in high school, but I knew that if I came in at three in the morning and my dad had a hike planned for six or a project for which he needed my help, I had better be up and dressed and ready to go anyway. I enjoyed those early mornings with my father. It should not surprise me, then, that underlying my own natural affinity for early hours are my father's teaching and my own pleasure in the time spent with him. Society, too, reinforces my position. Offices are open by 8 or 9, stores and even restaurants usually close by midnight. Apartment buildings sometimes enforce quiet hours at night. Hospitals ask visitors to leave. My position has been well-supported.

Once I understand my position better, I can question it a bit more. Is it true that "early to bed, early to rise makes a man healthy, wealthy, and wise?" Maybe. Or maybe not. The statement might sound true to me because of my background and my own internal clock, but does it apply universally? Now that I'm aware of why I believe it to be true, maybe I am more open to understanding my husband's position. I can see that he can conform to expectations, but he also truly does produce his best creative work much later than I could. While he can be up before dawn and handle an interview with aplomb, he thrives in late-night commentary. Once I engage in a little self-reflection, I can see the faults and inconsistencies in my insistence that I am "right." It's a silly argument, but if we let it, that point of conflict could be damaging to our relationship. Understanding myself first, I can understand my husband better, and we can find common ground.

And what is that common ground? How is it found? First, we find points where we agree. Every argument has some point of overlap. With health care, the overlap, again, is that all people of good will want their fellow human beings to thrive and be as healthy as possible. Starting from this understanding, what do I personally believe is the best way to achieve that goal? I need to think through my own ideas first and truly understand my position. Developing my thoughts on solutions is an easy step compared to trying to understand how I came to believe what I do. Just as I can look back over my experiences to see how they shaped my thoughts on bedtimes, I should be able to trace the foundations of my thoughts on health care. Once I fully under-stand my position, its pros and cons, and my reasons for holding it, I can better understand those who disagree with me. From that understanding, I can begin to seek the common ground. My ideological opponents and I can then approach our disagree-ment with humility—accepting that we might be wrong—and with graciousness and respect.

We can't use sarcasm or be rude or judgmental in our con-flict—or try to "own" the other side. As with my husband, I need to assume he's not out to get me and not take offense at some-thing he says. If I feel hurt or offended, I need to clarify—is that what he meant? Too often, in a disagreement, one or both parties will hold back, unwilling to speak with candor lest they risk either exposure or giving offense. In true Socratic dialogue, however, the rules are clear: Speak freely and extend grace to each other. Give your honest opinion and try not to either offend or take offense. Feel free to be assertive, even fierce, but stay away from insults and personal attacks.

Socratic dialogue isn't always gentle or smooth. It requires deep thinking, much self-criticism, and a rejection of beliefs that come too easily. Group think is especially dangerous. My students have all studied basic logical fallacies. Two that are easy for them to grasp are false appeal to authority and the bandwagon fallacy. Yet, our popular media and our government leaders resort to both regularly. Anytime the response is something like, "Well, X [leader or agency or school or source] said so" or "everyone else agrees…" we should immediately be skeptical. Does X indeed have the knowledge and authority to be a definitive resource? *Why* does everyone agree on that position? It is not easy to challenge a group.

I've been the mom with the baby who wouldn't sleep at night in a room of other mothers who all had the answer to making her sleep. But I didn't agree with that answer. How much easier it might have been had I simply agreed! Easier for me perhaps, though not necessarily for the child who still sleeps like she is wrestling dragons. Having a second child who closed his eyes the moment of the last tuck of the swaddling blanket was nicely affirming, yet how hard it was to think critically and carefully about my position on infant sleep in the face of all those other mothers the first time around. I knew they didn't have any special knowledge or background in infant sleep. I knew we were all listening to our mothers, our grandmothers, our older friends, our doctors, and a million "sleep experts" in books and online. We were all sorting through conflicting advice and trying to do our best. Yet, sometimes, groups that start out with many different opinions begin to coalesce around one particular idea. The more individuals come to agree with that position, the more right it seems to be. How does that one opinion first take hold? Maybe the first mom in the group had great success with a particular view on sleep training. Perhaps a few others, insecure about their ability to successfully parent their newborns, saw that success and wanted to emulate it. It doesn't take much to get a group opinion solidified around an idea; It takes so much more to stand against it. That doesn't mean you must automatically disagree with a belief *because* it is held by a group. Sometimes, groups are correct. Sometimes, the belief has been tested and tried and found sound. But any time you encounter a popular opinion that makes it easy to agree, you should take a second look at why you agree.

How do you do that? You start by testing that opinion against beliefs you already hold. Are there any inconsistencies? Does this popular opinion contradict something else that you believe? Can you honestly believe both at the same time, or must one of them be false? Where is the inconsistency? If you find a contradiction, then you test the two beliefs against other beliefs you hold and against your knowledge. If you need more information, more facts, you seek that out. When it came to my daughter's dreadful sleep, I didn't assume that either my beliefs about infant sleep or those of the groups around me were correct. I considered the other things I believed about newborns, tested the various opinions against the facts about infants and sleep that I already knew, and went searching for more information. In the end, I rejected the group consensus and held to my belief. I added to my knowledge, kept an open mind, and revisited the question whenever something new came before me.

Unfortunately, we don't seem to be practicing critical thinking much in this way today. Most schools no longer offer formal logic or teach logical fallacies and how to recognize them. Even literary analysis in schools is often confined to partial texts, even mere paragraphs. We are not teaching students to study context and understand an author's point of view, place in history, or even inconsistent beliefs of their own. Our students are taught to be "nice" and to be "kind," but sometimes that is simply interpreted as not being "mean" or not "fighting." And, as my mock trial students showed, not fighting means not arguing. Not arguing, however, doesn't dissolve conflict. If anything, conflict becomes internalized, absorbed into our unstated assumptions about the world. We can become desensitized to the internal inconsistencies in our own beliefs if we never have occasion to test them. Critical thinking means sometimes hard thinking, hard looks at our beliefs and assumptions, and sometimes hard decisions about what we want to do with what we find.

Like confronting bullies or speaking up for those who need a champion, we should be confronting our own beliefs and assumptions and providing a space for other voices to be heard. We must think about what defines an argument—a series of premises that lead to a conclusion. We must think about the difference between truth and validity. Should we trust an argument that is not logically valid, even if it supports our beliefs and appears to be true? What do we do with an argument that we know to be true yet remains unsupported by valid logic? We can learn some common logical fallacies and learn how to spot them in arguments—even when we are using them ourselves.

Critical thinking grows as we grow and mature. The ability to think deeply and carefully through a difficult subject, analyzing not only the facts as we understand them but also our own possible biases and uncertainties, is absolutely necessary for true reconciliation, problem-solving, and growth. Critical thinking is not merely the exercise of thought but requires the use of logic, reasoning, creativity, and skepticism. Socratic questioning is one method of engaging in critical thought. Socratic questioning, first and foremost, is the questioning of ourselves. Within Socratic questioning, we seek to come as close to absolute truth and certain knowledge as we can by asking questions about our beliefs and our set of known facts. It is not about questioning others while we rest secure in our own beliefs. Each new piece of knowledge, each new fact, each new feeling or set of beliefs should be tested against what we already know. When we find internal inconsistencies, we must decide which inconsistent belief is untrue based on how it fits with other facts we know.

This is the crucial element of debate that is missing today. We are quick to settle into our beliefs, easily supported in a myriad of places, especially online. Confirmation bias further convinces us that our understanding is the correct one. My children all have been homeschooled, at least in part. Any parent is probably aware of how quickly any child-related topic begins to drive your online experience. Homeschooling websites abound. Different theories on how to homeschool, which curricula to use, why homeschooling is important, and why not homeschooling is a terrible choice clutter my online world. One year of research and buying homeschool materials and my web searches were primed to move pro-homeschooling links to the top. Social media primed to suggest local homeschooling groups. Sixteen years later, I have to intentionally do the hard work of looking for information that is anti-homeschool. If I don't want that perspective, I never have to see it. My own views are endlessly mirrored back to me in academic studies, news articles, columns, blogs… Everywhere I look, I see the benefits of homeschooling. But surely homeschooling has some valid criticism. Studies exist that contradict the ones I want to believe. Most of the time, I don't really need that information, but it is important to me that I stay abreast of research and new data that is being presented. A decision made with the information available nearly two decades ago might not be the best given the information available today. It's my responsibility to look past the easy answers that confirm my belief. It is all the more true if I wish to debate the subject with someone else. I can apply this same thinking to things like breastfeeding versus bottle-feeding, the use of paper plates versus washing dishes for an event I'm holding, low-till versus no-till versus traditional tilling practices in farming, and even the trickier debates of our time, such as book "banning" and sex/ gender issues. The sources that support our views are always the ones that jump to the top of the queue, but we cannot become complacent and accept them without looking deeper.

It is easy to spend our time working to defend our beliefs and convince others of their rightness. And all of this is reinforced by the tone of news media, publicized political debates, and the people with whom we choose to surround ourselves. We seek to bolster our own set of closely held beliefs rather than test them. We read news media from "our side," which we label neutral. We have drinks and talk politics with people who share our geography, our socio-economic status, and our set of values. We rarely engage in thoughtful conflict with those with whom we disagree.

Critical thinking doesn't develop without intentionality. It must be taught and it must be nurtured. We must read widely and think deeply about what we have read. We must not be passive receivers of information, but rather, we must hold it up against what we already know and believe and decide where it belongs. We must be exposed regularly, normally, in our everyday lives to ideas and people and beliefs that are quite different from our own. We are tribal in nature and we seek others like ourselves. It has become the norm to consider diversity to mean the more obvious differences such as race, ethnicity, or gender, but viewpoint diversity, diversity of socio-economics, education, background, family of origin are harder to discern or catalogue. So we find ourselves in a racially diverse neighborhood or sharing an office with an even mix of genders, but somehow, we share most of the same beliefs. We don't need to dig deep and challenge ourselves.

Think about what we believe and why. Listen to what others say they believe and seek to understand their "why." Make Socratic questioning of yourself the first step in any conflict. Learn and practice Socratic dialogue with others. The more each individual begins to practice true critical thinking, the more the tide begins to turn and space opens up to engage in healthy conflict.

CHAPTER 2

Creativity and Wonder Redux

"It met the mythological search for romance by being a story and the philosophical search for truth by being a true story."
—G.K. CHESTERTON, *The Everlasting Man*[64]

"Wonder is the desire for knowledge."
—THOMAS AQUINAS[65]

"The purpose of a storyteller is not to tell you how to think, but to give you questions to think upon."
—BRANDON SANDERSON[66]

"Lord Bacon tells us that a prudent question is the half of knowledge. Whence comes this prudent question? we repeat. And we answer, From the imagination."
—GEORGE MACDONALD, *A Dish of Orts*[67]

What turns a young girl into writer Dorothy Parker (who said, "Creativity is a wild eye and a disciplined mind"[68])? What turns a young boy into Albert Einstein? Critical thinking begins in the imagination. Einstein famously said, "Imagination is more important than knowledge."[69] In context, he did not intend to suggest that knowledge is unimportant. He was explaining that because of his knowledge, experience, and ability to think critically and analyze information, he could intuit, or imagine, a result not yet verified and then test his theory. To think critically requires a sense of curiosity about seeking truth and wonder about the world around us and the people in it.

We prepare ourselves to think critically—and begin weaving in the third important strand in our rope— through stories. Thinking critically requires us to understand both ourselves and others around us. We must learn to discern the motivations and biases of others, and to do so, we need to be able to put ourselves in their shoes and grasp their perspective. Immersion in stories and building our imaginations when young gives us the innate openness to learning about others. We learn compassion and empathy for "the Other" in our lives by first feeling compassion and empathy for the characters in our stories. A young girl becomes a battle-weary old soldier spying on twelve beautiful princesses or a prince-turned-frog who tries to befriend the spoiled king's daughter. A teen boy feels the pain of a sister and daughter who is denied the right to fight alongside her kin in defense of her land, who dresses as a warrior and defeats a witch king by declaring, "I am no man!" Everyone learns the power of pity and mercy for a groveling Gollum.

We learn to wonder how the world works as we read a biography of Leonardo da Vinci, the power of words as we listen to Martin Luther King, Jr., and the need for beauty even in utility as we study the life and works of James Audubon. We question why John Adams could rely so heavily on the advice of his wife—yet agree to deny her the vote. We stand with Sydney Carter at the guillotine, and we puzzle over his motives and the workings of justice. We sit with Jo March and gasp as she rejects Laurie and try to decide if we agree. In those moments, in those stories, real and imagined, we learn how to think and reason, and we stretch our minds to absorb new thoughts and ideas.

It isn't enough to simply analyze new information as it is received. We must have a library of knowledge against which to weigh it. We must have experiences, feelings, and ideas against which this new information either holds or doesn't. We can't live the thousands of lifetimes it would take to accumulate the knowledge we need to think critically about everything we encounter. We do not all experience war or the hunger and desperation of poverty. Not everyone loses a parent at a young age or loses a friend while still in childhood. We are not all farmers or city dwellers, musicians, artists, or scientists. I was never a young boy or a young man. My sons will never experience high school as a teen girl. Yet, we can learn to understand those perspectives and add them to our mental library. We can think about legislation regarding immigration with some measure of understanding that doesn't come from our experience. We can ponder agriculture policy though we may never have been a farmer. Our perspectives can be widened through the stories we have read that grow and stretch our imaginations and our capacity for wonder.

Mitali Perkins, author of such wonderful children's and young adult literature as *Rickshaw Girl* and *You Bring the Distant Near*, writes about the importance of stories in developing our ability to see the Other in her non-fiction book *Steeped in Stories*. In our rush to be mindful of offense, we push aside "classic" literature that is out of step with cultural mores of the day. That may sometimes be right. But what do we do with Mark Twain and *Huckleberry Finn*? Is his story not worth reading because Twain used language that is (understandably) offensive today? But what lessons can *Huckleberry Finn* teach us today? Can we learn to see through his eyes? Or the eyes of Jim, who is fleeing slavery? If your family history is one of reservations and discrimination, can you read *Little House on the Prairie* and glean some understanding of the white settlers who pushed indigenous peoples off their land? As a descendant of a settler family, can you read *The Birchbark House* by Louise Erdrich and understand better the impact your story had on others and how that impact still matters today? Good literature should be able to draw us into the perspectives of the primary characters and leave us feeling as if we know them, no matter how unlike ourselves they are.

When I decided that I would pursue a law degree after college, I intended to eventually work in something related to child welfare or education. Part of that interest was fueled by my parents' challenges within the foster care system in Pennsylvania and their struggles as foster parents who eventually adopted my brothers from foster care. I had a front row seat to the dysfunction within the state child welfare system. I saw the caseworkers with far too many children in their care, foster parents who enjoyed the payouts more than the children, and incomprehensible hurdles for foster-adoptive parents, who watched abusive and dangerously neglectful biological parents skate past with a wave of the hand. I saw children who needed champions, parents—both biological and foster—who needed support, and case workers and administrators who needed clearer laws, sustainable mandates, and fewer cases. With that information in front of me, I knew I could find ways to help if I had my law degree.

But my interest really started long before my brother first walked into our home with his caseworker. Years of stories had introduced me to "orphans" of various sorts, and my heart already had been broken for them. I might not have known any foster children yet, but already I knew they needed nurturing, they needed discipline, they needed love. Influenced by stories and informed by my brothers' experiences, I wanted to help. I already knew in a heart-deep way that children whose early lives were stories of brokenness, loss, and trauma might not come to us with the sunshine of Anne Shirley but perhaps with the anger and resentment of Mary Lennox or the fear and distrust of Nat Blake in *Little Men*. I knew that as much as Anne soaked up any love and affection the Cuthberts offered, she also doubted and worried that it wouldn't last. The reality of fostering abused and neglected children is not, of course, the easy tale of a children's classic. I have that lived experience now, but stories gave me an entry point for empathy and understanding before my brothers ever brought those stories to me in all their painful reality.

Empathy and understanding may be an entry point, but I also needed to expand that understanding to engage in the real work of child welfare policy. My undergraduate concentration in Political Science was focused on women, children, and families. We read case studies, books on feminist legal theory and social welfare policy, legal documents and court cases—and stories. We read *Life for Me Ain't Been No Crystal Stair* by Susan Sheehan and *Always Running* by Luis J. Rodriquez, among many others. We didn't just read law and policy, academic tomes, and statistics. We read stories that demanded of us our imaginations, stories that pulled us beyond the general into the specific. For some of my classmates, this was a more challenging exercise than it was for others. Some of them pushed back on the stories, protesting that this type of personal story was mere anecdote—biased, unreliable, and not entirely relevant to serious study. Others of us dove right in.

The families in these stories lived and breathed and experienced the very policies and laws we were trying to study. From *Crystal Stair*, I could *see* Crystal and her son Daquan. I could hear Crystal's despair and desperation. Imagining Crystal, we could experience her struggles as she and her son both moved through the labyrinthian child welfare system. And experiencing those struggles with Crystal opened our minds to the very specific failures and faults in that system. We gained a deeper, richer, and more thoughtful understanding of the challenges facing children and families caught in the cycle of poverty, addiction, and abuse by immersing ourselves in their stories. Then, pulling back to a broader view, we connected what we had witnessed in our minds to policy documents, statistics, and analyses. We could move past stale solutions that had proved unworkable to new, more creative answers.

Not only do stories keep our imaginations alive and active as children, but they provide a gateway to better problem solving as adults. The more we stretch and grow our imaginations, our creative selves, as children, the more we have access to that part of ourselves when we are faced with adult problems requiring critical thinking. And the more we practice creativity, the more we continue to engage with stories as adults, the more we keep that muscle exercised.

The classic negotiating text, *Getting to Yes* by Roger Fisher and William Ury, builds on the idea that to reach a solution, one can expand the pie or find more resources to maximize joint gain. Negotiators, using their theories, seek creative ways to meet the real needs of every party to the conflict. They ask questions about the underlying interests of the parties that go deeper than the surface description of the conflict. What do the parties to the conflict ultimately want? Can those needs be complementary? Can one find ways to make "trades" that will benefit both parties and so give them the freedom to agree to a deal? At the macro-level of cultural conflict, imagination can aid critical thinking by helping us to see the could-be of a better world. At the micro-level of interpersonal conflict resolution, creativity can be used to identify unique values that can be maximized for all involved.

Had American leadership not been willing to think "outside the box" of US-Soviet escalation during the Cuban Missile Crisis, the world may have been consumed by nuclear war. The Soviets had sent a private proposal for a solution to the missile crisis that was then contradicted by a public declaration. The usual response from either side was a show of strength, of not backing down. The thought had been that any show of weakness would prompt the other side to take advantage. The normal course of action for President Kennedy would have been to respond to the public letter, ignoring the better way offered in the private correspondence. After all, the Soviets, the thinking went, would not want to be seen as weak if their public demands were not met. Fortunately for the world, one Kennedy advisor used what Robert McNamara later identified as empathy for the Soviet position and was willing to speak up against his colleagues' recommendations. And the president was willing to listen. Empathy—learned and practiced by putting oneself in the place of the other and viewing a situation through his eyes—and creativity in finding a solution based on that understanding. As a result, Kennedy responded to the private demands, missiles were removed from Cuba, and the threat of imminent nuclear war averted.

What would have happened if one advisor had not been able to see the situation from another perspective? What would have happened if President Kennedy and his other advisors had been unwilling to break their usual thought patterns about the Soviets? As former defense secretary McNamara tells it, that was exactly the problem in Vietnam: The US failed in empathy, rethinking their own position, and willingness to seek a creative solution to a seemingly intractable conflict.

On a smaller scale, how many sibling arguments resolve with a more lasting impact when we find creative solutions to conflict? Most of us have seen the pictures online of siblings sharing one large t-shirt labeled "our get-along shirt" and probably snickered a little. Whether you think it's a good idea or not, the shirt certainly offers a creative solution to sibling bickering. I've asked my children for ideas when we've encountered those dug-in sorts of problems that occur when siblings share close quarters. Sometimes, my parenting approach doesn't have the right answer, and my adult imagination fails. They've negotiated activity exchanges, snack portions, and chores in ways that would never have occurred to me. Being open to different solutions and to different viewpoints is an absolute necessity in changing our cultural approach to conflict.

I've also found that sometimes my children are okay with leaving a conflict unresolved. By that, I most certainly do not mean unaddressed. They instinctively know that ignoring an area of conflict altogether is not usually a helpful approach. But they are comfortable with leaving some conflicts open and unsettled. I've been told quite bluntly by all of them to stop trying to fix certain points of contention at various times. They retain an open-mindedness and sense of possibility that often dims as we lose our childlike ability to embrace wonder and the unknown. A conflict left undecided today isn't forever. A disagreement now could be resolved tomorrow—or a year from now—or never—and that is okay with them. Can it be that way with the rest of us?

We become more rigid in our thinking as we grow older, slightly more unwilling to bend. With years of experiences behind us, with rules and patterns we have learned to follow in both our public and private lives, and with expectations we have about the behavior and motivation of others, we sometimes find it difficult to see beyond what we think we know of the people we encounter. It becomes hard to imagine scenarios in which people behave differently, where outcomes are less certain, and where possibilities are endless. Sometimes, it's cynicism or bitterness, but often, it's simply the fog of everyday life. To process the influx of information, we automatically sift and sort people and events into pre-existing categories based on prior encounters. Sometimes, that is by race or religion or political party. Sometimes, we sort by experiences, such as "baseball parent" or "someone from *that* church." Or perhaps we sort by personal impacts, such as "liar," "mean girl," or "gym bro." They may not be conscious labeling, but our brains need a way to keep up with the constant flow of data in our busy lives, and attaching new events to older memories is one way to organize and process it all.

Unfortunately, we often stop there. Once I've placed Mrs. Jones in the box labeled "Church X," she is now imbued with all of the traits, good and bad, that I have unconsciously ascribed to people from Church X. If I am not careful, deliberate, in my future interactions with her, I may never replace that first label. Each and every interaction will be viewed through that lens.

How do we push through that fog? Keeping an open mind and being curious about others isn't easy as we navigate the complexities of relationships in work, school, neighborhoods, churches, and family. But curiosity about others, wonder, and genuine interest in knowing someone is an absolute necessity for a healthy culture of conflict and reconciliation. This is true whether we are considering interpersonal conflict at a familial level or societal fractures such as racism or political tribalism.

Curiosity is one of the keys that unlocks our ability to engage in the critical thinking necessary to resolve conflict. It must start with ourselves, again returning to the Socratic responsibility of checking our own internal beliefs. Curiosity starts with investigating information—and people—that challenge my thinking and understanding. When I worked with World Vision on human rights advocacy in the Middle East, I often encountered members of Congress who lacked curiosity. Busy men and women, they accepted the advice given to them by trusted staff and colleagues, despite the attempts by myself and others to provide information and context. Two incidents stand out in particular because the Members involved showed careful, creative, critical thinking. I once had a member of the House of Representatives jump in with both feet, ready to speak out against a piece of legislation most of her colleagues refused to even discuss with me. When I, baffled, asked her why and how she came to her conclusions against the word of her colleagues, she replied that she had "read the bill," and that caused her to do some investigating. She brought out maps and diagrams, showing me exactly what she had found. It took time and (minimal) effort to reach her decision to go against her colleagues, but mostly, it required her to ask a few questions and think creatively about the problems with the information she had been given.

The second instance involved the conflict at the border of Israel in Lebanon in 2006. Angry words were flying, and members of the House and Senate were falling over themselves to get out in front with trite, tired statements on the Middle East. Many NGOs (non-governmental organizations), such as World Vision, had both local and international staff on the ground aiding the people directly involved in the conflict zone, but few members were interested in talking with us—until Senator Ted Kennedy asked a handful of NGO representatives to come to his office so he could ask questions. We spent one afternoon with him, reporting on exactly what our staff were telling us. He asked question after question, seeking a deeper understanding of the situation from a human perspective. Of course, he had access to military intel that we lacked, as well as direct communication with Lebanese and Israeli government officials. But he knew that the people living and serving in the middle of the conflict had valuable insights *and stories,* a different perspective that could help him better understand and, in turn, combine that information into policy recommendations.

On a personal level, I started college feeling somewhat out of my depth. I knew the reputation MIT had earned for nerdiness, and I had already anticipated being surrounded by weird, geeky students. At the same time, I was determined to shake my own nerdy bookworm reputation and become more sophisticated, more urban. I had a definite bias against both geeks and rural "redneck" boys. You can imagine my feelings upon meeting my suitemate—tall, overly friendly, deep rural southern drawl, a dorky ballcap- and flannel-wearing engineer, and a son of a preacher, no less. Of course, you can imagine how I appeared to him: northern, flighty, a little stuck-up, a sorority girl who snagged a frat boy for a boyfriend my first week on campus. We had a lot of obvious stereotypes to either overcome or confirm.

By the time graduation rolled around, Mark was one of my dearest friends. We joked that we "met in the shower" because, truthfully, we did get to know one another when we couldn't quite seem to unsync our morning shower routine and ran into each other repeatedly in our shared bathroom. Those incredibly awkward conversations over the sinks and in the side by side (still very private!) shower stalls gave us the opening we needed to genuinely wonder about the other. Thanks in no small part to his genuine friendliness, I was able eventually to look past the good old boy exterior to see a sweet, deeply kind, and witty young man, and he found in me someone he could trust to talk to and to tease and counsel. That nerdy southern boy had a wickedly funny sense of humor, and the stuck-up sorority girl was much more insecure than she seemed in the hall. How many other friendships did I miss because I wasn't able to look past an accent or a style of dress? Mark, I think, probably missed out on very few. Even at eighteen, he possessed the rare gift of seeing the true person beneath whatever masks they wore. He taught me much about prejudices and curiosity by his example. Unfortunately, I've realized only years later how preconceived and unexamined labels impacted other relationships in negative ways, and I've worked not to repeat those mistakes.

Intentionally examining our filters is essential to fostering healthy conflict. In the digital age, we're bombarded with so much information that we can't help but come up with conscious and subconscious ways of sorting incoming information. We all do this every day in a hundred small ways. As people and news clips and images flash past us, we sort them more quickly than we can consciously process, allowing us to focus on what is important or necessary in the moment. We must do this, or we would be overwhelmed with data. Imagine walking through Times Square in New York City and having to think about and analyze each person, each advertisement, each storefront, vehicle, and sound individually? Instead, our brains simply sift the scene before us, bringing to our attention the car entering the crosswalk against the light, the pretty dress we might like to find for ourselves, the name of the restaurant for which we were searching. Practical as it is, all of that sifting confirms beliefs and biases we already hold. Every toddler screaming in the background of a restaurant adds to the belief that toddlers should not be in restaurants. Those toddlers sitting quietly with their parents fail to impress themselves in our subconscious, and our bias is unchallenged. It takes conscious effort to question ourselves and what we believe to be true.

Remaining curious and cultivating creativity pushes against those subconscious biases. Are all dog owners obnoxiously focused on their furbabies? Are all Italians loud? Are all homeschoolers weird and unsocialized and all public-school kids doomed to worldly hedonism? Are all Trump voters (or all Republicans) hateful white supremacists and all Harris voters (or all Democrats) arrogant Communist elitists? What logical fallacies must I commit to remain convinced of these beliefs? What must I do to question my belief? Maybe it's easy to do that with our dog pampering neighbor. What about crazy Uncle Chuck, who fuels up on Thanksgiving turkey and treats everyone to a full volume rant about how the Democrats and Washington are destroying the country? Must we explore our reaction to *him*? Must we be curious about him? What about Cousin Ashley, who refuses to attend Thanksgiving if Uncle Chuck is there because she says he stands for everything hateful and evil in the world, and she doesn't want to be around "toxic people?" Who do you invite? If you agree with Cousin Ashley, though *you* are a nicer person and don't post anti-MAGA memes on social media like she does, you might agree that Uncle Chuck is toxic, and maybe Thanksgiving will be more peaceful without him. But if you agree with Uncle Chuck, maybe you'll say good riddance to Ashley and her ridiculous insistence on tolerance that doesn't tolerate "hate."

The third option is to enter into relationship with *both* Chuck and Ashley with open curiosity and wonder. It would be acceptable to tell both of them that Thanksgiving dinner may not be the best place to hold court on politics, but that both are welcome to the table. Privately, you might ask Uncle Chuck about his beliefs, being willing to think honestly about your own beliefs in the process. Does anything he says make you think differently on some points? If you agree with Ashley, does anything you learn from Chuck cause you to question some of those points of agreement? Are your beliefs internally consistent? You might think creatively about how to host Thanksgiving dinner so that all feel welcome. What is the purpose of the meal? Why would you think to invite both in the first place? Is it important to "keep the peace" during the meal? If so, how can you ensure that happens?

Bringing Uncle Chuck and Ashley together for Thanksgiving dinner may not be the right solution. Perhaps the two of them are not willing to set aside their animosity to share a meal together. Critical thinking begins with an observation; in the case of conflict, the observation necessarily considers the source of the conflict. The observation leads to questioning how that observation aligns with one's own thoughts, feelings, and beliefs, as well as known facts. Curiosity and wonder about the nature of the opposing belief or the observation follows, along with creative thinking about how it can be so. A critical thinker then connects the dots, using inference, as well as both deductive and inductive reasoning, to draw conclusions about that which was observed. Existing knowledge is compared to the new information and the reasons considered to determine if the conclusions hold. No conclusion can be certain without further testing. Just as one does not draw scientific conclusions without being able to replicate results, one should not accept belief conclusions unless they hold consistent across different situations, times, and persons. Only after we have looked deeply into ourselves, thinking critically about an observation or new belief, can we then turn towards considering the source of the new information and perhaps consult with others for their perspectives.

Perhaps Uncle Chuck, for all of his rants, is someone who is bored and likes to "rile people up" for his own entertainment. As a source, maybe he doesn't actually believe everything he says. Perhaps Cousin Ashley is known for adopting new and popular opinions and defending them fiercely—even that memorable foray into Wiccan practices in tenth grade. The source matters. Maybe you *like* Cousin Ashley and were best friends in high school, while Uncle Chuck always pinches your cheek and calls you "Shorty." Our feelings are a valid reference point in thinking critically—as long as we are aware of our feelings and the reasons behind them. In the end, I might decide not to invite either, or to invite just Chuck or just Ashley, not necessarily because of their stated beliefs and opinions, but due to their willingness to be engaged in relationship, to be a good guest, and to be open to genuine conversation rather than using the Thanksgiving table as a podium.

When we are thinking creatively, being curious, wondering about the world, our beliefs, and our positions on areas of disagreement, we are willing to be wrong. We are *able* to be wrong because we know we are able to draw new conclusions. When we are curious, we seek truth. We don't need to hide in our caves with those who are like us. If we are curious, we can talk to both Chuck and Ashley and our identity isn't threatened by either of them. We can ask questions and pose scenarios in which one or the other might be right—or perhaps both be wrong.

Importantly, fostering a spirit of wonder and curiosity enables us to shine light on areas of conflict. We want to see what is hidden. We want to wrestle with new ideas and engage with people and their beliefs. Creativity allows us to recognize that our mirrors are fractured. Creativity accepts that the world may be different than what we believe. Creativity accepts the challenge opposing viewpoints offer and calls upon imagination, knowledge, and experience to evaluate and discern. When my children approach me with a conflict, I ask them to consider the position of the other first. The more curious they are, the more willing they are to consider their sibling's view. The more creative they are, the easier it is to do so.

One way we teach this skill is through literary analysis. Reading a speech, a non-fiction text, poem, or novel is an exercise in understanding viewpoints. Analyzing the work then examining the arguments, the beliefs, or the ideas it presents, gives us a chance to compare them to our own and to those of other works we have read. I have noticed a trend in schools today to conduct this type of literary analysis using only partial works. Rather than read all of Emerson's *Self-Reliance*, a high school student may be given a two or three paragraph passage to dissect. Rather than comparing entire novels, they might be asked to compare passages from two different books. This narrow selection does not give the students context for the passages they are asked to examine. How can they think critically about Emerson's ideas if they do not understand how he arrives at his conclusions? Can you adequately compare and contrast Elizabeth Bennett's ideas of marriage with those of Jane Eyre if you read only a few paragraphs from the beginning of Austen's novel and a few from the end of Brontë's? Will you understand the perspective of each? To truly understand, to place yourself in the shoes of the characters and the minds of the authors, and to develop your own understanding of the themes of marriage in early 1800s England, you need to immerse yourself in their views and ideas. To fully understand the views of an Uncle Chuck or Cousin Ashley, you need to consider the totality of the person, know the context, and imagine yourself in their shoes.

George MacDonald wrote that "imagination takes reason to the threshold of mystery and moral truth."[70] Vigen Guroian concludes MacDonald's thought by asserting that "it remains for the heart of courage with the will to believe and the vision of imagination to embrace the beauty of goodness and the strength of truth..."[71] Without creativity, without curiosity and wonder, we are left with cold reason that can never bring us to relationship and reconciliation.

CHAPTER 3
Facts AND Feelings

"Emotions have taught mankind to reason."
—LUC DE CLAPIERS, Marquis de Vauvenargues[72]

"The best lack all conviction, while the worst/Are
full of passionate intensity."
—WILLIAM BUTLER YEATS[73]

For most of my life, I've been buffeted by the wind and waves of facts versus feelings. One moment, I'm being chastised for being too emotional, for not thinking clearly, letting my feelings get in the way. The next, I'm disappointing someone for being too rational and cold and not feeling anything. Even my parents played tug of war with my reactions. My mother would cry that I was unfeeling and cold, just like my father, while in the same argument, my father would stalk off, telling me it was impossible to reason with me because I was so emotional, just like my mother! To this day, I flutter between responses to events, never quite certain I'm on the right side of facts versus feelings. But what is the right side? Or must there be one at all?

The debate isn't about facts versus feelings or about the left versus right brain, no matter what pop psychology might say. *Star Trek's* Spock makes for good fictional drama as he balances his human emotions and Vulcan logic, but in real life, we humans must learn to use both well. Making good decisions requires both factual knowledge and valid, thoughtful feelings. Our feelings simply are; they exist in a way that is neither inherently good nor intrinsically bad. What we do with those emotions is a choice. Critical thinking goes beyond mere logic to acknowledging and recognizing our emotions, how they might cloud our thinking, and how they influence our decisions. Aristotle defined this as *phronesis*, or practical wisdom—the wisdom of doing the right thing, or moral will.

Phronesis is the intersection of thoughts and ideas with judgment.[74] The ancient Greeks considered this practical wisdom as the point in which we think and act according to our values, moving past factual reasoning to contemplate the effect (for good or ill) of a belief or an action on humanity. To merely deliberate on the theoretical without care for impact would be to deny the heart. We have feelings for a reason. We can discern how a belief or an idea can help or harm others, not only ourselves. Critical thinking requires moral judgment as well as syllogisms and arguments.

Our emotions are as important to our ability to think critically as is our sense of logic and reason. It is when we use the tools we have gained through stories, through the development of our moral imagination, empathy, compassion, creativity, and wonder, that we are able to approach others with the openness and vulnerability necessary to solve problems and reconcile relationships. How else but with our emotions do we discern good from bad? Right and wrong are value judgments we base on a set of facts and beliefs, but it is with our emotions that we can know the rightness or wrongness of an act towards another.

Critical thinking isn't done in a vacuum, divorced from our emotions, experiences, and personalities. We bring all of that to the table when we analyze an argument or question an idea. Failing to consider our emotions leads to clouded judgment and inconsistent beliefs. The Greek use of *phronesis* to take more than head knowledge into consideration allows for the richness of experience to be weighed. Our emotions are not mere vapors, easily blown aside with a breath. They are part of who we are, born of our lived experiences, our thoughts, our conversations with others, the things we've read, and the beliefs we've formed. To pretend that our feelings have no place in critical thinking is an absurd, and dangerous, false dichotomy that creates an insurmountable barrier to healthy conflict.

Can we talk about education policy without the intrusion of our own memories of attending school? Those memories are not mere facts and figures but include sights, smells, and sounds that all convey emotion. To have a fully informed debate on school choice, curricula, teacher qualifications, or any number of education related topics, all parties to the discussion must be aware of and acknowledge their emotional responses. I failed in my quest to be valedictorian of my high school class by a fractional percentage due solely to the lack of athletic ability that earned me B's in gym class. The outrage I feel decades after graduation certainly informs my feelings about physical education policy. I can't have a reasoned discussion about the merits of including classes such as PE or music in the calculation of a student's grade point average without awareness of my bias, which comes directly from my disappointment in high school. Do I give in to that thirty-year-old emotion and defend my stance that PE should not count towards GPA? Or do I turn my critical thinking skills inward to examine my opinion, understand the impact of that negative emotion, and weigh the facts as I understand them now against the emotional response of a teenager?

Of course, my sixteen-year-old self was disappointed—and embarrassed—that her ineptitude with any sort of ball or gym equipment cost her an academic award. And no, that emotion shouldn't obscure facts or guide my conduct in the discussion.

However, that emotion was valid. It was a natural reaction to the situation, and it adds context to the debate. Should non-academic classes be weighted the same in calculating GPA for college and scholarship purposes? In addition to any statistics, practical arguments, and other facts, the emotional response of students might also be a factor to consider, which means my own feelings about the topic are worth considering. My feelings are also likely to interfere with my judgment of the other factors, and recognizing that helps to diminish my bias.

Unacknowledged feelings do not simply fade into the background as we deliberate. Rather, they can end up having an outsized impact on our conclusions because we aren't honestly and thoughtfully appraising the implications of those feelings. If I enter into the debate above without reflecting on my emotional response to the topic, I am likely to strongly defend my position that non-academic classes should not count. Emotions are best acknowledged rather than denied or ignored. Allowing "the Other" to bring their feelings and emotions into a discussion moves us closer to healthy conflict.

We tend to identify most strongly with the characteristics or beliefs we have that are most under attack. We instinctively rise to defend that part of ourselves. Despite my maiden name—Mazzocco—I've never felt particularly Italian-American, but you can be sure that I will get quite defensive over that Italian name when called a *dago* or friends joke about the Mafia. It's not a rational response but simply a human one. But that emotion is now part of any discussion I have around identity, Italian-American culture, or red-lining in certain cities in the first half of the last century.

As tension around race, religion, and gender grows in the United States, we can see even those who hold moderate views becoming more defensive and less objective. If there is a perception that a part of your identity is being attacked, you will almost always rise to defend it. Feeling defensive about your identity is a natural response when it seems like pop culture or mainstream media is criticizing it. Even if the criticism is less than it seems, once it is noticed at all, confirmation bias will continue to support the perception. And if you try to keep your feelings separate from "the facts," you will only succeed in convincing yourself that the facts are stronger than they actually are. Your feelings are still there, still influencing your thinking, still contributing to your reasoning—but without any check on them, without testing them against what is known. How do we identify the emotions that are influencing our thinking? How do we bring them into our reasoning as tools and not saboteurs?

Though necessary and even valuable, emotions can obviously get us into trouble and lead us away from healthy conflict. What we know of the brain tells us that during times of high emotions, we do lose the ability to think clearly and process information in rational and helpful ways. When our amygdala, that tiny cluster of neurons in the center of the brain responsible for processing emotions, is energized, our ability to use higher level thinking deteriorates.[75] Studies have shown that intense emotions, whether good or bad, affect our cognition. Positive emotions may have less of an effect than negative emotions, but a neutral emotional state performs best across cognitive tests.[76] In particular, our ability to access our working memory is negatively impacted by our emotional state. This persists in studies considering both a pre-existing emotional state and one that is induced as part of the testing. When we are experiencing strong emotions, good or bad, our ability to logically reason is worsened.

Our emotions impact our thinking in countless ways.[77] A feeling of disgust, for instance, prompts us to throw things away or leave a situation. Joy and anger tend to lead to action. And when we feel fear, we have a heightened perception of danger. When in danger or threatened, feeling afraid helps us by magnifying our understanding of risks, which potentially brings us safely out of danger. Unfortunately, that same response causes us to have a defensive posture towards any potential risk and lessens our ability to accurately assess the threat. When I hear politicians recommending their constituents arm themselves against the opposing party, I am reminded of how dangerous this could be for everyone. Fear is encouraged, which causes people to see even innocuous remarks as potential threats. With reasoning ability weakened by the strong emotional response, people become even less able to think critically about their opponent's arguments and ideas. When do we reach a tipping point on that fear? What happens when fear is accompanied by anger, anger that prompts action that is not guided by clear thinking? Yoda certainly knew of what he spoke when he said, "Fear is the path to the dark side." When we are afraid—real fears of real enemies or fear from a lie sold to us—we defend. We defend our person, identity, beliefs, and tribe. Feeling under attack, we grow angry in our defense. Yoda tells us, "Fear leads to anger. Anger leads to hate. Hate leads to suffering."[78] We should heed the wisdom of this small green puppet in a pop culture space epic because he speaks true. Much suffering could be averted if fear was either admitted and conquered or never given fuel in the first place.

This is how we become a culture in a state of high conflict. Once we begin appealing to emotions, we enter into a Mephistophelian bargain in which we find that the emotions are the ones driving the bus. We struggle to regain control of our own critical thinking, as well as control over the conflict. Do we appeal to disgust? Then, we begin to feel disgusted, and we struggle to relate to the person on the other side. We no longer empathize with them, even if we want to. All of our decision making is informed by our desire to remove ourselves from the other.

Disgust leads to shaming and guilt, and we further distance our-selves emotionally and cognitively from those with whom we disagree. And the further we remove ourselves, the harder it is to re-engage. We become more easily disgusted by them, their actions, or their beliefs. Our position seems stronger and more pure. And so the conflict rolls on, gaining energy from the in-creasingly heightened emotions.

Not only do these emotions fuel conflict by lowering our critical thinking skills, they also have the potential to build anx-iety in us. As I often tell my children, when they are angry or worried, they truly cannot think clearly. The fight or flight (or, more accurately, fight, flight, or freeze) response takes over, and we enter into a frantic loop of finding ways to fight or flee. As the hippocampus takes over physically, the stress response builds and we are ready for action. Unfortunately, being ready for phys-ical action means we are less ready for cognitive action.

So, how do we reconcile this conflict within our very per-sons? If emotions are a given part of the human experience, yet emotions interfere with clear reasoning and critical thinking, can we ever be truly thoughtful?

Emotions are personal, internal, and seemingly beyond our conscious control. Yet, are they really? We have labels for our emotions: anger, fear, envy, joy, sadness, humiliation, and satis-faction, just to name a few. Science, however, can only label emo-tions based on our reporting of them. Our descriptions may be universal, but our emotional experiences are vastly different and, to some extent, culturally informed. Just as the virtues—faithful-ness, love, justice, courage, kindness, and patience— are largely universal, yet take on different shades of meaning across cultures, so too emotions, though labeled the same, express themselves in vastly different ways. In that sense, emotions can be considered a cultural construct.[79] How we respond to situations, people, and threats is internal and personal, but how we interpret the emotions is intrinsically linked to our culture.

Those external markers can be changed. We can learn that while our past experiences may shape our internal response, we are not bound by our past interpretations. We are not doomed to continue responding the same way to the same emotional triggers. Cognitive behavioral therapy can help reshape emotional and physical reactions to trauma, for instance. Therapy doesn't erase past hurts or minimize past pain, but it helps form new responses to them in the present and reframe how we experience similar events in the future. Therapy can be absolutely necessary in some cases to help reshape responses and should always be considered for clinical depression, anxiety, or other mental health concerns. Sometimes, family, friends, or spiritual advisors are sufficient. If you do not have those supports in your life, or if you suspect more complicated issues to resolve, it's a courageous strength to seek professional help. Therapists use a variety of methods to help manage complex cognitive and emotional challenges, and not every therapist or every method is the right fit for every individual. It's okay to take the time to find the right practice rather than sticking with one that doesn't suit or giving up on therapy altogether.

In addition to learning ways to move beyond coping to reshaping our negative emotional responses, we can also learn to adapt or reinterpret our emotional responses as we move between cultures—including family and regional subcultures. We may grow up interpreting anger as an emotion best suppressed or denied, or perhaps we have been taught that anger is a strong and honorable response to injustice. Understanding our underlying emotions and how we personally internalize them is a necessary part in interacting honestly with others. We may not realize the cultural understanding underlying the reactions and responses of others, but if we are aware of our own, we can recognize the potential for misunderstandings. Just as we need to begin our Socratic questioning with our own beliefs, we need to first understand our emotional responses and where they originate to better understand others.

Our emotions can disrupt our thinking. They can cloud our judgment and cause us to misread both verbal and nonverbal cues from others. Negative emotions might raise our defenses, heighten anxiety, and lessen impulse control. Cliche though it might be, my response to being told to calm down is rarely positive. My hackles rise in defensiveness, I am immediately anxious about my perceived capabilities, and I definitely lose impulse control—at least verbally. The first time a teen son said the words, "Mom, chill out," was also the last. While I took calming breaths to remind myself to parent responsibly, his older sister gave him a verbal slap down. We aren't aware of every negative emotional association, but we can be aware enough to sense our reaction and work to slow it.

Even positive emotions interfere by inappropriately lowering our defenses and causing us to miss potential points of concern. While positive emotions assist in expanding our creativity and flexibility, they still interfere with our ability to reason logically. Being more open and vulnerable to the opinions and ideas of others is valuable but must not be at the expense of reason. My children are well aware of the power of putting me in a good mood before asking for a special privilege. I've caught them coaching each other before a big ask. More than once, when they were younger, I heard from the next room, "Teddy, you go ask mom if we can watch a movie. Do something cute and funny, and she'll say yes to you." Teddy is our "cute and funny" youngest and that was heavily exploited by his older siblings. I like to think I am someone who parents with logical and consistent rules and decisions, but did I fall for the "buttering up?" More times than I care to admit! Making decisions (even such as whether or not your children can watch a movie) while in a state of high emotion means making decisions without full use of reason and critical thinking skills.

But making decisions without considering our emotions also leaves us lacking. We *need* our emotions to fully make sense of the world. We need our emotions in order to empathize with others and see their perspective. We need our emotions in order to fully address our own concerns. We must understand our own emotional stake in an issue before we begin problem solving. Socratic questioning of our beliefs and ideas includes questioning how we feel about something and how our past feelings inform our current beliefs. If we are honest with ourselves, we come out with a better understanding of what we believe and why. The why is crucial for productive conversation with others. Not only does it help us present our positions more clearly, but understanding our own "why" helps us seek to understand the "why" behind another's position.

Dealing with emotions while attempting to solve problems, think critically, understand others, and resolve conflict is, quite frankly, a bit of a conundrum. In his book on Plato and the Dialogues of Socrates, British historian George Grote wrote that "belief does not follow proof," but rather that humans, in the course of their growth and development, tend to believe first and *then* seek proof.[80] And that is what we see: We feel a certain way and believe certain ideas that follow those emotions, and then we seek to prove that by reason and logic. That's not a criticism but an observation of our often illogical human condition. We are creatures of emotion—love and hate, disappointment, happiness and sorrow, despair, anger, and shame—and our beliefs spring naturally from those feelings, tangling with our experiences to form our opinions about the world and other people. We truly are "wonderfully and fearfully made," as David sings in Psalm 139, with all of our chaotic and inspiring and damaging emotions a part of our very beings. Our Creator Himself felt emotion. He saw Adam and realized he was lonely. He rescued the Israelites from slavery in Egypt in mercy, and He wept with the sisters of Lazarus. We *feel* because we are human.

Not only do we feel big emotions in response to our circumstances, whether we are happy to be reunited with a loved one or embarrassed when we fail a test or angry when we feel disrespected, but also our emotions can be in response to our setting. Color experts recommend certain paint colors for bedrooms versus kitchens because psychology has something to say about how color can impact our mood—our feelings. Remember how the mood of a city changed when the mayor decreed Tirana should become a rainbow? You may even pass out documents in blue folders during a meeting to convey stability and trustworthiness or wear a red "power tie" to project an air of dominance. To this day, my oldest refers to our house in Washington, D.C., as our "happy yellow house," and we have one common room in our current house painted yellow because we know that she associates it with good emotions. In American culture, we traditionally wear black to a funeral to express grief, and we tend to wear light, bright colors to a baby shower. In recent years, more people have requested of their loved ones that no one wear black to their funeral because they want their mourners to remember them with joy and gladness rather than profound sorrow. Even the color of the chairs around a conference table can set the emotional tone for a meeting that subconsciously affects our thinking. Oscar Wilde wrote eloquently of this, saying, "Mere colour, unspoiled by meaning and unallied with definite form, can speak to the soul in a thousand different ways."[81] We may not always recognize the impact of our surroundings, yet they affect and stir us nonetheless.

Place matters when it comes to our ability to think deeply about an issue and to resolve conflict in part because our emotions are impacted by our surroundings. Natural spaces raise levels of empathy and compassion, release creativity, and help increase our vulnerability. They calm high emotions, allowing us to think more logically. Beauty inspires, motivates, and brings joy. The positive impact of beautiful spaces is well-documented in everything from keeping youth out of jail to making workers more productive to facilitating healing in medical settings. The emotional impact of our *where* matters when it comes to *how* we approach others over a point of disagreement.

We are not merely our emotions, but we disregard our feelings to our peril. We need our emotions in order to make good decisions. We need to understand them and how they influence our thinking. Our emotions tend to focus our attention on ourselves and our desires. We seek to minimize negative feelings and expand our positive emotions. We tailor our actions to make *ourselves feel better.* Critical thinking separates us a bit from our emotions and turns some of our attention on others. We turn from trying to please ourselves to thinking about what makes a *situation better* for everyone. But what does help improve a scenario for everyone involved? Answering that question requires, yes, critical thinking—analysis, questioning, fact-seeking, fact-checking, and observation—but it also requires an understanding of the wants and needs of "the Other." We understand those by considering our own emotional responses. Ignoring our emotions means we are less capable of understanding others. And ignoring our emotions, stuffing them back down, hiding them away, does not mean they are gone. It doesn't mean we no longer feel them or feel their impact. Rather, when we ignore our feelings, they have a tendency to push their way back to the surface in uncomfortable and damaging ways.

Denying and then indulging our emotions inflicts damage in other ways. Blind allegiance to our passions does prevent us from seeing truth—and from truly seeing others. Our emotions keep our attention fixed on ourselves. We feel happy, sad, irritable, amused, bored, or angry, and we fixate on why. We ponder our feelings, what caused them, how we can change them, and what they might mean. When our emotions are guiding us, we tend to use our critical thinking skills to wonder about our feelings, about ourselves. We explore our emotions and pursue our thoughts about them and the ways they are affecting us. But when we recognize the biases that grow from our deepest feelings and the experiences that shaped them, we are able to use those emotions to see into the hearts of others and offer ourselves as partners and friends. We should not be afraid of our feelings but learn to use them wisely, as Aristotle taught, to seek understanding.

WEAVE YOUR OWN ROPE

1. Setting the Stage

"There is an emanation from the heart in genuine hospitality which cannot be described but is immediately felt and puts the stranger at once at his ease."
—WASHINGTON IRVING[82]

"Let not the emphasis of hospitality lie in bed and board... the soul worships truth and love, and honor and courtesy flow in all thy deeds."
—RALPH WALDO EMERSON[83]

"Eating together puts us on the same level...we admit our sameness, and we recognize our basic humanity. In this sense, eating is a safe space, a place where we are ourselves."
—JOHN PAUL LEDERACH, Journey Towards Reconciliation[84]

"A community is not merely a condition of physical proximity, no matter how admirable the layout of the shopping center and the streets, no matter if we demolish the horizontal slums and replace them with vertical ones. A community is the mental and spiritual condition of knowing that the place is shared, and that the people who share the place define and limit the possibilities of each other's lives. It is the knowledge that people have of each other, their concern for each other, their trust in each other, the freedom with which they come and go among themselves."
—WENDELL BERRY, The Long-legged House[85]

Place matters. We begin a story by saying, "Let me set the stage." We draw listeners into the setting, helping them to see where the action occurs, asking them to enter into the story. We know that matters. When my children were small, they would spend hours creating elaborate sets for their games, often doing more to arrange the barnyard or the dollhouse furniture just so than to actually engage in the ensuing play. The setting was important. But why?

We are created beings existing in a material world. We are not mere intellects or emotions. Our senses inform our feelings and our critical thinking. We have eyes to see flowers, ears to hear birdsong. We brush our fingertips across ripply bark of a maple and sniff the fresh cut hay on the wind, and we relish the taste of strawberries in June. We delight in the beautiful, and we sorrow at decay. We find rest in lovely spaces and can feel agitated or ill at ease when our surroundings are uncomfortable, distressed, or indicative of a lack of care. We find ourselves most open to knowing and understanding others when we feel comfortable and at home. When we can fully relax physically, we are able to be less guarded mentally and emotionally. Or perhaps I should say we can be more *appropriately* guarded mentally and emotionally. We are better able to accurately assess and respond to others when we are not physically—or physiologically—in a state of stress. Opening our hearts and minds to others happens more naturally.

Knowing our own place in the world, feeling rooted and secure in that place, whether our place of origin or a home we have made for ourselves, helps us to approach others with confidence and empathy. When we feel rootless or feel defensive of our home place, we struggle to connect with others in a healthy way. Trees may be felled because their roots are too shallow or the ground beneath them is undermined. As when we ourselves lack roots in a transient and temporary world, we are easily overcome by the storms of conflict. The ground beneath our feet is insecure and easily slides away, and we are consumed with keeping our footing. We need to know where we are from.

Knowing where we are from sometimes means facing uncomfortable or even traumatic history, but ultimately, being able to thoroughly understand our own roots helps us to understand others. I know where I am from. I am mildly obsessed with Ancestry.com, and my children roll their eyes when I point out—again—my great-grandmother's old house in Pennsylvania. I collect family stories and bits of memorabilia. Everyone knows that family heirlooms (or junk) will find a home with me. But my family history isn't without dysfunction, and part of remembering means grappling with the less pleasant pieces of the past. For me, it also means the discomfort of processing my own sense of disconnect throughout high school.

Writers and politicians alike often trade on their backgrounds. For some, that is legitimate fodder for their body of work. The inestimable Wendell Berry writes in gorgeous and moving poetry and prose alike of his rootedness in rural Kentucky. That is his lived experience, and he shares the wisdom and observations springing naturally from that soil. No false currency is his. But others create a narrative that sells out of the bits and pieces of their personal history that feel most marketable or poll the best. They tout Appalachia as their home yet have little connection to the people and places of the region.

I struggle with defining my "place." My childhood was spent in rural western Pennsylvania, but even as a child, I always felt on the cusp of flight. I left for college in Boston at barely seventeen, and I have never been back for any meaningful length of time. With parents divorcing when I was a young adult, I find that I struggle to know my "home base." Can I really say I am from this place when so little of my life was there? In many ways, I was a spectator to the struggles of the families around me. I saw tremendous poverty and lack of opportunity, some of that in my own family, but is that *my* story? Was that my place? Perhaps yes.

Perhaps no. I lived adjacent to my community, but as a child, I lived, in some ways, more fully through the stories I consumed. My place was Prince Edward Island, an English moor, and an imaginary land called Prydain. When I was given the gift of designing my bedroom in high school, I was overjoyed. Ever since, I have created "my place" everywhere I have lived. I may not have deep roots in a childhood home, but I do have family roots and a driving desire to define a home wherever I am.

Sometimes, I feel a disappointment that I am not tied to a special geography or culture. I longed to be an Emily *of* New Moon or live in a house with a name or be a part of a particular little town. We all want to belong somewhere. My own personal cultural rootedness has no easy label, however.

It doesn't need one. Hearing firsthand the stories from forced migrants and refugees, befriending so-called "third-culture kids" (the sons and daughters of diplomats, missionaries, and military service members who have grown up around the world), and myself owning my various labels has shown me that who I am and where I am from may have a complicated retelling, but the end result is simply me. Social media—and the news media—are far too consumed with labeling each of us. Every year, I notice more options when filling out forms that ask my ethnicity, religion, or gender. We are East Coast elites or Bible belters or urban poor or "deplorables." We are defined in public spaces by geography, appearance, faith, politics, heritage, and sexuality. But I am not a label. No one is. I can claim western Pennsylvania as my place of origin and do so without hesitation. I am not bound by the labels that might be so associated. I can relate to the people who are there now or grew up there. Am I a Steelers fan? Not really. My boys can tell me far more about the current (and past) team than I ever knew. But I can remember well my third-grade teacher, the junior varsity football coach, who had his class of twenty-two girls and eight boys make 3-D construction paper Steelers helmets for a craft project! I remember the thrill of coming out of the tunnels around Pittsburgh to see a clear sky and marveling at the lack of smog. Living now in central Maryland, again on the foothills of Appalachia, I find myself code-switching into my old accent more and more often. I rarely say "yinz," but my "these ones" and "those ones" are alive and well, and we have a wonderful "crick" on our farm, surrounded in places by "jaggerbushes." I still flinch when my Pittsburgh vowels and vocabulary quirks come out in professional settings because I am still that teenager at MIT being mocked because of my accent. It was thought to be "cute" at first because it seemed southern, but I turned out just to sound "like a hick." I'm rooted more deeply in that geography than I think, but I am also an alumna of two "elite" East Coast universities. Am I a hick? Or an elitist? Which spot do I claim?

I claim both. And neither. My place is my home, where I am surrounded by the flotsam and jetsam of a life lived in many places with many labels. I bear within me the history of West Virginia "hillbillies," Italian-American immigrants, and the Scots, the Welsh, and the English who built the farms and railroads of western Pennsylvania, and the many characters, real and imagined, from the thousands upon thousands of pages I digested through the years. I have chosen this piece of land, this geographical place, to put down roots for my family. The roots of our farm and of our church are part of the very history of this valley. It's not my history, but I am wrapping it into our family story moving forward. We will carry the legacy of this land with us, making a new story from the old one. As we have chosen new homes along the way, we have had to choose how to define our place and to carry that with us as we go.

That freedom to choose must come with the responsibility not to self-isolate. There is nothing inherently bad about moving into a neighborhood that feels comfortable, but what do you do when someone moves into your neighborhood who seems out of place? How do you choose a place yet not choose a label? These questions are ever more important as our population shifts and settles with job opportunities and education pulling us away from our places of origin. When we wanted to buy a house of our own in Washington, D.C., before our first child was born, we would have loved to live near close friends to create a community with them. Our budget, however, had to dictate our purchase. We chose a home that met our physical needs: Both of us could walk to work, my husband on Capitol Hill, and me at World Vision. We could walk to the Metro and a few shops. Most importantly, we could afford the mortgage! And so we began our little family in Northeast D.C. We could have easily created a community of people very much like us. It would have meant reaching beyond the physical boundaries of our neighborhood—and to a large extent, that's what we did. Our closest friends lived nowhere near us. Our church, though within a distance we could walk, was on Capitol Hill. Our daughter went to a playgroup on the Hill and then preschool. We had friends in other D.C. neighborhoods and in Virginia.

But we lived in Northeast D.C. On one side was an older couple who had raised their family in that house. Beside them, an elderly woman was born in her home. On our other side was a single man who had owned the house for ten years already and had a Section 8 apartment in his basement. We wanted our community to be our place, to find our place in our community, though we seemed to be quite different. We intentionally created our home, our place, there in our happy yellow house.

Our daughter and our son grew up as the only children on the block, surrounded by aging African-American families. They adored Mr. David, who lived in the basement next door. Miss

Pat was a living legend, the scary but oh-so-nice lady down the street. Mr. Charles and Miss Gertie laughed at their backyard antics and were merciful when they shattered their brand-new custom sunroom window by throwing "pebbles" at it to get their attention. And they still have the professional grade markers and the caricatures Mr. Gene, the graphic artist, gave them. We chose to open our home and our hearts to our physical neighbors. We didn't know them before we moved in. Our life experiences were vastly different. We were young and white and very much not from D.C. But when we left, we mourned because we belonged in that house and on that street.

How did that happen? It wasn't entirely organic, and we never became the best of friends. Aside from encountering folks outside as we walked or played, we did not have much overlap with our neighbors. And they all had busy lives with family and friends. What we did have was warmth and friendliness, helpfulness, and understanding. I could talk to Floyd about the shabby condition of our fence or the differences in raising boys versus girls. I could chat with Charles about his honey-do list when he retired before Gertie. And Pat and I could discuss education issues and the school across the street endlessly. Did we go deep into each other's lives? No. We were only there a few short years and perhaps that would have changed over time. We watched Floyd's kids become young adults and Charles and Gertie graduate grandchildren from high school while our children went from crawling to walking. I don't know how things would have evolved as our children grew older and we settled more comfortably into middle-aged life. We were intentionally building a foundation, though.

We started by simply being friendly. I say simply, but for most people in our culture today, being friendly can be challenging. We don't want to intrude or be obnoxious. We worry that we don't know them, so what can we say? It's easier, isn't it, when we see our neighbors dropping their kids off at the same school or run into them at the same grocery store? When we have obvious points of overlap, we are more comfortable at least saying hello. I am not the most socially adept sometimes, but I didn't want to be a stranger in this place where I lived (remember all those stories I read!), so I did say hello. I asked questions—easy ones like "Did the trash actually get taken last night?" or "What's your dog's name?" I complimented front gardens (my husband still has a little yard envy over Charles' front garden from our days in D.C.) and grandbabies. I joked about the odds of getting a bookstore on H Street and got mad about the trash left around the bus stop. We found common ground, and we stood there. I very much doubt that anyone on our block ever even contemplated voting the way my husband did. And his public job meant that most people could make some pretty good assumptions about his politics. We didn't find common ground in political labels, true, but we did find it in political issues. As we got to know each other and built a casual trust, we could talk education, healthcare, Social Security, or even gun control.

That didn't happen without conscious effort. I can't speak for my neighbors, but I can speak for us. We wanted to be neighbors. We wanted those casual, friendly relationships. And we knew those needed to be built, not assumed. But building isn't the same as engineering. Those conversations needed to come from the heart, even if they were as simple as asking why the buses were lined up differently across the street. Our only agenda could be that of growing into our new home alongside those who were already there. We had to genuinely want to get to know them. We had to be honestly engaged.

I try to create a space where all are welcomed in. Where all may find rest and a pleasant environment. I set the stage for that, but not through great expense and an eye for perfection. I am not a perfect hostess. My home is two hundred years old, and though it is a lovely house, its age is showing. And I still have children who live in this space. I am still not a professional chef. But I am someone who wants all of her guests to feel that they are entering a sacred space, a common ground sort of space, where they are welcome, regardless of labels.

Our home now, Fairlight Farm, does have an advantage when it comes to setting the stage for welcome. We have the privilege of stewarding over sixty acres that face south towards the heights of Virginia and Maryland over the Potomac River. We watch the play of light across the ridges that bracket the valley, and we track the spreading lines of shades of green up the hillsides as winter turns into spring. Our guests are not just welcomed into our home; they are welcomed into the beauty and serenity of the valley. Whether they stand on our porch and gaze across the fields or walk the trail down to the creek, you can see the stress fade, if only for those few moments. There is a joy and a contentment that being in nature brings, and it is as undeniable as it is well-researched.

Creating a welcoming space for others doesn't require perfection. In fact, let go of perfection altogether. Being "insta-worthy" can sometimes make us more stressed or tired than vulnerable and welcoming. Put together a platter of sandwich fixings or a plate of grocery store cookies if that is what you have time or money to do. Grocery store brand cookies work as well as Oreos. Plates from the secondhand store serve the same purpose as heirloom porcelain. Don't let the perfect be the enemy of the good. Your guests want *you*, not the good china.

Who do you invite? Our lives are busy. Full. Whether that's because we are working two jobs and caring for a sick parent or because we have children in seven different after school activities and our weekends are filled with piano recitals, travel ball, and birthday parties, our lives feel non-stop. By the time we're done talking to customers or parents at school drop-off, our relational tank is empty. It is easier to keep our voluntary social occasions to those we know well, who are similar to ourselves, and who require little effort to get to know and little emotional expenditure.

If we want to see a different culture of civic dialogue and reconciliation in our communities, however, we need to push past the discomfort of extending hospitality to those we don't know well or who aren't like us. Be hospitable, truly, to everyone. Create spaces where beauty thrives. Do not be dismissive of the importance of pleasing all of our senses and stress the value of a space that is welcoming and brings rest to others. Learn how beautiful spaces and natural spaces foster a sense of calm that allows us to breathe more deeply, let down our guard, and engage our logic rather than leaving us agitated or defensive.

We need to come to the table open to sharing it with those who come to sit beside us. The Christian faith includes a God who didn't stay in His lane, who didn't share a table only with those of His social and religious sphere. He is a God who broke bread with the outcasts, the poor, those who became wealthy on the backs of the poor, the unclean, and the Temple priests alike. And because He knew who He was, because He was rooted in His place, understanding His past, knowing His present, He was the same person, the same God, at every table.

So what does that mean for you? How do you weave this strand of Place?

Know who you are and where you are from.

Create roots for yourself and your family. That may be your hometown, with family and friends that have surrounded you and shaped you your entire life. Even if you no longer live there, you can point to those people and that geographic place as that which formed much of who you are today.

Or maybe you moved frequently as a child or now as an adult. Or maybe your home of origin is a minefield of trauma or despair. So, your roots are formed from the traditions and rituals you create. I found a church home within the Anglican tradition at a time when I felt rootless and restless in the chaos of law school life in New York City. Tied to the past by hundreds of years of liturgical tradition, tied to the millions around the globe each Sunday reciting the same liturgy, I felt a sense of place that gave me roots in the midst of upheaval. It was here that I met Madeleine L'Engle as a student in her Sunday School class; here in a lovely, sunbathed stone church, I found a tribe of people gathered around a masterful storyteller who invited us in and created a beautiful space for us to hear stories and for our stories to be heard.

Develop family traditions, even as a family of one. Surround yourself with the things that ground you and remind you of who you are. Research your family tree if that helps you understand your past. If you feel untethered or struggle to move past an unhealthy childhood or lack of connection, consider speaking with someone about that. A good therapist can give you the tools to work through that disconnectedness or help you understand your past in ways that can help ground you in the present.

Make decisions about what it looks like to you to be rooted—does that mean declining a job that would result in a move away from a place you love? Or taking a job knowing you are rooted in your connection to family and faith? Do you have a church with strong traditions that give you a sense of place and time? What about family history and rituals? If you move frequently, maybe being rooted is a combination of knowing yourself and your past, creating traditions that you carry with you to each new location. You are "home" when you set up your throw pillows on the couch and your spider plant on a windowsill and when you order your first cup of coffee at the closest coffee shop. Maybe it's when you get your library card in your new town or introduce yourself to the neighbors.

Do you have a strong sense of your own identity and all the bits and pieces that come from others? I am still learning how much of who I am are the labels I've worn, and how much is truly part of me. Understanding what it means to be rooted is a necessary component of a healthy culture of conflict and reconciliation.

Choose community where you are.

This is such a difficult thing to do these days. We are so transient. Whether we move because we can and because we are seeking the best place, the best job, the best schools, or the best environment, or whether we move because we must, to be near family that needs us or to find work, there is no question that our culture today is a mobile one, though the numbers suggest that is slowing. Research indicates that approximately two-thirds of Americans move away from their hometown for a variety of reasons, usually relating to jobs. But even within a general geographic area, people move. They move across town to send their children to a different school or to find a "better" community. Perhaps we need to think carefully about how and why we choose our new homes.

We did not choose to live in Northeast Washington, D.C., because of the community. We did not know anyone there. The schools were unknown. Our church at the time was outside the city altogether. But the neighborhood was what we needed. There we could have one car, and both of us could walk to work. Whatever childcare option we found for our soon-to-be-born oldest would be close to both home and work. We could afford the house and stay close to our jobs instead of living farther from work, necessitating long commuting hours and time away from each other and our daughter. For all of these reasons, we felt confident in our decision to move there. We could have moved to Northeast D.C. and maintained our communities elsewhere, going to them and bringing them to our home, an oasis in a location that was not our community. Our closest friends did not live nearby, and we certainly didn't stop being friends. But we also found a church that was closer. We walked everywhere and got to know our neighbors. We engaged with the local school long before our daughter was old enough for kindergarten to be on our radar. We frequented the local coffee shops so often that my oldest son once stubbornly insisted that we weren't going to go to *our* home to get hot chocolate after a long, cold walk and a little bribery, but that he meant he wanted to go to *Miss Mimi's house* (Miss Mimi being the owner of the Ethiopian coffee shop down the street). Was it an ideal physical community? Perhaps not. It *was* good. We loved our house, our neighbors, our coffee shop, the school principal, and the wonderful men in the corner shop across from us who treated our then-six-year-old with all the dignity her small self demanded when I let her go in to buy a popsicle alone. But it was also a place where cars were set on fire in the alley behind us with astonishing regularity. The return of "fireworks season" each May sometimes prompted me to hit the floor because I wasn't quite sure that first "pop-pop" wasn't gunfire. We *made* it our community and our home. We managed to move without having to sell our yellow house and our oldest two children still, to some degree, consider that home. They mourned the deaths of Mr. Charles, Ms. Gertie, and Miss Pat. Though they like the new, more upscale market across the street, they miss that little corner store it replaced. We made that home for them and rooted ourselves there.

Sometimes, we need to move. And we want what is best for ourselves and our families. Still, maybe we need to be more mindful of all of the things that make up a home and a community. Think about what would make a location a Place with a capital P. And wherever you end up, really *live* there. Meet your neighbors. Look past the political sign in their front yard and say hello. You can roll your eyes in private at what you see as ridiculous lawn décor, but chat with your neighbor when she is adding another concrete pig to her front garden. Host a block party, invite people over to swim, don't be afraid to run next door to ask for a cup of sugar. Spend time outside being a part of the space in which you reside. More than one country song laments the lack of front porches. Cliché or not, front porches can play an important role in community. If you have one, use it. If you don't, plop a lawn chair out front and enjoy a cup of coffee on a Saturday morning, waving to the neighbors as they pass by. Even a recent post on Nextdoor.com for D.C. neighborhoods lamented the loss of front porch time, as various posters chimed in to say that they try to keep that up because, yes, it does make a difference.

I don't speak much about our sojourn in Northern Virginia. I learned quickly that no matter how lovely our wooded backyard, no matter how fun a *cul de sac* could be for children, I was not a fan of suburban life. Our street, however, captured the essence of community in some important ways. We were sold on the house for three reasons. First and second are related. The backyard was lovely, with old, old oak trees, tulip poplars and pines, azaleas, rhododendrons, and a lovely shade garden with paths winding through the trees. There was an old wooden playhouse for the kids and a gazebo for us. Behind the yard? Acres upon acres of a beautifully landscaped cemetery. I could feel, at least a little, like I was back home in the country. After years of urban living, I could have my trees again. But the third reason was the icing on the cake. The day we showed up for the home inspection, the area was experiencing the tail end of a hurricane, with pouring rain and flooded streets. Neighborhood children were out of school due to flooding—and they were running amok in the street, splashing in the water, floating toy boats in the gutters, and having water fights. The realtor, also a neighbor, swooped our daughter away and introduced her to a few of the kids. We didn't see her again for an hour. She returned soaked to the skin and laughing. Halloween, we discovered the following month, was as much for the adults on the street as it was for the kids. Firepits, adult beverages, costumes—it was almost a block party from one end to the other. The older couples on the street, their children long grown, still decorated and waited eagerly for trick-or-treaters. A few months later, we received the flier for a neighbor's annual Easter egg hunt. We were unsure if we should go, being new. Oh, no, we were told, you have to go. For over twenty years, they had hosted a neighborhood wide Easter egg hunt. The older children were proud to be hiders, and those in elementary school and younger went in organized waves to hunt. Prizes were awarded, snacks were enjoyed, and the neighbors mingled and caught up on each other's lives. While these activities do not alone make community, do not secure a space to hear and to be heard, they are a step in that process. And a necessary one.

If you are a business owner or pastor, how do you develop your space into the kind of Place that builds community? Maybe you host open houses at your office or retail store. You sponsor Little League teams and place ads in the high school yearbook. You might encourage your town—or your block in a larger city—to host an annual sidewalk sale and spring festival. Think creatively about how you can engage with the people and businesses around you. As a church, open up your social hall or classrooms to outside groups. Host book clubs that are welcoming to community members. Make a spaghetti dinner an annual tradition or an Easter egg hunt for the neighborhood. Sponsor a game booth at the local fair or provide snacks for a weekend soccer game. Your community is your people—your congregation, your employees, your customers—but it is also the place where *you* are. Become a part of that space.

Invite people in.

Invite people in. When, you might ask? Between getting home from my job at 6:30 pm, making dinner, overseeing homework, and putting my children to bed before collapsing into bed myself? On the weekend, between working that second job to keep up with the bills, taking my children to their extracurriculars, and trying to get enough laundry done to keep us clothed for the week?

Or maybe you already host often. You might have a close group of friends who meet twice a month for dinner or a regular book club at your house. Your social calendar and your emotional tank are full. How can I ask you to invite more people into that fullness?

And if you can find the time and energy, whom do you invite? What about your new neighbor with the obnoxious bumper sticker? The elderly couple at church who live in that fancy house across town? The single mom that never seems to get her kid to robotics club on time? Do they get invited in? The only agenda you need in order to provide a welcome is that welcome itself. We are called to share our lives and our table with those with whom we disagree, with our friends, with the stranger, and even with the enemy.

When we lived in D.C., we wanted to be more than just neighbors who talked over a fence. After a couple of years of smiles and waves and outdoor conversations, it was more than time to invite them in. For us, that means a party. An open house sort of party that starts in the afternoon and goes into the night. With food and drinks and music and everyone we know. A holiday open house was the perfect excuse to throw open the doors to our neighbors. And our friends from church. And our friends from work and school and children's activities. We didn't hold an event for our church friends and another one for the neighbors and yet a third for our work community. Our closest friends came early and stayed late. The neighbors who came stopped by for lesser amounts of time. From the outside, one wouldn't call it a raging success if the goal was immediately to draw closer to our neighbors, but long before the following December, our neighbors were asking if we planned to host another party. Which we did and to which they came.

Inviting others into your place means bearing your labels lightly. I can't say we leave them at the door because our labels are part of who we are. Again, labels are *part* of who we are. And if we only invite in the people whose labels match our own, we will miss out on all of those who have so much to offer us from all the other parts of themselves, as well as their labeled bits and pieces. Social media is replete with angry diatribes against Choose-Your-Label-Here, but have those keyboard culture warriors ever invited those Labels in?

Invite those people: Offer your neighbor a drink while you are both grilling in your neighboring backyards; open up your annual summer barbeque to your coworkers or the parents of your children's friends or the weird new neighbors with what seem to be three generations living in one house; or post an invite to your book club on your neighborhood social media page.

As a church leader, organize a downtown clean-up and invite the business owner at the end of the block with the Pride flag over his door. Town leadership? Host a town hall for local businesses, schools, and houses of worship to discuss ways to engage local children in the community in safe and healthy ways. Find ways to invite each other into your space for conversation about shared goals and common problems.

Create a welcoming space, a pleasant and sustaining environment, beauty.

Our house in D.C. wasn't a large house. Our furniture was IKEA, yard sale, and hand-me-downs, well-loved by two rambunctious toddlers. We are not chefs or decorators, and our budget was "do it as cheaply as you can." So why did we host eighty people? Why did we invite even a few work colleagues? Why did people want to come back? It wasn't about the furniture, the food, or the decorations—but in some very important ways, it was exactly the furniture, the food, and the décor.

We arranged our hodge-podge of furniture so those who needed it could find a place to sit. When we welcomed in someone we thought could use a comfortable seat, whether a pregnant friend or an elderly neighbor, we led them to where they would be most at ease. We put seats in groups and made sure we had at least a few places for cups and plates to rest. We used lamps and dimmers on the overhead lights—enough light to see but not enough to be harsh.

We had plenty of food—hot and cold, rich or spicy, as well as milder flavors. We chose foods that meant something to us: I had learned to make hummus working with peacebuilders and aid workers in the Middle East, and my husband chose meat and cheese for a charcuterie board. We had wine from Macedonia, where my husband had lived as he worked to set up an internship program in the post-Yugoslavia Macedonian Parliament. I made the ham and potatoes I enjoyed growing up. We didn't try anything unfamiliar to us or anything we didn't already make and love. Our table was set with an abundance of foods we already enjoyed and wanted to share with friends. And we had so much of it. I learned early in life to set out a vast spread for a party, and I did my family proud. From many years of gatherings of extended family, I knew how to keep the food coming! And we had coffee and cocktails, sodas, water, and a giant punch bowl because somehow punch bowls make it seem like something special. What we didn't have was a caterer or a fancy array of exotic foods. We didn't need an expensive meal to have a fabulous meal. Almost two decades later and I am still trying to recreate the potatoes I accidentally made for that first open house.

Our décor was just… what we had: photos of our family, artwork carefully collected on our travels—nothing pricey, nothing noteworthy, but loved by us–family knick-knacks gathered along the way. And books. So many books. These were things we loved—things that told our guests a little bit about us. Coasters from Bogota. A painting from Haiti. Depression glass from my grandmother. Too many boldly colored throw pillows because I like feeling surrounded by them. A few toys because with toddlers in the house, you will usually find that toys tend to hide in dark corners and multiply, reappearing just after you thought you had them all safely tucked away. That was our home, and we welcomed people into it. We added fresh flowers for the party and lit a few candles for ambiance and scent.

And that was our party, our home. Our guests were carefully curated only in the sense that we asked each other for names and addresses. We liked the people we invited, and we thought maybe some of them would like each other too.

It has been many years since that first holiday open house, and we still host them most years. Much of the guest list is the same, and there are new names added. I realized last year, as I wandered through the dining room checking on food supplies, that I hadn't talked to anyone in several minutes. Looking around, I saw friends, old and new, young and old, chatting, laughing, sharing stories. Our guest list is still neighbors, old friends, work colleagues, and church friends—people who do not always know one another before they arrive, but somehow, every year, new friends are made. To me, that is the essence of welcome: Our guests are well-come to our home.

It is that same pleasant and sustaining environment you can create at your church, business, and office. If you want to change the way our society views conflict, if you want to engage in healthy civic dialogue, and if you want to see reconciliation win, then you must engage with others in places of warmth and welcome, places of comfort and rest, and places of beauty that delight the senses. This lets people know they are valued and that you want them to come. They feel more like honored guests and less like potential adversaries.

Use the beauty of the natural world—inside and out.

Not everyone can live—or wants to live—on sixty-two acres, over an hour from the city. Their homes may be more modern or more minimalist. Perhaps they prefer vases of fresh greenery to the lilacs I have on my table, and perhaps they have window shades to block the view of their kitchen from the neighbors. But nature is not absent from the city or the suburbs. The natural world helps us to relax, release stress, and be more vulnerable and empathetic.[86] Knowing that, we can find ways to make it a part of our lives, even in the midst of urban noise. Research shows that having green plants in our living space is not only good for our physical health, but their presence in our homes has been shown to reduce our mental, as well as physical, stress.[87]

In short, plants make us happy. Studies have shown increased attention and focus, better memory, and more productivity when we share our interior space with living plants.[88] Research about the air purifying qualities of houseplants is inconclusive, but not so studies on the mind and soul purifying qualities—and the downsides of not having them. We are part of the natural world ourselves, and we thrive when we are reminded of that. No matter our fondness for interior design—whether modern and minimalist or grandmother chic or farmhouse rustic—we are soothed and inspired by nature.

To create a space where we can hear and be heard, we must include nature. If you cannot or do not wish to go to a natural setting, bring nature into yours. Biophilia, an affinity for the natural world, and biophilic design are emerging areas of research over the past decade or so. We instinctively relax more and are happier in settings that are truly natural—or mimic the natural as much as possible. This extends inside to having green plants, of course, but also the shape of our rooms and our furniture, the colors we use, and the forms we see. A genuinely inviting space, a space that encourages rest and vulnerability, is one that recalls us to Creation.

As a host in your own home, you can decide how to decorate. You can add flowers to the table, or a plethora of plants. Moreover, you can use natural fibers, colors from nature, and organic shapes that soothe. You can live in a tiny apartment on the edge of the city yet fill your home with reminders of the world outside. Does that mean decorating like your grandmother in 1985? With floral prints and earth tones? Unless that's what you love, then of course not. If you are minimalist or like Scandi style, go for it. You will be a better host, express hospitality best, be more welcoming and more open when you are in a place that you love. We are not all Martha Stewart or *Home and Garden*. Not everyone drools over Pinterest boards of elegant dining room tables. But we can all be comfortable in our space, and we can all find ways to make our space warm and welcoming—and part of that is bringing the natural world in.

Mid-century modern designs, Scandinavian style—they are seen as minimalist and, as the name implies, modern. In particular, mid-century modern embraces the space race and the new materials of a modern world. But part of what makes them enduring is that they remind us of the natural world. Heywood-Wakefield is a prominent designer of the mid-century modern period, and they drew extensively on the natural world. They used natural materials, clean lines that were reminiscent of the forms of trees, streams, and smooth stones. Like their contemporaries, they focused on warm colors and organic shapes. Mid-century modern builders used large windows and walls of glass, along with blended spaces, to bring nature inside. Similarly, the seemingly futuristic, minimalist look of Scandinavian style actually has nature at its heart, with natural woods, organic forms, and shapes and colors that reflect the beauty of long winters in the north. People are drawn to these styles because of the ease and comfort they represent.

Bringing nature inside doesn't have to mean decorating with pastels and flowers or turning your living room into a greenhouse. It simply means to be mindful of the restfulness and restorative powers of the natural world and finding ways to incorporate that into your home with your own style. I kill houseplants. I have a few that I'm trying to coddle at the moment, but my track record isn't great. Thanks to one of my sons and a fascination with air plants a few years ago, I thought I would try adding some green that way. I've managed to kill at least a half dozen air plants in the last few years, but I have a few hanging in there. Even in college, I nursed a shamrock plant in my dorm. I am not the sort of person who enjoys mucking around with houseplants, repotting them as they grow, turning them in the sun, spritzing their leaves, and, as I recently learned you are supposed to do, dust their leaves periodically. I will probably never be someone who would think to dust the leaves of a plant. But I enjoy my little green pets. There is joy in seeing my array of somewhat straggly plants in my kitchen window. Find ways to experience the joy of nature no matter where you live.

Want flowers for your dinner table? Dandelions count! Violets, ground ivy, chicory—you don't need a florist's bouquet to bring delight to the senses. Do mothers reject the flowers clutched in the chubby, sweaty hands of a toddler, or do they see the beauty and the love conveyed? People feel welcomed, special, cared for, and loved when we take the time to set the table with a vase of flowers. I use the term vase lightly. I've put flowers—and feathers and grass and branches—in a can, an old mug with a missing handle, a jar, and a juice box decorated by my preschooler, and every time it brightened the table, it made the meal a little more festive and a little more joyful. And made my guests feel a little more relaxed, a little more special.

Be vulnerable and host the stranger.

My kids have played on a variety of sports teams over the years and in the different places we've lived. Most teams have some sort of end of season gathering. Most of the time, ours have been at the field. It's a fun time for the kids to let off steam, celebrate their season, and eat junk food. The parents mingle. A little. Mostly, people chat with the other parents that they already know. Maybe they know them from school or the neighborhood. Often, the parents divide into a few different little clusters and, for the most part, remain in them. That's been fine. Again, we have busy lives. I'll never see most of these parents again when new teams form for the next season. We don't have much in common. I'll enjoy my hot dog and coke and move on. But for the past two years, we've done things a little bit differently.

At the end of each season, we invite my son's team, coached by my husband, to the farm for a picnic, a fire, and swimming (spring season!). The kids on the team and their siblings swim or play flashlight tag, getting to know one another better and having fun. The parents, freed from the awkward rituals of post-game chitchat, mingle in a friendlier, more open way. The groups shift and adjust as people walk off to get another burger or glass of tea. Some stake a claim to the chairs around the firepit and hold court for the evening as their audience moves and changes around them. Though a few tend to draw together and hold themselves apart from the chaos, most parents mingle freely and linger well after the food is gone, and the children are punch-drunk with sugar and feral freedom in the dark. After multiple seasons, our end of season party is no longer just our team. We host a few others alongside ours, and the kids and parents who played together in the past catch up with one another. For the most part, we rarely see one another outside of soccer. Out of context, I might not even recognize most of them. But for those evenings, we are a little community gathered around food and fire to celebrate a fun soccer season. Conversation doesn't tend to go too deep, but it manages a sincerity and personalness that goes beyond soccer field small talk. It may still be the shallow conversation of acquaintances rather than close friends but gone is the superficiality of the field. Opening our home is a signal that we are opening our hearts to this community, and that openness is reciprocated every time.

You don't have to host thirty kids and their families for a soccer picnic, but if you want to be part of moving from division to reconciliation, think of ways to host that work for you. If you have a book club, can you open the invitation to those you don't know? I met a lifelong friend ten years ago when I decided to send an open invite for a mom and daughter book club. Our daughters remain cordial and friendly, but their younger brothers are fast friends, as are we. What about a dinner or a picnic for your team at work? Coffee for the preschool moms? Think of ways to engage your broader community. Do you want to plan a community garden? A service day? Rather than gather in a meeting room at the local library, offer to host in your home. You will be surprised at the difference the change in environment makes.

With the ease we now seem to have with video meetings thanks to the rise of Zoom during the pandemic, sometimes it feels more efficient to just schedule a group online. Though effective enough and easier for those who are busy, online meetings lack the warmth of in-person gatherings. You can certainly build relationships online. I do not argue that point. But when gathered in person, particularly in a personal setting, groups break down barriers much more quickly. Body language and tiny changes in expression and tone of voice are more revealing in person. But more than that, people who are guests are more receptive to personal connection. There is a give and take of hosting that paves the way for more candid conversation.

Not every Zoom meeting can move to your home, but when you have the option, consider it. School committee meetings, neighborhood planning sessions, office holiday parties—these can all happen at home. Look for ways to open your home. Seek out opportunities to invite in the stranger, the mere acquaintance. Have lemonade on your porch and call out to the unknown neighbors to join you on a hot summer evening. Welcoming others, serving them, and being vulnerable in opening your door all help weave the fabric of community. Those who sit at the table together find it more difficult to be enemies and easier to consider becoming partners. For those of us who lament the culture of distrust in our society, opening our homes and offering a seat at our table is one small—but oh so large—step in building a diverse and healthy community that is able to weather conflict, solve problems, and be reconciled.

2. Sharing Stories and Sharing Ourselves

"You're never going to kill storytelling, because it's built in the human plan. We come with it."
—MARGARET ATWOOD[89]

"Stories are not mere flights of fantasy or instruments of political power and control. They link us to our past, provide us with critical insight into the present and enable us to envision our lives not just as they are but as they should be or might become. Imaginative knowledge is not something you have today and discard tomorrow. It is a way of perceiving the world and relating to it."
—AZAR NAFISI, *The Republic of Imagination*[90]

"Because we fail to listen to each other's stories, we are becoming a fragmented human race."
—MADELEINE L'ENGLE, *Sold Into Egypt: Joseph's Journey Into Human Being*[91]

Have you ever gone from assuming you were going to dislike a new acquaintance to developing a deep friendship instead? Every time I pass the sign for Friendly Hall on our kitchen porch, I think of Josephine and her Yankee Captain and wonder at their story of moving from enemy to beloved. How did that happen? Their shared experiences were part of that, I'm sure. I'm also certain that stories played a role in their relationship, just as they do in ours. My law school roommate, the one who determined she would dislike me due to all of my "pink, Christian stuff," became a best friend thanks to long evenings in our apartment swapping stories. Stories move us from strangers to friends—or, in some unfortunate cases, from strangers to enemies. Of course, we grow our friendships in many ways. We share meals, do favors for one another, watch our children play sports, go to a ball game or a club. But as we do those things, we tell stories. We start with the most basic stories—where are you from? We tell a funny story about our son or a dog or a co-worker. Gradually, our stories get richer and tell more about who we are and who we have been. With our closest friends, they can finish for us the stories we tell a thousand times, the ones that go to the very heart of our identity. And we hear their stories. We know their stories as well as we know our own, and that is how we know our friends.

I know I love stories. I love stories because they tell me who I am. They help me make sense of an often confusing world. And they open my imagination to new people and new places. We are all storytellers in one way or another because we are all part of the Great Story by the Author of the universe. We are created in His image, and thus, we tell stories. Like Jesus, the Jewish storyteller and teacher from Galilee, we tell stories to help people understand. Stories help them to understand us almost as if they have lived beside us all along. But even as I say we are created to be storytellers, some of us have forgotten that. We tend to grow up and believe we must put aside the childishness of stories.

Stories are more than tools to convey information. Stories color our understanding of the past, shape our sense of the present, and guide our vision for the future. As Azar Nafisi, author of *Reading Lolita in Tehran*, writes in *Republic of Imagination*, imaginative knowledge is how we decipher the world around us. The acclaimed children's author Katherine Paterson says, "Stories help us to see what is true and that visions of truth are nourishing to the human spirit."[92] She also reminds us that stories heal—and that the word *heal* comes from a root meaning "to make whole." Thus, we need stories to nourish us and make us whole.[93] Healing stories lead us to a deeper, richer, more mature knowledge of ourselves, our world, and the other people who inhabit it.

A story that fails to do those things is not a proper use of a story at all. But, one might argue, it is important to know the bad stuff, to understand evil and the muck of the real world. I agree most emphatically. Yet stories that tell of the worst of humanity can also help make us whole as they lead us into deeper comprehension and empathy. Children know this, and few of them shy away from difficult or disturbing stories unless prompted and trained by worried parents. Our world is difficult and disturbing for vast numbers of children, after all. And even the most coddled, privileged, or cocooned children know fear, worry, sadness, anger, and hatred. They feel tension in their parents, get angry with siblings, are jealous of a friend. They want and need stories that are real, in the very realest sense of the word, as they seek to grow and understand the world.

Attending the HopeWords Writers Conference in Bluefield, West Virginia, my middle son, thirteen, listened intently to the speakers, making notes, and laughing at their jokes. He was especially fond of the talks given by an author he loves, who was as funny and witty and charming as you would expect from his fiction. But when I asked him his favorite session, his answer was immediate and surprising. "I liked Mitali Perkins and what she said about books not telling readers what to think or feel. I hate children's books that lecture or try to explain how I should feel about something." Later that evening, I found my introverted son in conversation with Mitali Perkins, telling her how he appreciated what she said.

His older brother complains bitterly to me any time he has to do some form of literary analysis (and for a high school junior studying for the AP English exams, that's fairly frequent). How do we know, he wants me to explain, what an author "really means" by a sentence, a phrase, or an illustration? Do authors really think through all of the symbolism they wish to use and then work it into their story somehow? Is the reader really expected to sift through all the words and identify each symbol and what the author intended for them all to mean? While I do not have the strength of will of Katherine Paterson, who apparently managed not to tell her children it was merely for the sake of achieving a diploma, I also think that we do search for symbolic meaning in stories.[94] That is part of how we find meaning in the world. We may not have to explain in three paragraphs why an author may have their protagonist dressed in blue, but we do, even subconsciously, take note of such things as they help bring order to our understanding. A storyteller who *explains* their symbols is, as my son expressed in his thoughts about Mitali Perkins, manipulating the reader. A reader—or listener—ought to be able to interpret the story as they need to. How many times have I read *A Wrinkle in Time,* liking Meg, *being* Meg Murray in all of her awkwardness and oddness and *outsiderness,* longing to fit in, yet not enough to be someone different? My son, on the other hand, started his book report with, "First there's Meg. She's normal." While, yes, that says a great deal about our family, I also see that he wasn't reading *Wrinkle* in the same way that I had. He also loves the book—but not because he can become Meg Murray. The richness of L'Engle's story captures his imagination as thoroughly as it did mine, but what he takes away from it is not the same.

In the homeschool program in which all of my children have been enrolled at one point or another, seventh and eighth graders learn to write persuasive essays using *The Lost Tools of Writing*. They read various novels and then produce increasingly more developed (and interesting) essays, learning to utilize such tools as alliteration, comparison, and parallelism. To organize their thoughts and choose topics for their essays, the students are taught to decide on an "issue" or a question about a character's actions. They then find examples in the text that are Affirmative, Negative, or Interesting to support or refute their thesis. I've always been amazed at the way these students perceive the stories they are discussing. They can take the same issue and the same text, yet they arrive at very different conclusions. What they understand about a novel such as *Where the Red Fern Grows* might depend on their life experiences prior to reading the book, as well as other books read, movies watched, and conversations had. For instance, no one in our immediate family is a serious hunter, and our dog is purely a spoiled pet, but my children are familiar with hunting and hunting dogs from other family and friends. Classmates with different backgrounds are going to relate to the main characters differently than my son, and he will take away different lessons from the story than they might. One of my sons has adamantly refused to acknowledge any greater symbolism in the *Chronicles of Narnia*. It's not that he doesn't see it as possible, but more that he chooses to simply enjoy the stories. Yes, Aslan can be a Christ figure, but can he not love the story and the sacrifice and the grace and mercy and love without thinking that Aslan is Jesus? Is the story any less good and true and beautiful because he chooses not to analyze it? Of course not.

I know that the lessons I learn from a book like *To Kill A Mockingbird* are probably not those gathered by my children, now so many decades removed from Jim Crow laws, desegregation, and the Civil Rights Movement. I learned of those things from those just a little bit older than myself, that history was recent and raw. Today that is the distant past, yet to my children's generation, it feels as if events in *To Kill A Mockingbird* are part of the same distant past as Dr. Martin Luther King, Jr. and Ruby Bridges. I have realized that it is difficult for them to see the changes from the time of the book, which was during the youth of their great-grandparents, to the activism of their grandparents, and then the mixing and settling and growing pains of my youth. To them, those intervening years mean little. So, as I read Harper Lee in the 1980s, a rural northern white child, I saw the story through the filter that was the sea change of the 1960s. My much more cosmopolitan children of the 2000s do not share the same filter. And they wonder, how would a child of color in 1980s Mississippi view the story? Or one of my son's preschool classmates in Washington, D.C. in 2010, a preschool in which he was the only white child? Same compelling story. Same bewitching prose. Same injustice. Same Scout. But we bring to stories *our* stories. Like tossing handfuls of wildflower seeds into a field, what is revealed in the mixing is unique to every time and place.

We need stories in our lives—from birth to death stories are as necessary as air and water. They root us in time and place and give us history. They help us know ourselves and give us an identity. They teach us lessons of compassion and empathy, helping us walk in the shoes of others and see through their eyes, and stories provide the fuel for our imaginations. We must teach our children to be storytellers, to love stories, and to listen for them. And we must remind ourselves how to do the same when the world encourages us to leave stories behind in childhood. How do we weave this strand? How do we use the wavy panes of stories to help us become people who thrive in a pluralistic community where conflict propels us forward rather than holding us hostage?

Tell the family stories that help build your identity

"We are braver and wiser because they existed, those strong women and strong men... We are who we are because they were who they were. It's wise to know where you come from, who called your name."

—MAYA ANGELOU[95]

Tell your family stories to your children, even before they know the characters. Retell their favorites—and your favorites. Tell of your childhood escapades, and if you have siblings, share their stories, as well. Children love to hear stories about aunts and uncles as children. They find it unbelievable that these grown-ups once fought over the LEGO bricks or schemed to peek at Christmas gifts. Talk about your grandfather who fought in WWII or your grandmother who left home after high school to work at the seaside, two states away. Your memories become stories for your children, and they help your children understand who you are and who they are. Hearing the story of how you broke something precious when you were six helps them believe that their own mistake can be forgiven, too. Knowing that you had a dog that you loved gives them a tighter emotional bond to you when their beloved pet passes away. Stories about great-aunts and uncles they will never have the opportunity to meet give them an anchor to history.

I never met my great-grandmother's parents, but from family stories, I know that she came from an old and wealthy farm family that was well-connected and well-established in their county. Therefore, I, too, come from a family that was once well-respected and rooted in a particular place. Likewise, learning that my great-grandmother regularly corresponded with her cousins in Wales, though we are not sure they ever even met in person, gave me a sense of belonging that extended across an ocean and across a century. We wish she had shared more of that relationship with us and told us their story to add to our own. But, her not sharing that information led to a new family story—all about how Great-Grandma somehow never told her children and grandchildren how well she knew her Welsh cousins and kept in touch with them, and why on earth did she not tell?! We share, too, the story of one "Mrs. Stephens." We do not know Mrs. Stephens. We can find no record of Mrs. Stephens in any family documentation. There is no known Mrs. Stephens in our family history. Except—a beautifully framed, quite large photograph labeled Mrs. Stephens was found in my great-grandmother's upstairs after she passed away. Mrs. Stephens was elegantly dressed in the style of the late nineteenth century and her portrait was extravagantly framed. We even found a smaller copy of the photo. But there was no date and no identifying information other than "Mrs. Stephens." My great-grandmother died in 1990, yet here we are, over thirty years later, still cracking up with laughter when we tell the great-great-grandchildren about the illustrious Mrs. Stephens.

Who are you? When you lie awake in the quiet dark of 3 am, with no children, no spouse, no pets, parents, or coworkers, when the world goes still for just a few moments, who are you? What stories play in the movie theater of your mind? Who are the actors making an appearance time and again?

Those 3 am movies are too often replays of moments we wish we could forget—or do over—but sometimes, too, they play the story of our lives. We relive a favorite childhood memory and grieve anew the loss of a grandparent. And as we fall back into a last sleep before dawn, our minds commit again those moments to memory, refreshed and reshaped by the present. Our stories begin with the world we first know, our family, as we learn to make sense of people, relationships, and connection. Eventually, we add to our identity the stories we read and claim for ourselves. But before we identify with Anne Shirley or Emily Starr, Tom Sawyer, or Huck Finn, we try to find our place in our family stories.

What do your family stories tell you about yourself? Who are you? I always clung to family stories, repeating them, asking for details, wanting to know. Some of that, I am sure, comes from the sense of *not-belonging* that comes from abandonment and adoption. Who am I? The family tree of my biological father back to colonial America is all online in the West Virginia county where they were born. I can poke around in that family tree, taking surreptitious peeks at branches and leaves that tell me stories I hadn't heard before. I knew I had a great-aunt, a sister of my grandmother, who was a professional wrestler. I found her on that genealogy site and was able to find pictures and read stories about her life. I've added her to my family lore. My children and I have examined her photos, tracing her features to find any family resemblance. Who am I? I have some roots in rural West Virginia. My grandfather did, in fact, have a still. And long after he divorced my grandmother and moved back home, he did, in perfect West Virginia cliché, marry a cousin. But is that *my* story?

No, not really. But also, yes, it is. I did not grow up in the mountains of West Virginia. I do not know those hills and hollers. The family there are strangers to me. However, I *am* partly formed of the young marriage and tumultuous break-up of my parents. I was shaped by my mother's attempts to stay in a relationship with a family that was saddened by their son's and brother's behavior. And I am imbued with some of the essence of the stories I have gathered—hoarded really—about them. Their stories shaped them, and that, in turn, shaped me.

I am also formed by the stories of my parents' families, experiences, and hopes and dreams. Hearing those stories told and retold gives children the belonging and security they need as they grow and mature into healthy adults. My unrootedness is balanced by the richness of the family stories I heard at all those chaotic gatherings over the years. I needed those stories to ground myself in a particular place and time among particular people. My grandfather drew imaginary creatures and played piano by ear? *That's* where I get my creative streak from! My grandmother was also a fussbudget? A-ha! That explains why I had the traits that prompted her to call me Granny Gert when I was a preschooler. Our children need to know where they are from before they can figure out where they are going. They need to know that they belong somewhere.

We all crave that sense of belonging. We need to know our people, our tribe. That childhood identity provides the foundation for healthy relationships in adulthood. If we know who we are, if we know our history, we find it easier to make prudent decisions about our voluntary associations in adulthood. We have the freedom and confidence to make friends, to choose groups with which we want to be identified.

If your parents came from another country, teach your children about their journey and their first home. Maybe you grew up speaking only English at home, but you and your children can learn the language of their grandparents together. Maybe you can travel to that country and meet relatives there or visit the family town or church. Maybe that isn't possible for a number of reasons. But still, you can tell the stories. Tell them of where, who, and why. Talk of the trip to their new country. Tell the story of how your parents met and tell the stories of other relatives they may never get to know. A child may grow up in suburban Virginia and be fully American, fully embracing the world in which they live, but still feel they belong also to a city in Southeast Asia. Tell them those stories. They will need to know the past so they can understand their present and grow into their future.

Help them research family roots, even the ones that you would rather forget. Let them know their family history and learn from all of it, heroes and villains alike. Visit the cemeteries where family are buried. If they do that as small children—looking for the grave of their great-great-great-uncle who fought in WWI or the tiny headstone that marks the resting place of a beloved child from long ago—they will grow up with a deeper understanding of generational history and a deeper connection to a place, even one that is far from where they live, and a deeper appreciation for those who lived and died and changed the world of their time, little by little.

If your family of origin left trauma and despair in its wake, find the good and the true amidst the pain and deceit. Look in your memory for those people who helped you and tell those stories. Did a teacher encourage you to dream big despite being told at home you were small? Tell that story. Did a great-great-great-great-grandmother brave a trip across the ocean to escape persecution? Tell of her courage, even if those who came after her did not live up to her example. Those stories of pain and heartache, of injustice, despair, and brokenness can open doorways to healing and love, mercy, hope, and wholeness. We cannot teach our children the good, the true, and the beautiful if they do not know of the ugliness that lurks in our world, too. Our family stories are a mix of good and bad, heroes and villains, beauty and pain, just like the world in which our children grow up. Give them a view that shows beauty amidst the ugliness through the restoration glass of family stories. Their first glimpses of the triumph of the good over evil come at home, where in that safe place, they can learn that good can win and that hope can defeat despair.

Tell the personal stories of your children and listen to them tell their own.

Not only do you tell family stories; you also tell their stories. Tell them about the funny things they did as babies. Talk about how Aunt Sue had to look at their newborn feet to see if they inherited the family toes or how their cousin greeted their arrival by throwing his toys in the crib demanding, "Baby *play!*" Describe how they were chosen with love out of foster care or longed for for so long before their arrival—or how they were a joyful surprise. Repeat the family lore about fierce water fights in the backyard and how the middle brother wouldn't go to sleep until his big sister told him goodnight.

Write down the best stories to remember them or create photo books that tell the story of their babyhood. Children need to hear those stories. They need to know who they are. They need to know how they fit into their world when their world is still small. When they leave home, the world is suddenly a big—and slightly terrifying—place. Who are they, and how do they fit? If they have a history of stories that tell them just that, they can face that scary world with a little more confidence, an inner strength that helps them navigate adulthood.

Children in foster care, who are often unsure of their roots and not able to trust their family histories, will often cling to their personal stories. They want to know who they are and what they can do. If you know these children, you can help them strengthen their sense of self by telling them their stories. You might not have stories of babyhood or funny sayings they had as toddlers, but you can tell them about how happy you were to meet them. You can describe their favorite food or favorite movie. You can tell them how much you loved to read to them or how much they loved it when you made up voices for all the characters. As an adult, it may grieve you to watch them struggle with choices or want "everything pink" because they didn't have anything their favorite color before now, but you can tell those stories in ways that give them hope, that create good memories that give them a sense of connection and identity.

And, finally, don't just *tell* personal stories. Listen to their stories as well. Anyone who has spent any amount of time around a preschooler knows that they can tell the longest, strangest, most convoluted stories of anyone, often cracking themselves up with their own humor as they go. It's tempting to cut them off, to impatiently want them to "get to the point." Only, the point is the story itself—the telling of it, the hearing of it. The point is the shared laughter, the high five at the end, and the knowing nod of sympathy. I am not always a good listener to my children. As toddlers or teens, they sometimes begin long-winded stories and explanations just as I am ready to walk out the door or can barely keep my eyes open at night. I have one child particularly adept at suddenly starting to tell a story just as my favorite song will begin to play as we drive somewhere. The temptation to tune out, to interrupt, or to listen more to my inner monologue, begging them to finish, is strong. But I listen most of the time. I've been treated to many a fifteen-minute, apparently hysterically funny, story from a three-year-old that concludes with a question I cannot answer because I never did quite understand the subject of the story. I've blinked at a teen who abruptly stops talking before they've gotten close to what I would consider a satisfactory conclusion.

But, I listen. I listen to their stories because that's how they tell me who they are. Creating that space for storytelling means giving them confidence in sharing themselves with others. It helps them settle more securely into a sense of self. They feel seen and heard when you pause in your day and listen to your not-quite-four-year-old tell you for the seventeenth time since Monday about how *Amelia knows how to read.* Yes, I knew after the first telling that Amelia could now read, that my child was not especially happy about that, and that she was mad, *mad,* MAD about that. I had heard that *Amelia's* class had more fun and *Amelia's* class thought my daughter's class was for the *babies.* But I listened again because that not-quite-four-year-old was telling a story about more than Amelia's reading ability. She was also telling me a little bit about herself, about how she thought about herself and her inability to read like her friend. She was giving me a glimpse of her heart. So I listened, again, to the same story, and one day I noticed she had added a new sentence, this one about how she had been practicing her letter sounds and how good she was. Now, I could hear her frustration about trying to keep up—but I could also hear her determination and her pride in her own accomplishments. I listened again the next day and I heard pride for her friend's accomplishment. Letting her tell that same story again and again was a way to let her work through her feelings and find her footing again. She was strong and capable, and she was enough right then, even though she couldn't quite read as well as Amelia. And she could be Amelia's friend because Amelia's different strengths didn't make her less or her friend more. A decade and a half later, I find myself revisiting the same sort of story with a child who knows I will listen—and she will feel heard.

Do not forget fairy stories.

Who we are is complicated at the best of times. I may think my identity is of my own making. That I am the me I was created to be and no other. Yet, the reality is a bit more complex. The closer I am to my Creator, the more I am stripped away to the true essence of myself, but short of heaven, we are none of us that real. We begin with that self, but we add to it the stories of our childhood, the wicked witches and evil kings, monsters and dragons, as well as the fairytale princesses, brave knights, and wise guardians. Whether our childhood is one of trauma and pain or a fairytale of its own, we are changed by what we live. We may begin to see ourselves as an entertainer or an adventurer. We might identify as charmed or as damaged. Who we are becomes an amalgam of who others believe us to be.

Eventually, we add to that the characters in the stories we read, the ones we wish we could be. We are Meg, Jo, Beth, and Amy March combined, along with a little Laurie and Aunt March. We're King Arthur, Guinevere, Lancelot, Sara Crewe, Robin Hood, King Richard, and Harry Potter. Some days, we are more Peter Pevensie, stalwart and brave, and other days, we feel more like Edmund as we brood over the wrongs we perceive. We might be inspired by Marie Curie or Mae Jemison, Thomas Edison, or "Doc" Edgerton, or dream of making the world more beautiful like Miss Rumphius, create art like Degas or Calder. And as we marinate in the lives of these characters, real and fictional, we begin to absorb them into our very selves. We learn to value hard work, patience, courage, temperance, loyalty, charity, creativity, goodness, and beauty. We understand better why selfishness, greed, cowardice, anger, and impatience should be shunned.

Even as we learn it is better to avoid those traits, we learn, too, to comprehend them. Why is Lancelot both good and bad? Why does Peter forgive Edmund? In our first exposure to Robin Hood and to King Richard the Lionheart and his sniveling little brother Prince John, the roles of good and evil are clearly drawn. We fight alongside Robin Hood while he dodges the selfish and petty Sheriff of Nottingham and helps the poor; we cheer for the larger than life brave and handsome King Richard; and we despise the evil, conniving weasel that is Prince John. When we read longer, richer stories of Robin Hood and the true histories of the time, we start to understand the conflict between Richard and John. We ponder motivation, wonder if the story could be different.

In other words, we are beginning our journey of empathy. Stories lead children into deeper relationship with the feelings and motivations of others. The more characters they know, the more emotions and thoughts they see reflected. The best stories draw us into the characters, good and bad, and let us live in those lives for a moment, see through their eyes, and poke around in their thoughts.

So, how do you start your children on the path to those kinds of stories? You start with fairy stories. Much has been written on the power and value of fairy tales, from G.K. Chesterton to Junius Johnson's *On Teaching Fairy Stories*. Some have argued that fairy tales are not necessary—perhaps even bad for children. They can be violent, dark, frightening. They celebrate magic. Fairy tales aren't real and don't reflect real people and real values. And yes, good fairy tales are often frightening. Our world is frightening. A child may live in a beautiful home filled with soft carpets, cozy beds, nutritious food, and fun toys. They can be secure and healthy and see nothing evil or dangerous in their everyday lives. Yet, still, children have nightmares. They still suspect a monster lurks under the bed or behind the draperies. Babies startle at unfamiliar noises and cry—not from the volume, but from the unknown. If you live in an urban environment, you know that children can become accustomed to all sorts of loud noises—the squeal of bus brakes, the crash of a dumpster, and the constant sound of traffic. But introduce a new sound, an unknown noise, and the baby will flinch or even begin to cry. The fear of the unknown, the unseen, grows in us from birth. Children *know* that the dark is real. They don't want their adults trying to tell them it is not. They want their adults telling them what to do about it.

Fairytales deal head on with the dark. The dark is there, evil is real, the forest is menacing, and the witch is truly wicked. Children can shiver in fear as the hero trudges slowly along that forest path, with danger rustling in the underbrush alongside. But they can also be fiercely angry at the wicked queen trying to trick the princess. Fairytales help them learn when to get angry, what forms injustice and evil take, and how to identify a hero—and how to *be* a hero. Fairytales strip away the covering of the known, the details of life as children experience it, to get to the heart of good vs evil. The bad guy is simply the bad guy. The characters are fantastical, magical, and unreal. The villain isn't the bus driver or the mailman; the villain is a dragon, a tyrannical prince, or a terrible sorceress. Chesterton reminds us that children have always known dragons exist—but fairytales give children St. George to slay the dragon.[96] If dragons exist to terrify, if St. George exists to defeat them, then children can defeat their dragons, too.

So read fairytales. Read *The Wild Swans, The Princess and the Goblin, The Hobbit, Prince Caspian,* and even *Cinderella.* Let children discover dragons and evil stepmothers, goblins, and orcs. Let them dream of being a wise and faithful little sister, a brave young princess and her rescuer, an adventurous and clever hobbit, or the fierce and determined mouse Reepicheep. Give them metaphorical swords (or maybe help them make swords of their own!). Read aloud the versions that have rich and descriptive language, and do not be afraid of the darkness.

I have to add a special note about the Mouse-endorsed versions of classic tales. My children have enjoyed those animated stories of *Cinderella* and *Mulan* and *Beauty and the Beast*, and I make no apologies to those who find them unacceptable for various reasons. I also make no apologies to those who love the Mouse for my next words: Do not replace the good, true, beautiful, and *hard* fairytales with those. Just as we don't give our children candy bars in place of dinner, we should not give our children pop culture fairytales in place of the richness of classic fairy stories. Yes, they can be frightening. The language can be challenging. The heroes are complicated. Some older versions of *Cinderella* are quite bloody. The transformation of the Beast into someone Beauty can love is sophisticated, dealing with emotions for which children don't yet have names—but the emotions are real even so.

It's okay for children to read and watch retellings of fairy stories that smooth over the rough edges and erase the more challenging aspects. Sometimes, easy entertainment is fine. But don't stop there. If you watch the animated *Cinderella* and read a lighter version of the tale, then also take a look at an older Grimm version—and then go to the library and explore versions of *Cinderella* from around the world. If you read aloud, choose the versions with richer language and more complex characterizations than a child may be ready to read on their own. If they read a children's adapted version of King Arthur, you can read aloud from a more advanced version.

Often, too, we begin to stop reading aloud as our children become readers themselves. We let them read books at their tested "reading level" and forget that their intellectual and emotional levels may be far beyond their skill at decoding words. Long before they easily can read Tolkien for themselves, children can fall in love with the story as read by parents or grandparents. Will they understand every nuance and appreciate all of Tolkien's gorgeous use of words or his elaborate world-building? Likely not, though I am quite sure they'll surprise you with their understanding and insights. One of my children chose to be Faramir for Halloween the year he was six. With so many heroic characters to choose from, why did he choose a more obscure Tolkien hero, not one of the Fellowship? Because, he explained, Faramir was really the BEST character because he understood the nature of the One Ring and chose not to be tempted by it. Children will surprise you with what they can glean from stories if we only trust them enough to read with them.

Read stories that show the good, the true, and the beautiful about the world.

When children love stories and listen for stories and tell stories, they are eager to learn about the wider world through stories. My daughter is our only child who has been to the Middle East, and that was when she was too young to remember, but all of them have more than a glancing understanding of that part of our world. Because of my work in peace and humanitarian advocacy for Israel-Palestine, they heard my stories—or rather, the stories of those with whom I worked. They heard stories of Palestinian Christians whose families had tended olive groves in the land for hundreds of years, who could answer "Jesus" when asked how their families came to be Christian—and meant the actual living man Jesus of Nazareth who walked that land two thousand years ago among their ancestors. They learned of refugees seeking a home in that place and of refugees forced to leave theirs. They heard about Shepherds Field and the Old City of Jerusalem. They read, too, of the Roman occupation of Persia, Alexander the Great, Assyrians, Babylon, great empires, and great learning and commerce.

We read stories that brought the world in which I worked to life for them. Some were directly related to that work—the beautiful *Sitti's Secrets* by Naomi Shihab Nye and *One City, Two Brothers* by Chris Smith, about brotherhood, peace, and self-lessness—and others were from the broader region, including ancient Persia. We read fairytales and folktales from Lebanon, Egypt, Iraq, and Israel. We went through many versions of *Arabian Nights*. Did my children watch *Aladdin*? They did. They also had read enough to begin to "correct" the animated movie when they watched it a second time. As my children grew older, they found other books about the Middle East. My daughter read more by Naomi Shihab Nye. My boys and I found Daniel Nayeri's *The Many Assassinations of Samir* and *Everything Sad is Untrue*. As a senior in high school, my daughter wrote a scholarship-winning short story set amidst the turmoil in Iran. Her idea sprang from classes she was then taking, but she was confident in her writing because she was already familiar with the world beyond her home on the East Coast of the US through *stories*.

Yes, the news is important. We must learn to digest and understand the straightforward facts of any given circumstance. But our deeper human understanding comes from stories. We learn more about people and places and their history and their motivations from their stories than we can gather from our daily news recap. When we are familiar with the history of China, for instance, through not only textbook history but also through folktales, fairy stories, and children's books, we have better context for contemporary events. We must read stories written by people from within their own culture—but we can also learn much from those on the outside.

Frances Hodgson Burnett's *A Little Princess,* like *A Secret Garden*, tells of colonial India at the turn of the nineteenth century from a very British perspective. Neither book is particularly objective when describing the Indian population among which the English lived. Do they really teach us about life in India in 1890? Arguably, they do. They tell us quite plainly of English attitudes and injustices. Perhaps Mary Lennox and Sara Crewe of the stories do not realize the harm in how they speak of or treat their servants, but modern children can see. And they can gain an understanding of how colonialism has a negative impact on cultures that can far outlast any military occupation. If you are going to read *A Little Princess,* however, then also read stories by Indian authors who can speak into the oppression and injustice of colonialism. Mitali Perkins treats this in depth in her book *Steeped in Stories.* We can use stories like this as springboards for further discussion and understanding.

We can read *Cry, the Beloved Country* and *Things Fall Apart*—and also Joseph Conrad's *Heart of Darkness.* The three books handle the realities of colonialism in African countries very differently. While Conrad writes from a Polish-British perspective that is contemporary to the events described, Nigerian author Chinua Achebe writes from within the culture but from a time after *Things Fall Apart,* as does South African author Alan Paton in *Cry, the Beloved Country.* What can all three novels help us understand about Nigeria, the countries that have formed around the Congo River, and South Africa today and in the past? How do the different authors tell those stories?

Stories put things in perspective, shape context, and give us insight into places and people we do not otherwise encounter in our everyday lives. Find those stories. Find them for your children in folktale collections and picture books. Look online for lists of good books by authors from around the world. As your children get older, help them find novels, fictionalized historical works, and biographies that teach them about the world. And find those books for yourself. Don't be afraid to dip your toes into the waters of young adult fiction—and even those beautiful picture books—to let you see China or Vietnam or Australia, Germany, Russia, Iraq, Ecuador, or Haiti. When you read those stories, begin to *see* those places in your mind, and begin to understand some of the history, you can read the news and hear true stories beyond the facts and the bias with which they may be presented.

Use stories of other people to prepare us to really hear the stories of those around us.

Likewise, read stories of other people. Let yourself become the characters, see the world through their eyes. Charlotte Mason, a British educator and reformer in the nineteenth century, promoted the idea of what she termed "living books," books that are "fit and beautiful expression of inspiring ideas and pictures of life." [96] Living books, in her understanding, are books that are filled with ideas and not just facts, books that fire the imagination and draw the reader into the lives of the people—or animals—in them.

Living books, whether fiction or nonfiction, introduce us to people, helping us feel what they feel, viewing their world through their eyes. I have never been to the American West, and I certainly never owned a horse. But in first grade, I read every *Billy and Blaze* book in my elementary school library, and I lived every one of them. I could practically feel the soft hair of Blaze as I hugged that horse's neck. I knew what it felt like to race along a pasture. I could smell the leather of Blaze's saddle. I knew Billy's desperate longing for a horse like it was my own—even though I had only ever vaguely wanted a horse and only because my classmate Tracy rode horses and wore cowboy boots and braids and cool Jordache jeans. I even wrote my own Blaze story. Decades later, watching two of my sons ride, I feel a little niggle of *déjà vu* every now and then, and I realize that sense of reliving comes from *Billy and Blaze*. I felt pride with Billy, and fear and joy and anger. I was sometimes a lonely little kid, and I longed for something like Blaze—a friend, a confidante, and the freedom to ride out past the boundaries of my yard. I wanted to explore, and I wanted a companion with whom to explore. I wanted the *feelings* of Billy and his horse more than I wanted the horse itself.

That's what living books do. They help us name and understand emotions—first our own and then those of others. First, I could *be* Pocahontas, and she could help me understand when I felt out of place, scared, or helpless. She could help me understand how to be brave in the face of the unknown. But after that, I could begin to see what she saw. I could feel her sense of disorientation, fear, and helplessness. I could enter into her pride in her place of belonging, her sorrow at being far from home, and her courage. Even a children's book that romanticized a very tragic story could give me entry into that world. A seven-year-old may not be old enough to understand the starkest realities of European colonialism in the Americas, but by making friends with the storybook Pocahontas at seven, I was able at thirteen and twenty and thirty-three to better understand the life she actually lived.

Living books, such as well-written stories of Pocahontas, even if simplified and sanitized for young readers, help us enter into the lives of others, and those easier versions pave the way for us to digest more challenging information. Still, reading what Charlotte Mason deemed "twaddle," which is essentially the junk food for the mind when it comes to books, is part of the reading life for most lovers of story. As first graders, we might be enamored with the *Rainbow Fairies* or then fall in love with *Star Wars* fanfic in middle school. Maybe we like rom-coms or political thrillers. A well-written story in any genre can engage our minds and our hearts, and sometimes, we read just to be entertained. However, we should never give up on good stories. If you don't have the time or inclination to read a two-volume biography of Robert Frost (true story—that incredibly in-depth look at the poet's life kept my sanity intact through the first month or so of motherhood with a baby who had to sleep upright!), or if you are not a particularly strong and fast reader or don't care for it as a pastime, you can still find ways to engage with stories about others. Audiobooks engage our brains much like physical books and can be a restorative way to pass the time on a stressful commute. Shorter works, such as essays and profiles, are living stories, as well.

Sometimes, it is easier to immerse yourself in childhood favorites. Go ahead and re-read Tom Sawyer as an adult. Revisit Narnia or Avonlea or even spend time with Ramona Quimby. Even picture books can give us insight into the thoughts and feelings of others. If you don't want to read them alone, share those books from childhood with your children. Maybe they need to get to know Ramona and know that someone else sees the world as the same crazy place as Ramona. Or maybe they need to understand Ramona because they have a quirky, loud, rambunctious kid in their life, and they just can't understand her. Don't just read the words on the page. Books are the perfect conversation starter. I admit to occasionally choosing a read-aloud because I felt I had a child who needed to "meet" a particular character, whether to help them to be heard or maybe to help them hear someone else.

To Kill A Mockingbird wrestles with the labels bestowed by race, as well as class and mental illness. The reader grows in empathy and understanding alongside Scout and Jem as they navigate childhood amidst the prejudices of their Southern town.

But more than learning the viewpoint of the young, relatively privileged, white protagonists in *Mockingbird,* one glimpses the world through the eyes of poor Black Tom Robinson, accused of rape, and of MayEllen, trying so hard to escape her violent existence of abuse and poverty. Harper Lee masterfully manages to create empathy for the woman responsible for the ruination of the lives of Tom and his young family. The very best of stories allow us the uneasy view of life from the perspectives of multiple, conflicting characters. I can hate MayEllen for framing Tom, but I can also pity her for the circumstances of her life that led her to do it. And I am better for it.

Reading living children's books that draw us into the world of the characters, their minds and emotions, prepares us to hear the real-life stories of the people around us. We can more easily step into the shoes of the refugee family in the news or the farmer down the road if we have that experience of stepping into the shoes of our favorite characters. Read those books to your children, but then take them out into your community to get to know the stories of the people they encounter. Introduce them to the woman who delivers the mail or the man who works at the coffee shop. Help them make friends on their soccer team by modeling the behavior you wish to see from them. Talk with them about what you observe about people. Maybe ask if they noticed anyone looking tired today or sad or if a teammate was happy or excited. Help them identify the emotions they observe.

As adults, take time to listen to the stories of others, even if they are hard to hear or you disagree. Teach empathy to your children by being empathetic. Invite that crazy uncle to Thanksgiving and listen to his stories. It's okay to direct the conversation away from controversial topics over turkey and pie, but if you hear him as he tells his stories, you learn more about who he is and what he believes, aside from what you consider his despicable political opinions. If you can hear him and learn to know him a little more, perhaps later, as you sit by the fire, you won't be as afraid to broach the topic of politics and ask him what he thinks and why. And, if he has felt heard around the table as he talked about his buddies who lost their jobs and can't pay their medical bills, then maybe he will feel less defensive and calmer as he tries to tell why he votes the way he does. No guarantees! Not everyone is able to be respectful, no matter how much respect you offer, and not everyone is willing to extend to you the courtesy and empathy you give. And some people truly are "toxic," though I believe that word is much abused. Still, you will be surprised at how many people you find who are eager to have a meaningful conversation about very difficult topics if only they feel they will be heard. And hearing them starts with knowing how to hear them—which starts with empathy. And empathy is learned well through stories.

In *The Rock That Is Higher, Story as Truth*, Madeleine L'Engle grapples with the implications of the Bible if seen as literal or not. In that discussion, she compares this to the tension in how we hear the stories of others. There is a Truth beyond all the stories, but that truth is *in* the stories. We need to learn to hear the thread of truth, the good and the beautiful, no matter the interpretation. My memories of my own childhood, of stories told then, and of my children's childhood are haphazard at times. I'll begin a story, only to have corrections shouted from various corners. But it's *my* story. Not, as our post-post-modern world tries to say, "my truth," for there is only one great Truth. But it is my story, my memory, feelings, and ideas. When you listen to stories of those on different sides of a conflict, you will hear different stories that often do not line up with one another. You must learn to listen to the *truth* that threads through them all.

3. Thinking Critically for Conflict and Reconciliation

"How unreasonable people are! They never use the freedoms they have, but demand the ones they do not have; They have freedom of thought—they demand freedom of speech."
—SØREN KIERKEGAARD, *Either/Or*[98]

"People can be extremely intelligent, have taken a critical thinking course, and know logic inside and out. Yet they may just become clever debaters, not critical thinkers, because they are unwilling to look at their own biases."
—CAROL WADE[99]

"Critical thinking is not something you do once with an issue and then drop it. It requires that we update our knowledge as new information comes in."
—DANIEL LEVITIN[100]

"Nothing in life is to be feared, it is only to be understood. Now is the time to understand more, so that we may fear less."
—MARIE CURIE[101]

I read a news article recently in which a fairly well-known news media personality declared herself "haunted" by the realization, mid-dinner, that some of her well-educated, engaging companions held different political views from her own. "Haunted." She was aghast that they might be from *the other side* and she hadn't known! She was uncomfortable continuing her acquaintance with them, and though she felt they must exist in a bubble and refuse to learn "facts" that would show them how wrong they were, she, too, seemed decidedly uninterested in hearing a different point of view. She seemed, in fact, afraid to do so. Afraid of these folks who appeared "normal" but then held such appalling views—views that were never really discussed.

We are often afraid to show our authentic selves. Sometimes, it's because we are worried about how we will be perceived. Will they still like us if they get to know us better? Will we still be included? Will we still belong? Human nature is such that we want to be liked. We need to be part of a family or community. So we adapt, just a little bit, to find our place in the group. In a healthy family or community group, everyone shifts and adjusts a bit in order to fit together harmoniously. Not so much that one becomes something she is not, but we change just enough, soften our edges some, and file down the rough parts so that we may slide along smoothly.

Sometimes, though, we go too far. We don't just sand off the more abrasive bits, but we start carving ourselves up, changing our shape to fit in. We gloss over the areas that don't match up, keep quiet about opinions that might show that we aren't really part of the crowd. Or perhaps we hold back because we fear division or anger on the part of others. We tell ourselves we don't want to make trouble or cause a scene. It's easy to stuff down our personal thoughts and keep to the shallow end for the sake of harmony. After all, we want to be *nice*.

The words above attributed to Madame Marie Curie are needed in this world of fraught emotions, especially around identity and politics. How do we move forward with conversations when we are wrapped in fear, lack of understanding, anger, and distrust? There is sorrow, too, in that emotional stewpot. Most of us want connection. We want dialogue and problem solving.

Few areas of knowledge are sacrosanct or fully understood, marked "the end," the file closed. Whether the nature of the cosmos or the hidden meaning in the poetry of Emily Dickinson, everything remains open to new information, deeper comprehension, and more thoughtful consideration. We cannot rely on mastery of a subject to inform our beliefs. We can't close a file in our mind; rather, we should be willing to hear and think about what is said by others who know a little more. We must be less fearful—more courageous in examining ourselves, our beliefs, and our biases.

The COVID pandemic will forever define an era in global history. We will be grappling with the implications of policies, behaviors, and attitudes that arose over the course of those years for decades to come. What struck me most was the repeated use of the phrase "the science shows" or "the science is." Though not an engineer, I did study for four challenging years with some of the best scientific minds in the world. "The science" is a misnomer or misdirection at best. We do not know "the science" about anything really. But what about gravity, you ask, or photosynthesis? Surely we *know* about those. Yes—and no. We know many facts about gravity or how plants turn sunlight into energy, but we do not know everything. Gravity, in particular, is quite mysterious. We do not, in fact, know much about it at all. There is no such thing as "settled" science. The very nature of science is to question. Do we know that light is a particle? And a wave? What does that mean? How do we know those facts? What if we are wrong? Atoms are the smallest units. Well, actually, atoms are protons, electrons, and neutrons. So *those* are the smallest units. Except protons and neutrons are made up in part of quarks. Is there something smaller than a quark? Perhaps. Though quarks and leptons being the smallest units of matter is generally considered "settled," the term is used much more loosely than a lay understanding suggests. For research purposes, you can consider that "settled;" meanwhile, other scientists are working to discover something smaller. That's the wonder and beauty of science: We can always keep researching, questioning, and seeking. We can still discover an infinity of wonders in the world around us.

And that is exactly how we need to consider every other area of knowledge. Yes, some things are "settled" as far as everyday life is concerned. We have to live with some questions seemingly answered as we go about our ordinary course of business. I certainly "know" that my friends who claim to be married are truly married. I have no reason to doubt that and would never demand to see a certificate of marriage to consider that a fact. If confronted with a woman who claims (plausibly!) *also* to be married to a friend's husband, I would need to take another look at what I think I know and believe to be true. But in the absence of such a claim, I would simply "know" my friends are married. I also "know" the boundaries of my farm. For most purposes, I trust the boundaries as we were shown, marked with paint and vanishing fence lines. I do not need to probe further or think more critically about my property lines most days. Yet if someone would begin to develop the field to our north, you can be sure I would have a professional surveyor on site to prove, as well as possible, the exact border of that north field. No beliefs or facts should be so sacred to us that we are unwilling to examine them carefully in light of new information.

We are quick today to voice our opinions and to declare our right to do so—and our right to ignore those who do not share our opinions. The internet is full of articles that affirm our desire to remove ourselves from those who disagree with us. We find all sorts of advice on how to create a family of our choosing and how to cut off those who might make us uncomfortable. And, yes, certainly, we have the right to do that. We do have freedom of speech in the United States and can boldly and loudly declare our beliefs on every platform we have. But all too often, those platforms become players in the great conflicts of our lives.

I lead a fledgling organization dedicated to putting these principles into practice. The Fairlight Forum was instituted to "create a space to hear and be heard" in a manner inspired in part by the *salons* of the Enlightenment. Here on our farm, in the shadow of the ridges that once saw the bloody result of division, we desire to bring together people who seek Truth, who are willing to wrestle with the Other on those topics that have brought us into a cultural moment of high conflict—race, gender, religion, economics, politics, and so on. If we are to thrive as families and communities and a nation—and even be a world at peace—we must accept that we do not and will not always agree. We can hold to our beliefs and yet still be one larger community. That is the nature of pluralism. One out of many, as heralded by the United States in our motto. To maintain that peacefully, we must be able to disagree and not demonize. We must strive for *healthy* conflict that welcomes questions and debate that upholds the dignity of the opposing sides. We must welcome "the Other" into our space, listen, question, and let us take the time to see each other through the perspective-shifting of empathy and human dignity.

So what do we do?

Be quick to hear, slow to speak.

For a long while, I had a little note hanging up in our family room that quoted James 1:19 ("So then, my beloved brethren, let every man be swift to hear, slow to speak, slow to wrath; for the wrath of man does not produce the righteousness of God." James 1:19-20). In a family of opinionated, stubborn arguers, I felt we all needed the reminder to be "quick to hear, slow to speak, and slow to anger." It's not easy advice to follow, whether you are fighting with a sibling or reading an antagonistic post on social media. Easy or not, this is the posture that must be cultivated to allow space for critical thinking to grow.

Being quick to hear or to listen is an ever-increasing challenge in lives that are full of noise. How do we ever discern what needs our attention? How do we tune our ears to hear what is important? We may have a podcast on our earbuds, children bickering in the next room, and a spouse wondering about weekend plans. We have co-workers who seem just to chatter two cubicles over but are also discussing shared projects. Our boss wants our attention, our children need us, our parents, friends, and neighbors all vie for a moment of listening. But we also feel guilty for not paying more attention to the news or learning about important issues in the world, so we are also listening to a news snippet or a talking head on a political website.

Being quick to listen may mean that we are trying to listen to *everything*. How can I know what is important? What if I miss what matters? Aren't we *supposed* to listen? To pay attention? Friends rave about the audiobooks they listen to on the way to work or the podcast you just *have* to check out. Everyone is listening to something all of the time. And there is never enough time to listen to it all. If I listen to news media with a right-leaning slant, I am supposed to balance that with media with a left-leaning slant, right? And I should be feeding my mind with rich literature and thoughtful writing. Never mind music. And conversation with friends. Is there ever a time for silence?

Silence comes when we remember to be slow to speak. That is our time to consider what we are hearing. To ponder, as Mary did in the wake of the whirlwind that was a teenage birth away from home and a visit from esteemed Wise Men from far away. Before Mary could ponder, before she could think on what she was experiencing, she first listened. She listened to the shepherds

who came to worship and the kings who came to present rich offerings. She listened to the animals around her and the bustle of
a small town overflowing with guests for the census-taking. She
listened to the ring of metal weapons against stone and the com-
manding shouts of occupying soldiers. Our world seems noisy,
but so was first-century Palestine. How did she know what to
attend to, what sounds, what voices were important to hear and
understand? We can probably safely assume that the mother of
Christ prayed; that she first, in silence, listened for the small, still
voice of her God.

As a follower of Christ, His should be the first voice to
which I, too, listen. In prayer and meditation, we can quiet the
outside noise, still our thoughts, and be silent. Into that silence
speaks the Word of God, Scripture we have read, prayers said
by us and for us, and the sound of Creation that calms, soothes,
and brings joy into sorrow or worry. Other faith traditions likewise teach those moments of stillness—whether guided medita-
tions, silent reflections, or other prayers. Therapists, too, suggest
those acts to lead us into times of quietude, where the noise of
the streets recedes, and we can rest our minds, hush troubling
thoughts, and find clarity in chaos.

Prayer and meditation not only benefit us in the moment,
but the positive effects continue throughout the day by clearing
out some of the mental and emotional clutter that has accumulated and reducing negative thoughts. As our blood pressure
lowers and our physical stress responses ease, our minds are better equipped to process our information overload. Studies have
demonstrated over and over again that people who regularly engage in prayer or meditation have lower resting heart rates, lower
blood pressure, better sleep, fewer headaches, and even reduced
chronic pain.[101] Prayer and meditation help reduce anxiety, lower stress, and help us grieve. When we pray and meditate, when

we let ourselves sit in contemplative silence, we become more patient, more self-aware, and more creative. Whether you pray as a Christian believer or not, the time spent in that stillness acts as a detox for the mental and emotional junk food that we consume, however unwillingly in some cases, throughout the day.

With clear minds and calm emotions, we are able to hear the treasure amongst the dross. We have better resources to sift through the news to find the facts of value. We have more energy and patience to listen—really listen—with understanding. I know that I find it far easier to control my anger when I spend time in prayer. I am less *reactive* in conflict and more prone to taking the time—and attention—to try to understand the perspective of someone who seems to stand on the other side of nearly every issue I hold dear. I have better judgment about when it is time to speak and when things are better left unsaid.

I am sometimes impulsive, erring on the side of putting everything on the table right away without taking the time to assess the situation, listen to others, and be still and listen to God or even my own mind. Even when it is right to (eventually) speak, an emotional brain dump usually isn't the best approach! When I listen first and speak later, I do a better job of choosing my words, I temper my emotions, and I speak directly to what someone is saying. I hear, so they feel heard.

We may joke about saying "bomb" on an airplane, but we often have little self-control when it comes to dropping verbal bombs into areas of conflict in our lives. All too often, we allow ourselves to blurt out, "That's crazy!" or "How can you—!" We blithely assume that those around us share our opinions, so we do not stop to think before we condemn opposing beliefs or, worse, mock them. We speak quickly and often fail to listen at all. Our throwaway comments may be as innocent as we say we intend, but if they deepen existing divides, they nonetheless cause harm. We can't begin to engage in healthy dialogue if we are unmindful of the impact of our words.

So, we are swift to hear and slow to speak—what of anger? It shouldn't astonish anyone that listening before speaking aids our attempts at being slow to anger. Taking the time to really hear what is being said, to process even the nonverbal cues, to ponder the meaning behind the words has the not so surprising result of empathy. Empathy is not shorthand for giving someone the benefit of the doubt or for not holding them accountable. Nor is empathy the same as pity. Empathy means that we deeply understand and are sensitive to the feelings of others. Where compassion suggests that we feel *for* someone, whether we understand their feelings or not, and sympathy means that we feel along *with* someone, empathy says we *understand* their emotions. We do not have to agree with them, or like them, or consider them good, but we have gained an understanding of them. We know something of the "why" behind their feelings, thoughts, and actions.

Empathy doesn't erase reasons for anger. In Scripture, Jesus, arguably the most empathetic human one could encounter thanks to the omniscience of the Divine, got angry. He could understand the motivations of others—and find their actions condemnable. But he didn't overthrow the tables of the money-changers in the temple in a fit of pique. Of course, he understood the motivations of the priests, the sellers of doves, and the money changers. Those motivations were actually what drove his anger. The desire for money, the greed, and the selfishness that turned the Court of the Gentiles from a place where all could worship into a corrupt and commotion-filled marketplace were the real problems, not merely the somewhat necessary act of changing money or selling animals for sacrifice. So Jesus came to His anger through a deeper understanding of the motives behind the acts.

In the same way, if we are listening and pondering before we speak, we may be slow to anger as we sift through the information provided, but we may still get angry. Only now, our anger has a reason and a purpose. We are able to know what we think and why, and we can decide, reasonably and rationally, how we want to respond. Sometimes, our response still looks emotional, but it is formed from the critical thinking that happened during our time of listening and waiting.

And that is why James 1:19 comes first when we ask what we can do to engage in critical thinking: We must be quick to listen, slow to speak, and slow to anger (or any emotional response). We use that time of listening to better understand others, develop empathy, and examine our own beliefs and biases. Only then should we speak.

Examine yourself first before judging others.

As much as we might want to dive into fixing all of society's ills, our first subject is our own mind. We all carry around bundles of beliefs mixed up with a collection of facts, passing thoughts, and experiences, along with some lies, misunderstandings, and false premises. We bring these to all of our conversations and relationships, sometimes boldly flinging them onto the table and staring down any who dare protest, sometimes tucking them discreetly under our chair lest we expose ourselves or give offense. Whether or not we deal with our bundles in a healthy manner, neither hiding them in the shadows nor defying others to challenge them, we need to fully understand what they contain before we enter into dialogue with others.

If you have strong opinions about politics, examine them. Why do you support a particular candidate? What are your motives? Do you fully understand their positions on controversial topics? What about on other matters? Do you agree with all of them? Why or why not? How important are certain issues to you? What about their person? Do you respect them and find them worthy of being a leader? All good questions to ask yourself.

But you must dig a little deeper. Ask questions about your own beliefs. You agree with the candidate on an issue—why? What, exactly, do you believe? What is your understanding of the issue? Can that be reconciled with other things you believe or know to be true? If not, what do you do? Too often, we decide to just hang out in the uncomfortable space where our core beliefs are in conflict. We want to believe both, so we simply... do.

Unfortunately, that inner disconnect paradoxically can often make us defend those incompatible beliefs that much more intensely. The unease keeps those beliefs on high alert, and we tend to be more emotionally invested in them. Sensing the inconsistency, our minds try to fill in the gaps, so to speak. Our brain doesn't like inconsistency, so it loops around itself, trying to find ways to make opposing ideas live together.

No one else can break through the noise of our own minds in turmoil. That job belongs to each of us alone. We are the only ones who can address the inconsistencies head-on and discover if they can be reconciled or if they must be discarded or changed. We cannot hope to have an honest dialogue with others about difficult subjects if we are not able, first, to be honest with ourselves.

Just like when we engage in Socratic dialogue with others, our first step is to acknowledge that all opinions and beliefs must be on the table. We cannot approach an honest understanding if we hold back certain beliefs as too precious for consideration. And yes, this applies even to our most deeply held religious beliefs. If they cannot stand up to scrutiny, should we still believe them?

Challenging our religious beliefs does not mean that we must discard them if we are left with doubts. Socrates did not intend that questioning would always discover the absolute truth. In fact, truth was something he believed could *not* be reached. The best we can do is keep examining ourselves, keep asking questions, keep discarding those ideas that fail to measure up, and keep edging closer to what is Truth. Doubts do not discredit faith. They show us what we do not know or do not understand—yet. I live suspended between doubt and belief, and that is okay. Nothing I know of the world has yet to prove inconsistent with my faith, so I can hold onto that as good and true. I can periodically examine my core faith beliefs against what else I know to be true, and I am confident my faith will continue to stand up against such examination.

Other beliefs? I am confident of some—that I've questioned, tested, and based on the facts as I know and understand them, they hold true and remain consistent with my other beliefs. Does that mean I'm done? Most emphatically, no. As new facts present themselves, we need to hold them up to our beliefs and test them against one another. If the facts prove accurate to the best of our knowledge, how do they support or challenge what we already know? Once we begin to take certain subjects or ideas off the table, we can no longer trust ourselves to be honest in our search for truth. In this world, nothing is forever certain, and we need to hold onto our beliefs loosely. Our goal should always be that of seeking the truth. If we cling too tightly to our beliefs, we risk missing the truth, missing information that leads to deeper understanding.

Clinging to our beliefs with closed hands and closed minds, we often see those who challenge our beliefs as enemies. How can we partner with someone we firmly believe to be wrong, who holds ideas we have no intention of examining more closely? If we want to engage in honest dialogue with others, we must be able to see them as potential partners, if not also friends. That has to start with accepting that our own beliefs are just as vulnerable as those of others. Humility is a difficult virtue to practice, especially when our emotions are high, and our values are being challenged, but if we want robust civic dialogue, healthy conflict, and the potential for reconciliation, we have to be willing to humbly examine ourselves before turning our questions on others.

Social media makes it all too easy to declare our opinions to the world in terms that are more akin to emphatic statements of fact than personal understanding. We can always share our opinions and the reasons we hold them, but we must always be mindful that we are sharing an *opinion*. And by sharing it, we intend to signal that we are willing to *think* about that opinion more critically. We have the freedom to broadcast our beliefs, but we should never forget the responsibility to think about them, too.

Social media can be a tool for sharing information about difficult topics, but it should not be a platform for strident declarations of absolutes. How much more can we connect to others, build community, and create a culture of productive, rather than destructive, conflict by asking questions rather than definitively tossing out labels? Be careful, thoughtful, in your use of social media, seeking to learn before you lay down judgment.

Know why you are having a discussion.

Why do we seek dialogue with others? When it's easy, and we are enjoying our conversation, we do so for the sake of deepening relationships. But what happens when we encounter someone who suddenly begins a monologue on a divisive issue? Or when we are asked to sit at the table with someone we believe to be on the wrong side of a local debate? Or when we are trying to satisfy our family, half of whom want to invite that crazy uncle to

Thanksgiving and half of whom say they won't come if he does? What, then, is our goal in dialogue?

Arguably, our ultimate goal is the same—to seek Truth. We should not engage in dialogue in order to win an argument or advance some goal we hold in the background. Our aim should be for both of us to inch closer to a true understanding. If we approach each other with an open mind, engaging for the sake of learning, we stand a much better chance of achieving, if not resolution, at least a state of peace. We should never enter into a debate for the sake of strengthening our own position. Truth may not be reachable in a given discussion, but the quest for it is the goal. Every discussion should be one that leads closer to truth and further from uncertainty. I do not know with absolute certainty who will make the best president of the United States. I can have a strong opinion backed with clear and convincing evidence, but I cannot know the truth. Every discussion I have on the topic should be one of *seeking* truth—and not declaring it.

We don't always want to have a Socratic debate. Sometimes, our goal is mere civility. Even civility requires us to know how to engage, however, which must start with understanding why. The mom at school drop-off who can't stop complaining—loudly to anyone who will listen—about the way a teacher handles the drop-off process might be someone with whom you need to work on a class party. It would be tempting to maintain a civil approach and avoid all appearance of conflict. But that isn't how we make progress in building healthy communities. Avoiding small conflicts can seem like a victory for civility, but it also allows our ability to metabolize larger conflicts to weaken.

Our society cannot seem to decide how we should approach conflict. We flip between sweeping issues under the rug, with false smiles and pleasant greetings, and demonizing those with whom we disagree, refusing all contact except the occasional flaming post on social media. Avoiding smaller conflicts can sometimes feel necessary to help us achieve other goals—such as a smoothly run fifth-grade Halloween party—but in the long term, sidestepping those minor points of contention prevents us from developing the connections that will lead to richer and stronger communities that are capable of handling the more difficult questions of our time.

So how *do* we handle that acquaintance or co-worker—or family member—with whom we just want to keep the peace? We start by not blindsiding someone with a discussion they may not be prepared to have. Ask if you can talk about what they've said; try to bring it up at a time when it's relevant, and you have the space to hold a conversation. In the middle of setting up for that class party is probably not the best time to broach a contentious topic. But maybe afterward, during the downtime of clean-up, it might be okay to suggest a cup of coffee and a few minutes to chat.

Healthy conflict is curious and seeks better understanding, rather than seeking to prove oneself right, convince someone else of your rightness, or highlight the conflict itself. Approach the subject with humility. Remember, you might not be right. Or only partly right. Maybe your beliefs need to be tweaked a little, too. If your honest goal is restoration and community, you do not need to be as concerned with being more right than "the Other." Instead, you are focused on *understanding* "the Other."

Easier said than done in many cases, especially when we don't have a partner in the dialogue but an adversary. Sometimes, our beginning isn't with the subject of the conflict at all. Sometimes, we need first to disarm our would-be opponent. In the case of the other fifth-grade mom, how could you disarm her and reach a place where the conflict can be brought to the table? If you suggest grabbing coffee to relax after that class party, you have a chance to get to know her a bit and *let her get to know you.* Who are you away from your group identities? Who are you when you are extending hospitality to friend or stranger—even the hospitality of a coffee shop?

And who is she? She is the mom of one of your child's classmates. That's a great starting point for finding common ground, but I would not linger there in that easy shared group identity. Maybe you can learn much about her if you go deeper into parenting stories and begin to push beyond where you sit as class parents. Maybe you need to move the conversation to career, hobbies, hometown, or travel. What can you share that opens the door to understanding?

If you are able to see her clearly as a fellow human being, with good and bad all mixed in, who shares some ideas and identities with you, you can approach the contentious topic. Remembering humility, begin with "I" statements. "I feel uncomfortable," "I was surprised when…" Remember that your goal is understanding and truth, so ask for comments that help move you to that goal: "Did I miss something? I'm wondering if I am understanding the situation well." Remembering that you want to start on common ground, ask if she has been doing pick-up for a long time or if she knows the teacher in question. Comment on your own observations that might be reflected in her response to the situation or how you view the pick-up process. No matter how differently you see the situation, you do have a shared experience. Affirm that. "School pick-up can be crazy! I often wonder how they keep their cool and if maybe they could do things differently?"

You can do all of those things and still be met with hostility and rancor. No matter how gracious or open you are, healthy conflict depends on both parties. Sometimes, all we can do is try to understand, remain open to changing our own minds, and show empathy to "the Other." We can keep our own biases and emotional responses in check and not succumb to group identities, defensiveness, or disdain.

Remember to keep your emotions to their proper role.

Feelings are real. They provide us with invaluable knowledge about ourselves and our relationship to an issue. We ignore them at our own risk. But our emotions do not get to hog center stage in conflict. They are bit players, a Greek chorus that give context but remain in the background. Keep your emotions in check when you approach a challenging conversation. Ponder their meaning, pay attention to what they are telling you, understand how they may be affecting your reasoning, but do not give them time at the microphone.

It can be helpful to spend time deliberating on your emotions and seeking to define them more precisely. Is it anger you feel or irritation or disgust? Are you sad, or are you ashamed? Most neurotypical adults can readily classify their emotions into one of several easy categories. We are familiar with the vocabulary of feelings, and we are comfortable using the words. Even if recognizing and defining emotions is more difficult for you, being willing to learn is a necessary step in maturity and in handling conflict.

There is certainly no dearth of books and other resources on emotional intelligence crowding bookshelves and websites today. Experts abound who can help us name our feelings and accept them. It is harder to trace them back to their origins and harder still to move ourselves through our emotions to clarity on the other side. One way to do that effectively is to dig down into the definitions a bit. A feelings wheel or an emotions wheel—two different forms that offer similar yet not the same insights—may be a familiar tool. Schools are now often using such visual aids to help children learn to identify and address their emotions, for instance. An emotions wheel labels our core or primary emotions, such as fear, disgust, anger, happiness, and surprise. Surrounding those are our secondary and tertiary emotions that flow from the core. The further out you go on the emotions wheel, the more specificity you have for clearly defining your feelings. The original emotions wheel is shaped like flower petals with the space between each labeled with the emotional state that comes from the blend of the feelings to each side.

These tools are an effective aid in becoming more aware of our emotions, their origins, and how to handle them. We may think we are feeling sad, but if we dig a little deeper, we may come to realize that we are actually disappointed and perhaps a little hurt. Or our anger is actually driven by envy or contempt. When we confront those specific emotions, we are better equipped to uncover their genesis. If I'm not just angry but am feeling envious, I can look at the why behind that and then begin to assess the validity of that feeling. What might have seemed like anger and might have fueled more conflict can now be addressed directly and perhaps internally.

When we take our seats at the table to engage in dialogue, we can choose to put that emotion on the table with its proper label. "I thought I was angry about the new development plans near the school, but I think I need to reassess. The plans look fantastic, and honestly, I'm a bit envious of the amenities in the planned neighborhood. That might be coloring my opinions about the negative impact of the proposal." You are now in a place to move forward with a productive discussion about the new zoning regulations because you are aware of your own bias.

Critical thinking requires us to be aware of our biases and those things that impact our reason. Learning how to reach further in understanding our emotions is part of identifying bias-es and hidden motives. Sometimes, our misunderstood or sup-pressed emotions prevent us from the vulnerability we need to handle potential conflict. Fear can be related to anxiety, but it can also be connected to a sense of insecurity or inferiority. Sur-prise might lead to confusion or a sense of being overwhelmed. We may be angry because we hate something, or our anger may have grown out of a sense of unresolved aggravation. Each of those will push us to react differently to someone else in a tense situation. Being able to clearly communicate our own emotional factors in a conflict paves the way for open communication all around and makes it more likely that our problem-solving will be effective.

Teach logic, learn logic.

This is a difficult one for those of us who have left school in the distant past. Formal logic is rarely taught in school today, mostly left to IB programs, classical schools, and those weird homeschoolers. Confession: I am one of the latter, and yes, my children have learned formal logic. I, on the other hand, had only a brief foray into formal logic as part of a college philosophy course. Most of my knowledge and understanding today comes from helping my children through their logic courses. Since all of them have been fairly self-sufficient in that regard, I still have only cursory knowledge of all of the formal proofs. But what I do understand is how an argument works, how to break an ar-gument down into its premises, and how to trace those premises to a valid conclusion. I can assess the truth of the statements and determine the truth of the conclusion.

Completing a textbook on formal logic isn't necessary for us to understand and effectively use logic in our arguments. A valid argument is one with such a structure that if the premises are true, the conclusion must be true. A sound argument is a valid argument with true premises. And truth is where it gets tricky. The truth of a statement is often what is at the heart of a conflict. The more we can get clarity around the framing of the argument, the more chance we have to debate the actual issues at hand. When arguments are obscured by ill logic, it can be hard to know what we are truly debating. Being able to parse an argument correctly, identifying the premises and their proper conclusion, is an invaluable skill in a conflict.

I have always been a terrible person with whom to watch political debates or speeches. Most years, I no longer watch political debates at all, though I try to stay in the room for the State of the Union. I can barely focus on the topics because I am too busy yelling at the television about the poor use of logic. My family has essentially banned me from watching it with them because I sit fuming and muttering things like, "That doesn't even make sense! How can they say that? There is no link from one statement to the next! It's just one logical fallacy after another!" I was first shushed, then finally outright banished, by my long-suffering husband, who has had many years of having to actually pay attention to these debates and speeches as part of his job. I was, apparently, a little distracting. But I cannot even hear the ideas presented if the arguments used are invalid.

Take time to learn how to structure an argument and how to identify those invalid arguments. Learning formal logic as an adult is probably not going to be especially useful. Studies have shown that while middle school students can improve logical thinking through the study of formal logic, the results are mixed for university students. Instead, research concludes that adults can improve their reasoning ability through logic puzzles, word games, chess, and even reading mysteries. Creative activities, whether painting or knitting or planning a flower garden, all help us develop logical thinking skills.

I love having flower gardens. In high school, I meticulously planned and planted what was probably a 200-square-foot garden with a stone path and a railroad tie border. I had roses, climbing flowers, and a variety of colors and heights. I considered hours of sunlight versus shade, plants that would grow well next to one another, what would spread rapidly, and what needed space. For a few years, I had an absolutely lovely garden, and I imagined I would have even more when I was an adult in my own home. I now have over sixty acres, three of which are more manicured acres, surrounding our historic house. I have the wide front porch with stone steps, a stone pool house that was once a well house, quaint wooden fences, brick sidewalks... And pre-existing landscaping that becomes more overgrown and unkempt by the year. Oh, we do maintenance. And my son faithfully makes mountains of mulch for me every year. My boys planted roses, and one of my sons has a thriving patch of mint varieties. Still, I have yet to create my masterful flower beds that take advantage of those stone steps and beautiful porches. I am paralyzed in the planning stages. Those of you who do create those artistic, flourishing flower gardens are thinking more logically than you probably realize. You are making decisions based on many competing factors that are both utilitarian and creative.

We are not all going to study higher level mathematics, formal logic, or computer science. Some people are writers or gardeners or mechanics. They use logic, deductive and inductive reasoning, in their lives and careers as well. Cultivate those skills in different areas of your life. Play with words, challenge yourself to an online game of chess, get a puzzle book for your spare time, plot a garden, or outline an argument for where to go on summer vacation. Train your brain to look for clear pathways from one statement or premise to the next and to identify conditional if-then statements. When you hear such statements, ask yourself if they actually make sense. Does the "then" automatically flow from the "if?"

Much of what people consider common sense is actually simply sound logic. What people would once call "street smart versus book smart" often meant someone who could think logically and reason well versus someone who knew a great deal of facts but not how to use them. With so much data flying at us today, we don't always stop to use our common sense to analyze it. We simply file things away in whatever category seems best and move on. In some ways, we are all a little bit more "book smart" than we used to be because we all have a wealth of knowledge in our pockets through our phones. We can quickly tell you the capital of Kazakhstan or the definition of *abjure*. We can look up the weather forecast for the next two weeks, the price of seed corn by the 50lb bag, and the best time of year for planting, but few of us can take that information and determine exactly how to plant a 17-acre field. The logical thinking that a farmer does to determine what to plant and how and when is not readily available to most of us anymore—but we can all still learn to do better!

We should also learn to identify logical fallacies—those arguments that appear to make sense on the surface but are actually quite flawed. They are easily disproved with a little matter-of-fact reasoning. Logical fallacies were first categorized, labeled, and defined by Hindu scholars in the late BCE and early CE and by Aristotle in his *Sophistical Refutations*. But logical fallacies, faulty, ambiguous reasoning, are simply part of human communication. You are likely familiar with most, though perhaps not by name. You might know *slippery slope, ad hominem, red herring,* or *straw man*. Social media posts often use *appeals to authority* and *bandwagon fallacies* to convince people that their arguments are correct. Look for arguments that say "most people believe" or "scientists say." We take more seriously a suggestion that we drink a certain juice or stop eating a certain food if we read about it on a website labeled "fitness and nutrition," even if we do not know the authors, their training, or their knowledge. We accept pronouncements from teachers and schools because we are conditioned to accept teachers as authorities. We are more likely to agree to a proposed book ban because all of our friends have been posting in support. With so much to absorb, we shortcut our reasoning to accept the authority of others or the group's acceptance of an idea. We hear an *appeal to pity*, and we are moved to action, although we know little about the actual circumstances. We fall prey to *sunk cost* fallacies when we make decisions based on the time or money we have already put into something. Being conscious of the more common fallacies helps us avoid them.

Compromise—it's not a bad word.

Politicians love *false dilemma* fallacies, or *false dichotomy*, which presents a situation in which it appears only two options exist—options which usually represent extreme opposites. If you oppose the Affordable Care Act, you must not care about the poor, the sick, and the elderly. If you support any gun control laws, you want to take all guns away from citizens. We've all heard versions of this and are sometimes guilty of these. When we care passionately about an issue, we instinctively frame it in the starkest terms possible. *If you care,* we cry, *you would do something! And* this *is the something that you would do!* We know other options might exist, but shouldn't we press for the *best* solution? Shouldn't we push for the *most*? When you negotiate, you don't start with the minimum you are willing to accept, right? You ask for the moon! Unfortunately, our opinions about controversial topics are not the same as haggling for a raise. When we push an extreme position, we alienate our would-be partners. When we force people into an all or nothing situation, we find ourselves on opposite sides of a chasm from those who cannot accept either all or nothing.

Compromise doesn't mean compromising your convictions. It means noting that other options exist between the two extremes. It means recognizing that most either-or situations are really false dilemmas. We don't need to either give more money to schools or hate children. We don't have to accept that you either fully embrace the latest agenda or you hate a particular group of people. In the case of Israel-Palestine, you do not have to be pro-Israel and hate the Palestinian people or be pro-Palestine and wish to erase Israel. Always, always, be skeptical of anyone who suggests you must choose one position or the other. You will find that they are usually presenting you with a false dilemma.

Just for fun... the next time you scroll Facebook or watch a political debate, make a tally of every logical fallacy you encounter. The internet has many lists of common fallacies available. It can bring a little levity to a world that feels ever more irrational and divided.

Living in a pluralistic society and an increasingly global community means agreeing to compromise as a way of life. Sometimes, that means the overarching questions of rights and responsibilities, the individual versus the common good. Sometimes, it means no nut products in personal school lunches or coming back into the office post-pandemic at least three days per week. Compromise is not a bad word. It does not signify weakness of intellect or of will. Compromise means strength. It means working together to seek the truth and solve a problem. It means solutions are more important than self.

We can hold to our own principles. We can believe we are morally and factually in the right. Yet we can still compromise in an effort to maintain open dialogue and move, however slowly, closer to truth. Few questions are truly either/or, no matter how strongly we believe our own position to be the only true answer. Conflict and Compromise; two words whose meanings have taken on such heaviness. To be in conflict on an issue simply means to hold views in opposition. To compromise simply means to find a way to an agreement through mutual concessions. Perhaps you give more, or perhaps you give less, but in compromise, you meet somewhere between your two positions. You create the space to meet by finding common ground. Common ground may only be a vaguely similar goal with very dissimilar means of achieving said goal, but that is enough ground on which to meet.

I don't suggest we compromise with evil. I don't suggest we find common ground in the degradation of human dignity. I do, however, believe we need to be very careful about what we allow to be labeled evil. Disagreements, even ones that stir the deepest anger in us, do not make an opponent evil. Serbian and Croatian military and militias did unspeakable harm to one another in the fiercely explosive breakup of the former Yugoslavia. Many of the complaints of both sides prior to the violence had merit. Once the label of evil was applied, however, there was no longer any desire to find any common ground for compromise. Could the war have been avoided? We can never be certain, but consider how easily people dismiss others today with labels like "Nazi" or "demoncrat." These words grant them permission to withhold honest, earnest debate, legitimacy to denying compromise. History has shown us the end of that road. Do we want to follow it again?

A special note for parents: Equip your children to think critically.

It is hard to watch your children go out into the world and not know what influences they are going to encounter. This is a tender point with parents, I have found. We naturally want our children to become adults who share our faith or think like we do. After all, we hold our particular personal beliefs because we think they are right! But our children aren't always going to grow up to be like us. It is tempting sometimes for parents to want to surround their children with people who think and believe as they do, to make sure they are given the "right" information so they can learn the "right" facts. However, as economist Thomas Sowell writes in *Intellectuals and Society*:

> Critics of ideological indoctrination in schools and colleges often attack the particular ideological conclusions, but that is beside the point educationally. Even if we were to assume, for the sake of argument, that all the conclusions reached by all the various "studies" are both logically and factually valid, that still does not get to the heart of the educational issue. Even if students were to leave these "studies" with 100 percent correct conclusions about issues A, B and C, that would in no way equip them intellectually with the tools needed to confront very different issues X, Y and Z that are likely to arise over the course of their future years. For that they would need knowledge and experience in how to analyze and weigh conflicting viewpoints.[102]

The best we can do for our children is to equip them to reason well. We should give them the tools of logic, a rich vocabulary, and as much knowledge of the world as possible. Read to them, debate issues with them, and expose them to good thinking. We cannot control the outcome, but we can help ensure that our children become adults who care, think, and come to their own best conclusions about what is good, true, and beautiful.

Epilogue

Our world is divided, but it's been divided before in the days of overt segregation, by landowner versus landless, male versus female, slave versus free, and feudal lord versus peasant. We've been divided by tribe, race, language, and religion. We have overcome various barriers, distinctions, and divisions before, and we can do so again. People want to connect. They want to be part of communities, families, and relationships. Creating the space for stories to be told and connections formed, learning to hear and apprehend the stories of others while sharing our own, and thinking deeply and critically about our beliefs before challenging the beliefs of others—these are the three strands that weave together to form a lifeline out of dysfunctional, ever-spiraling conflict.

Inviting your political sign loving neighbor to share a beer on the front porch isn't going to change the world, but it might change your neighborhood. Teaching your children to love stories doesn't mean the next election cycle will be free of drama, but maybe the one in twenty years will be. Or maybe the first-grade class president elections will be. And training yourself to listen to and really hear the stories of others? That can change your family, which can change their workplace, neighborhood, and school. Stopping yourself before defending a position you haven't fully explored can save a friendship or alter the course of a school board meeting.

The Camp David Accords didn't resolve the conflict in the Middle East—and may even have contributed to some of it; so, too, our individual actions may seem insignificant when we look at the troubles our world faces today. But it is the acts of each individual that creates a culture, and we can find again a culture of healthy conflict in community with one another. Every time we invite the stranger in and listen to their story, every time we say, "I hadn't thought of it that way, maybe you are right," every time we are slow to speak and quick to listen, we toss another pebble into the water and send the ripples out into society. Our small offerings are the only things that can change the tone of our culture. We *are* our culture. It isn't something "out there" or something we see in the distance. We create the culture around us by our own actions and our own attitudes. So make the change you can.

All of us desire to be from a place, to be part of a community. Comfort, history, tradition, and rituals are all part of that. Place can be ephemeral, but it can be people or the church or a tradition or a liturgy. Yet there is also something in us that longs for an actual physical place. When we think of heaven, we think of a place. We think of a mansion with many rooms, streets paved with gold, and a new Earth—but we always assume there's *a place*. We are body and spirit, and both our body and spirit long for a home. Create those places for yourself and for your loved ones. Help your community create those places of belonging, beauty, rest, and relationship.

Listen to people and their stories. Start at home. Flex your story muscles by reading fairytales to your children and rereading your childhood favorites. Listen to crazy Uncle Chuck and Cousin Ashley. People today feel free to reject their family of origin for many and varied reasons. They declare that they are easily and better replaced with friends that are chosen. But isn't family how we first learn to get along with others? Some created families are absolutely wonderful and necessary, and some natural families absolutely deserve the boot. Toxicity and abuse are real and terrible things. But it's not what pop culture is selling today. Reject that which tells you that you don't have to feel uncomfortable. Sometimes, we absolutely must feel uncomfortable in order to learn, understand, and love one another. It is only then that we can become people who can weather conflict and grow stronger for it.

Our world is divided, but it is a beautiful world. When you stop for a moment and *listen*, you hear music that reaches into the hearts of others around the globe. You hear birdsong and windsong that speak to a creation that defies the damaging touch of careless humankind. You hear stories that tell of courage, faithfulness, kindness, and great love. And you hear the voices of others crying out for peace, reconciliation, and healing. Add your voice to the music, the stories and the cries for peace. And the world *will* hear. And the world will heal. See the world through the perspective shaping waves and whorls of restoration glass, and it will be an even more beautiful place.

WORKS CITED

Introduction

1. Madeleine L'Engle, *The Irrational Season*. (San Francisco: Harper & Row, 1977), 85.

2. John Dewey, "Morals are *human,*" *Human Nature and Conduct: An Introduction to Social Psychology* (New York: Modern Library, 1922), 300.

3. Adam Piore, *Technologists are trying to fix the "filter bubble" problem that tech helped create,* MIT Technology Review, (technologyreview.com/2018/08/22/2167/technologists-are-trying-to-fix-the-filter-bubble-problem-that-tech-helped-create/ (August 22, 2018).

4. Andrew Peterson, *The God of the Garden,* (Brentwood: B&H Publishing, 2021). 160.

The Need for Place

5. Henri J. M. Nouwen, *Reaching Out: The Three Movements of the Spiritual Life,* (New York: Doubleday, 1975), 71.

6. John Muir, *The Yosemite,* (New York: The Century Company., 1912), 256. (accessed online, vault.sierraclub.org/john_muir_exhibit/writings/the_yosemite/ 8/9/2024)

7. Ralph Ellison, *Invisible Man,* (New York: Vintage Books, 1982), 564.

8. E.B. White, *Here is New York,* (New York: The Little Bookroom, 1999), 35-36.

The Need for Stories

9. Umberto Eco, *The Island of the Day Before,* (Orlando: Harcourt Inc., 1994), 207

10. Paulo Coelho, *Stories and Reflections,* paulocoelhoblog.com/2008/12/15/todays-question-by-stephane/ (August 9, 2024).

11. G.K. Chesterton, *Orthodoxy,* (San Francisco: Ignatius Press, 1995), 66.

12. Robyn, Fivush, Marshal Duke, Jennifer G., "Do you know...? The power of family history in adolescent identity and well-being." *Journal of Family Life* (February 2010); accessed online https://ncph.org/wp-content/uploads/2013/12/The-power-of-family-history-in-adolescent-identity.pdf (August 9, 2024).

13. BYU Family History Library, "Raising Family Historians: Capturing the Hearts of Future Geneaologists." https://familyhistory.lib.byu.edu/0000018f-9d4e-d757-a1cf-ffde0e3e0001/raising-family-historians-handout-pdf Accessed August 10, 2024.

14. Daniel Nayeri, *Everything Sad is Untrue: A True Story* (Montclair: Levine Querido, 2020), 37.

15. Aleks Krotoski, "Storytelling: Digital Technology Allows Us to Tell Tales in Innovative New Ways," *The Guardian*, Aug. 6, 2011 (https://www.theguardian.com/technology/2011/aug/07/digital-media-storytelling-internet)

16. Nayeri, *Everything Sad is Untrue*, 300-301.

17. Gregory Cajete, "Children, myth and storytelling: An Indigenous perspective." *Global Studies of Childhood*, 7(2), 113-130. (https://journals.sagepub.com/doi/full/10.1177/2043610617703832) (August 9, 2024)

The Need for Critical Thinking

18. *Attributed to* Sir Francis Bacon (1605) https://www.criticalthinking.org (August 9, 2024)

19. *Oxford Learner's Dictionaries,* (Oxford University Press, 2024), https://www.oxfordlearnersdictionaries.com/us/definition/english/critical-thinking (August 9, 2024).

20. Helen Lee Buoygues, "Teaching Critical Thinking in K-12: Where There's a Will But Not Always a Way," Re-Boot Foundation, June 2022. https://reboot-foundation.org/wp-content/uploads/2022/07/Reboot-White-Paper_NAEP-5.pdf (August 9, 2024).

21. Carnegie Mellon University, Eberly Center, "Students Don't Demonstrate Critical Thinking," https://www.cmu.edu/teaching/solveproblem/strat-criticalthinking/criticalthinking-01.html (August 9, 2024).

22. Mike Caulfield, https://hapgood.us/2019/06/19/sift-the-four-moves/ Accessed August 10, 2024. This blog post outlines the SIFT, or Four Moves, method developed by Mike Caulfield at the

University of Washington's Center for an Informed Public. SIFT stands for Stop, Investigate the source, Find better coverage, and Trace…back to the original context.

23. Charlie Warzel, "Don't Go Down the Rabbit Hole," New York Times, Feb. 18, 2021. (https://www.nytimes.com/2021/02/18/opinion/fake-news-media-attention.html

24. Klein, Jürgen, "Francis Bacon", *The Stanford Encyclopedia of Philosophy* (Fall 2020 Edition), Edward N. Zalta (ed.), <https://plato.stanford.edu/archives/fall2020/entries/francis-bacon/

25. Oliver Wendell Holmes, Jr., "The Path of Law," 10 Harvard Law Review 457 (1897). https://moglen.law.columbia.edu/LCS/palaw.pdf

26. Jacques Bailly, University of Vermont, https://www.uvm.edu/~jbailly/courses/clas21/notes/apologies.html (accessed September 27, 2024).

27. Madeleine L'Engle, *The Irrational Season*, 68.

28. Amanda Ripley, *High Conflict*, (New York: Simon and Schuster, 2021).

Part One: The Power of Place: Chapter One: Hospitality All Around

29. Harper Lee, *To Kill A Mockingbird*, (New York: Warner Books, 1982), 24.

30. Eleanor Roosevelt, *Eleanor Roosevelt's Book of Common Sense Etiquette*, (New York: Macmillan Company, 1962), Chapter 12.

31. Cambridge Dictionaries, https://dictionary.cambridge.org/us/dictionary/english/hospitality (August 9, 2024).

32. Gemma Tipton, "Céad Míe Fáilte? The True Meaning of Hospitality," *The Irish* Times, Apr. 30, 2018. https://www.irishtimes.com/culture/art-and-design/visual-art/cead-mile-failte-the-true-meaning-of-hospitality-1.3474075

Part One: The Power of Place: Chapter Two: The Nurturing of Nature

33. Linnie Marsh Wolf, ed., *John of the Mountains: The Unpublished Journals of John Muir*, (University of Wisconsin Press: Madison, 1938), page 317.

34. Shakespeare, William. *Troilus and Cressida*. Edited by Barbara A. Mowat and Paul Werstine, Folger Shakespeare Library, Simon & Schuster, 2008, Act 3, Scene 3.

35. Wendell Berry, "The Peace of Wild Things." *The Peace of Wild Things*. (New York: Penquin, 2018).

36. National Capital Planning Commission, *About Washington's Parks and Open Spaces*, 15 (https://www.ncpc.gov/docs/CapitalSpace_Washingtons_Parks_and_Open_Space.pdf) (August 9, 2024)

37. Kathleen Wolf and Mary Ann Rozance, *Green Cities: Good Health*, University of Washington, College of the Environment, Aug. 16, 2018. https://depts.washington.edu/hhwb/Thm_Community.html

38. Tate Williams, "Meeting the Need for Green," In the Garden Cemetery: The Revival of America's First Urban Parks. American Forests. Jun. 2, 2014. https://www.americanforests.org/article/in-the-garden-cemetery-the-revival-of-americas-first-urban-parks/ (August 9, 2024).

39. Marielle Segarra, "Spending Time in a Forest Can Boost Health and Lower Stress," NPR. Oct. 24, 2023. https://www.npr.org/2023/08/22/1195337204/a-guide-to-forest-bathing

40. https://glencree.ie

41. Brandon Hambler and Alistair Little and Wilhelm Verwoerd, "Cultivating Peace: An Exploration of the Role of Nature-Based Activities in Conflict Transformation" (February 10, 2018). Transitional Justice Institute Research Paper No. 19-03, Available at SSRN: https://ssrn.com/abstract=3121690 or http://dx.doi.org/10.2139/ssrn.3121690

42. Madeleine L'Engle, *The Irrational Season*, 11.

Part One: Chapter Three: Community and Space: Place

43. Alice Waters, *40 Years of Chez Panisse, The Power of Gathering*, (New York: Clarkson Potter, 2011)

44. Wendell Berry, *The Need To Be Whole*, (Shoemaker and Company, 2022) 31.

Part Two: Chapter One: Shared Foundations and Cultural Rootedness

45. Eugene Peterson, *Christ Plays in Ten Thousand Places, A Conversation in Spiritual Theology,* (Grand Rapids: William B. Eerdmans Publishing Company)

46. Tahir Shah, *In Arabian Nights: A Caravan of Moroccan Dreams,* (New York: Bantam, 2009).

47. Nayeri, *Everything Sad is Untrue,* 333.

48. Eudora Welty, *One Writer's Beginnings,* (Cambridge: Harvard University Press, 1984). 14

49. Madeleine L'Engle, *A Circle of Quiet,* (New York: HarperOne, 1984) 121.

50. Madeleine L'Engle, *Walking on Water: Reflections on Faith and Art,* (New York: North Point Press, 1995), 45-46.

51. Amin Maalouf, *In the Name of Identity,* (New York: Arcade Publishing, 2012).

52. *The Princess Bride.* Directed by Rob Reiner, MGM, 1987. *Amazon. com Prime Video.*

Part Two: Chapter Two: Imagination and Art, Creativity and Wonder

53. Vigen Goroian, *Tending the Heart of Virtue,* (New York, Oxford University Press, 2023), 134.

54. Kate DiCamillo, @KateDiCamillo. "Because when we read together, we open our hearts to a story…" Facebook, Jan. 30, 2024.

55. Sir Francis Bacon, *The Collected Works of Sir Francis Bacon (Unexpurgated Edition),* (New York: Halcyon Press Ltd., 2009). Kindle accessed August 10, 2024).

56. G.K. Chesterton, "The Red Angels," *Tremendous Trifles.* (Kindle Scribe, Prabhat Prakashan, 2020), 70. (accessed August 10, 2024).

Part Two: Chapter Three: Morals, Empathy, Vulnerability, and Virtue

57. Chautona Havig, *Clock Tower Bound,* Kindle, 2024, 243.

58. Nayeri, *Everything Sad Is Untrue, 237.*

59. Helen Hayes, *A Gift of Joy*, (New York: M. Evans and Company, 1965),

Part Three: Chapter One: Critical Thinking and Socratic Questioning

60. Plato, Cratylus 428D, Tufts University, http://data.perseus.org/citations/urn:cts:greekLit:tlg0059.tlg005.perseus-eng1:428d

61. Plato, Apology, 38a, Tufts University, Perseus Digital Library. http://data.perseus.org/citations/urn:cts:greekLit:tlg0059.tlg002.perseus-eng1:38a

62. Holmes, *The Path of Law*

63. Ward Farnsworth, *The Socratic Method: A Practitioner's Handbook*, (Boston: Godine, 2021)

Part Three: Chapter Two: Creativity and Wonder Redux

64. G. K. Chesterton, *The Everlasting Man.* Project Gutenberg of Australia e-book, 0100311h.html, August 2020. https://gutenberg.net.au/ebooks01/0100311h.html

65. St. Thomas Aquinas, *Summa Theologica, I-II, 32, viii.* Dominican Sisters of Saint Cecilia, "Desire and Wonder: Essential Elements in Catechesis," https://www.nashvilledominican.org/desire-wonder-essential-elements-catechesis/#:~:text=Thomas%20defines%20wonder%20(admiratio)%20as,in%20a%20deliberate%20and%20purposeful (Accessed August 10, 2024).

66. Brandon Sanderson, *The Way of Kings*, (New York: Tor Books, 2014), 806.

67. George MacDonald, *A Dish of Orts*, Project Gutenberg, EBook #9393, last updated Oct. 10, 2016. https://www.gutenberg.org/files/9393/9393-h/9393-h.htm

68. New York State Writers Institute, "Poetry Friday: What Fresh Hell Is This?," *The Conversation.* (Aug. 13, 2021). https://www.nyswritersinstitute.org/post/poetry-friday-what-fresh-hell-is-this (Accessed August 10, 2024).

69. Albert Einstein. "What Life Means to Einstein." Interview by George Sylvester Viereck. *The Saturday Evening Post*, Oct. 26, 1929. 117. https://www.saturdayeveningpost.com/wp-content/uploads/satevepost/what_life_means_to_einstein.pdf (Accessed August 10, 2024)

70. Reitsema, Edith M. "How Imagination Engages Your Heart and Moral Character," *Artway. https://artway.eu/content. php?id=1701&lang=en&action=show (Accessed August 10, 2024).*

71. Guroian, *Tending the Heart of Virtue,* 134.

Part Three: Chapter Three: Facts AND Feelings

72. Luc de Clapiers, Marquess de Vauvenargues, *Reflections and Maxims of Vauvenargues,* (London: Humphrey Milford, 1940), 45. Open Library OL6418842M, https://openlibrary.org/books/OL6418842M/The_Reflections_and_Maxims_of_Luc_de_Clapiers_Marquis_of_Vauvenargues (Accessed August 10, 2024).

73. William Butler Yeats, "The Second Coming," *Collected Poems,* (New York: MacMillan Company, 1933)

74. Richard Nordquist. "What Is Phronesis?" ThoughtCo, Apr. 5, 2023, thoughtco.com/phronesis-rhetoric-1691510.

75. Lauren Spigelmyer, "The Amygdala." *The Behavior Hub.* Nov. 2. 2020. https://www.thebehaviorhub.com/blog/2020/11/2/the-amygdala

76. Jung N, Wranke C, Hamburger K, Knauff M. How emotions affect logical reasoning: evidence from experiments with mood-manipulated participants, spider phobics, and people with exam anxiety. Front Psychol. 2014 Jun 10;5:570. doi: 10.3389/fpsyg.2014.00570. PMID: 24959160; PMCID: PMC4050437.

77. Rubin Khoddam, "Everything You Need to Know About Emotional Reasoning." *Psychology Today.* Sept. 13, 2023. https://www.psychologytoday.com/us/blog/the-addiction-connection/202309/everything-you-need-to-know-about-emotional-reasoning

78. George Lucas, *Star Wars, Episode 1, The Phantom Menace.* Lucasfilm Ltd., 1999.

79. Jozefien De Leersnyder, Batja Mesquita, and Michael Boiger, 'What Has Culture Got to Do with Emotions? (A Lot)', in Michele J. Gelfand, Chi-yue Chiu, and Ying-yi Hong (eds), *Handbook of Advances in Culture and Psychology, Volume 8* (New York, 2021; online edn, Oxford Academic, Mar. 18, 2021. https://doi.org/10.1093/oso/9780190079741.003.0002, accessed 21 Aug. 2024.

80. George Grote, *Plato and Other Companions of Sokrates* vol. 1. (London: John Murray, 1865), 258. https://www.gutenberg.org/files/40435/40435-h/40435-h.htm#v1page388 Accessed August 10, 2024.

81. Oscar Wilde, "The Critic As Artist, Part II," *Intentions,* (New York: Brentano's, 1905), 199-200.

Weave Your Own Rope: Setting the Stage

82. Washington Irving, *The Sketchbook Vol. II,* (New York: G.P. Putnam, 1861), 247-248.

83. Ralph Waldo Emerson, "Society and Solitude," *The Works of Ralph Waldo Emerson, in 12 Vols, Fireside Edition,* (Boston and New York, 1909). Vol. 7.

84. John Paul Lederach, *The Journey Toward Reconciliation,* (Scottdale: Herald Press, 1999), 134.

85. Wendell Berry, "The Loss of the Future," *The Long-legged House,* (Berkeley: Counterpoint, 1969).

86. Kirsten Weir, "Nurtured by Nature." *APA Monitor on Psychology,* Vol. 51, No. 3. April/May 2020, 50. https://www.psychologytoday.com/us/blog/the-addiction-connection/202309/everything-you-need-to-know-about-emotional-reasoning

87. Angela Haupt, "Your Houseplants Have Some Powerful Health Benefits," *Time,* March 2, 2023. https://time.com/6258638/indoor-plants-health-benefits/

88. Stephanie Langmaid, "Health Benefits of Houseplants," WedMD, Sept. 22, 2023. https://www.webmd.com/a-to-z-guides/ss/slideshow-health-benefits-houseplants

Weave Your Own Rope: Sharing Stories and Sharing Ourselves

89. Margaret Atwood, "Margaret Atwood on Serial Fiction and the Future of the Book." Interview with Lily Rothman. *Time.* Oct. 8, 2012. https://entertainment.time.com/2012/10/08/margaret-atwood-on-serial-fiction-and-the-future-of-the-book/?fbclid=IwZXh0bgNhZW0CMTEAAR1CaEVTc8NqIJ7qOa3S121y9KsP73SWH7SwgWg66XRI4BfdE_KMBzQ_c8E_aem_zrdu0uWVsLQTk-Ekb988ig

90. Azar Nafisi, *The Republic of Imagination: A Life in Books.* (New York: Penguin Books, 2015), 3.

91. Madeleine L'Engle, *The Genesis Trilogy: Sold into Egypt*, (New York: Shaw, 2001), 411.

92. Katherine Paterson, *The Spying Heart*, (New York: Lodestar Books, 1989), 131.

93. Katherine Paterson, *The Spying Heart*, 134.

94. Katherine Paterson, *The Spying Heart*, 144.

95. Maya Angelou, "Was This Maya Angelou's Final Interview?" *Ebony*, May 30, 2014. https://www.ebony.com/was-this-maya-angelous-final-interview-987/ (Accessed August 10, 2024).

96. Chesterton, *The Red Angels*, 70.

97. Charlotte Mason, *Original Homeschooling Series: Parents and Children, Vol. II*, (Simply Charlotte Mason), 263.

Weave Your Own Rope: Thinking Critically for Conflict and Resolution

98. Søren Kierkegaard, *Either/Or.* Translated by Howard V. Hong and Edna V. Hong, Edited by Howard V. Hong and Edna H. Hong. (Princeton: Princeton University Press, 1987), 19.

99. Carole Wade, credited to Carole Wade, TeachThought, https://www.teachthought.com/critical-thinking/quotes-critical-thinking/ (Accessed August 10, 2024). Possibly paraphrased from Carole Wade and Carol Tavris, *Critical and Creative Thinking*, (New York: Harper Collins, 1993), 14. "That is why intelligent people are not always critical thinkers. Clever debaters can learn to poke holes in the arguments of others, while twisting facts or conveniently ignoring arguments that might contradict their own positions."

100. Daniel Levitin, *Field Guide to Lies: Critical Thinking in the Information Age*, (New York: Dutton, 2016).

101. Marie Curie, attributed to. https://www.mariecurie.org.uk/who/our-history/marie-curie-the-scientist#:~:text=Marie%20Curie%20quotes&text=We%20must%20have%20perseverance%20and,is%20only%20to%20be%20understood.%22

102. Thomas Sowell, *Intellectuals and Society*, (New York: Basic Books, 2012). Quoted on Goodreads.com https://www.goodreads.com/work/quotes/8518862-intellectuals-and-society (Accessed August 10, 2024).

Epilogue

103. Henri Nouwen, *Reaching Out,* 65-66.

104. Denise Thorton, *Digging in the Driftless, https://digginginthedriftless. com/2010/09/17/what-you-don't-know-about-vintage-glass/ Accessed August 10, 2024*

BOOKS MENTIONED

Louisa May Alcott
Little Women
Little Men

Lloyd Alexander
The Chronicles of Prydain series

Heather Amery
Poppy and Sam Complete Book of Farmyard Tales

Jane Austen
Pride and Prejudice

Rev. W. Awdry
Thomas the Tank Engine Complete Collection

L. Frank Baum
The Wizard of Oz

Claire Huchet Bishop
Twenty and Ten

Ruby Bridges
Through My Eyes

Emliy Brontë
Jane Eyre

Virginia Lee Burton
Mike Mulligan and His Steam Shovel
The Little House

Elias Chacour
Blood Brothers

Shirley Climo
The Persian Cinderella

Barbara Cooney
   Miss Rumphius
   The Ox-Cart Man
   Roxaboxen

Christopher Paul Curtis
   The Watsons Go to Birmingham

Charles Dickens
   A Tale of Two Cities

Louise Erdrich
   The Birchbark House series

Majorie Flack
   Story of Ping
   Angus and the Cat

Anne Frank
   Anne Frank: The Diary of a Young Girl

Don Freeman
   Corduroy series

Kenneth Grahame
   The Reluctant Dragon

Margaret Hodges
   Saint George and the Dragon

Crockett Johnson
   Harold and the Purple Crayon

Junius Johnson
   On Teaching Fairy Stories

Jack Ezra Keats
   The Snowy Day
   The Little Drummer Boy
   Pet Show

Kathryn Kenny / Julie Campbell
   Trixie Belden (series)

Madeleine L'Engle
> *Wrinkle in Time (series)*
> *Walking on Water*
> *The Rock That Is Higher: Story as Truth*
> *The Crosswicks Journals*
> *Ring of Endless Light*

Munro Leaf
> *The Story of Ferdinand*

Harper Lee
> *To Kill A Mockingbird*

Dr. Qing Li
> *Forest Bathing, How Trees Can Help You Find Health and Happiness*

Robert McCloskey
> *Lentil*
> *Homer Price*
> *Make Way for Ducklings*
> *Blueberries for Sal*
> *One Morning in Maine*
> *Time of Wonder*

Lucy Maude Montgomery
> *Anne of Green Gables*
> *Emily of New Moon*
> *Rilla of Ingleside*

Brandon Mull
> *Fablehaven series*

Robert Munsch
> *The Paper Bag Princess*

Daniel Nayeri
> *Everything Sad is Untrue*
> *The Many Assassinations of Samir, The Seller of Dreams*

Naomi Shihab Nye
> *Sitti's Secrets*

Katherine Paterson
> *Bridge to Terabithia*
> *Lyddie*

Mitali Perkins
> *Rickshaw Girl*
> *You Bring the Distant Near*
> *Steeped in Stories*

Chris Smith
> *One City, Two Brothers*

William Steig
> *Amos and Boris*

Corrie ten Boom
> *The Hiding Place*

J.R.R. Tolkien
> *Lord of the Rings trilogy*
> *The Hobbit*
> *Sir Gawain and the Green Knight*

E.B. White
> *Here Is New York*

Laura Ingalls Wilder
> *Little House on the Prairie (series)*

Anonymous
> *One Thousand and One Arabian Nights*